AWAKENING
YOUR INNER
GENIUS

SEAN PATRICK

Published in the United States by Oculus Publishers, Inc.

www.oculuspublishers.com

For general information on our other products and services please contact our Customer Care Department at help@oculuspublishers.com.

ISBN 978-1-938895-15-9

WISE I/A No 12110601

Design: Piratas and Kiersten Lief

Printed in USA

Written by Sean Patrick

First Edition

For Sarah, Lenox, Mom, and Dad

CONTENTS

THE GREAT MYSTERY
OF GENIUS

"Thousands of geniuses live and die undiscovered—either by themselves or by others."

-Mark Twain

If I could write one sentence that would magically increase your IQ by thirty points, would you be interested in reading that sentence?

Probably. But why? What would be in it for you? Do you think it would help you make more money? Make a name for yourself? Find love, happiness, or fulfillment?

I've asked many people these questions and their answers are invariable. "Of course it would." The cultural correlation is undeniable: we've been indoctrinated to believe that the higher the IQ, the more likely one is to succeed in life. Hence, we assume that the scientists that win Nobel Prizes, the businesspeople that go from rags to millions, the authors that write runaway bestsellers, register in the highest ranges of IQ simply because they're enjoying sweet successes.

Well, a tremendous amount of research has been done into the scientific correlation between IQ and real-life success, and a very different picture has emerged.

IQ and success are related...to a point. Sure, someone with an IQ of 150 (a "genius" by all normal standards) is going to do much better in life than someone with an IQ of 80 (nearly "mentally disabled"). Similarly, a person with an IQ of 130 ("near genius") has a significant upper hand in life when compared to a person with an IQ of 100 ("average").

But here's the catch: the relation between IQ and success follows the law of diminishing returns. That is, when you compare two people of relatively high IQs, you can no longer predict success by IQ alone. A scientist with an IQ of 130 is just as likely to rise to the top of his discipline as one with an IQ of 180.

Dr. Liam Hudson, a British psychologist that headed up Cambridge's Research Unit of Intellectual Development in the sixties, compared IQ to basketball. If you're five foot five, your prospects of becoming even an NBA bench warmer are slim-to-none. The fact is if you're less than six feet tall, you can pretty much forget about your dreams to challenge King James in his court.

Statistical data shows us that you have to be at least seventy-two inches tall to be allowed on the ride, and each inch you push over that is probably better for you. There comes a point, however, when height just doesn't matter much anymore. Just because someone is seven feet tall doesn't mean he's a better player than someone who's six foot six (Michael Jordan's height). The point is you only have to be tall *enough* to have a shot at the pros.

The same pattern is true of intelligence and success in life. You only have to be smart *enough* to fulfill the intellectual requirements for success. History's greatest achievers—practical, savvy people that did big things and changed the world—are heralded as the greatest geniuses to ever have walked the earth, but while many of them had remarkably high IQs, many others were just smart enough.

If we can't explain their success in terms of IQ alone, what else did they possess that allowed them to rise to such heights?

Most people would answer along the lines of "extraordinary inherent talent." And they would be wrong.

Call in the inspired bard, Demodocus.
God has given the man the gift of song.

That's one of the many god-given gifts of characters in the *Odyssey*. We've learned much since it was written—we've decoded human DNA and discovered our place in the universe—but we still marvel at the abilities of geniuses in the same way as the ancient Greeks did.

Whether we listen to a sonata of Beethoven's, watch highlight reels of Michael Jordan, or learn a law of Newton's, we view extraordinary human skills as gifts granted by unknown forces for unknown reasons. Such an explanation is convenient, but is it correct?

For the last two centuries, behavioral scientists have studied that question through focused research on great performers of all types: business managers, chess players, swimmers, surgeons, jet pilots, violinists, salespeople, writers, and many others. Their findings, numbering in the hundreds, have led to conclusions that fly straight in the teeth of what "everybody knows" about ability.

The studies conclusively disproved the notion that great performance stems primarily from a natural "gift" or talent. While some people display innate talents for certain activities early on, amazingly average people have become champions in all manner of endeavors. Many such top performers overcame their average—or even below-average—intellects and nonexistent aptitudes to develop outstanding abilities in disciplines such as chess, music, business, and medicine.

Examples of such remarkable transformations abound throughout history. Henry Ford failed in business several times and was flat broke five times before he founded the Ford Motor Company. In his youth, Thomas Edison's teachers told him he was "too stupid to learn anything." Beethoven was so awkward on the violin that his teachers believed him hopeless as a composer.

The world of sports reveals similar findings. Many athletes viewed as superhuman in their abilities were found to have little or no inherent advantage over their peers when they first began their journeys to greatness. Michael Jordan didn't make his sophomore team because he was deemed too short and average to play at that level. Stan Smith, a world-class tennis player and winner of Wimbledon, the U.S. Open, and eight Davis cups, was once rejected for the lowly position of a ball boy because the event organizers felt he was too clumsy and uncoordinated.

How do we explain such unintuitive findings?

While many theories were put forth, there was one common factor that researchers recognized in all great performers: they practiced so hard and intensely that it hurt.

Ted Williams, a baseball legend considered the most "gifted" hitter of his time, was believed to have natural abilities far beyond ordinary men, including eagle-like vision, extraordinary hand-eye coordination, and uncanny hitting instincts. Williams later said that such stories were all "a lot of bull." He had a much better explanation for his superior skills.

Williams began his path to greatness at the age of seven, when he decided to dedicate his entire life to one singular task: hitting a baseball as perfectly as possible. Starting at that young age, Williams spent every free minute he had at San Diego's old North Park field hitting balls, every day, year after year after year. His childhood friends recall finding him on that field smashing balls with the outer shells completely beaten off, with a splintered bat, and with blistered, bleeding hands. He would spend his lunch money to hire other kids to shag his balls so he could hit as many as possible every day. When the city turned off the field's lights, he would go home and swing a rolled-up newspaper in the mirror until he went to bed.

This obsession continued throughout Williams' entire professional career, and it's no surprise that he excelled because of it. For "The Kid," as he was known, greatness was a long, grueling process—not a gift from the beyond (a claim that he found insulting).

Studies of people with extraordinary abilities, like Ted Williams, have given rise to what Swedish psychologist Dr. K. Anders Ericsson called the "10,000 hour" rule. The rule's premise is that, regardless of whether one has an innate aptitude for an activity or not, mastery of it takes around ten thousand hours of focused, intentional practice. Analyzing the lives of geniuses in a wide range of intellectual, artistic, and athletic pursuits confirms this concept. From Mozart to Bobby Fischer to Bill Gates to the Beatles, their diverse journeys from nothing toward excellence in their respective fields shared a common denominator: the accumulation of ten thousand hours of unwavering "exercise" of their crafts.

To put that number in perspective, if you practiced an activity four hours per day, seven days per week, it would take you about seven years to reach ten thousand hours. That kind of dedication can only come from the heart—a true love and passion for the activity.

So, what does all this tell us? First, that the seed of greatness exists in every human being. Whether it sprouts or not is our choice. Second, that there are no such things as natural-born under- or overachievers—there are simply people who tap into their true potentials and people who don't. What is generally recognized as "great talent" is, in almost all cases, nothing more than the outward manifestations of an unwavering dedication to a process.

Thus, the advice of "work toward your ten thousand hours" sounds completely reasonable. Right? But there's a problem. There are millions of people who work incredibly hard, yet have little success to show for it. Is ten thousand hours too simple of a prescription for greatness?

Yes. It overlooks another aspect of great achievement that cannot be ignored: *opportunities*—conditions that often appear to be plain old dumb luck.

—————

As Malcolm Gladwell explains in *Outliers*, in many ways, the opportunities presented to one are just as important to success as one's own inherent talents and willingness to put in thousands of hours of work. For instance, if your dream is to become a professional athlete, it's quite possible that you won't be able to work hard enough to overcome a most devious obstacle: your birthday. How could that possibly be a hurdle?

Easy. Most sports enforce age cut-offs—that is, the ages that determine whether you can play another year in your current age bracket as a "senior," or whether you have to move up and be a "freshman" in the next.

In Canadian junior hockey leagues, the age cutoff was formerly January 1 (it's now December 31). The closer your birthday was to January 2, the better. Why? Well, let's say you were playing in the Bantam category, which is for children aged 13 – 14. If your birthday was in December, you were going to get two years of play at this level. You were going to turn fifteen and have to move immediately into the next category, Midget (which is for kids aged 15 – 16). If your birthday was January 2, however, you'd get an entire additional year to play in Bantam (and every other age group) because when the ages were checked on January 1, you were still fourteen years old.

An extra year of play against players younger than you is a *huge* advantage. Your body becomes bigger, stronger, and faster every day, giving you an opportunity to truly stand out from your birthday-handicapped peers. This extra developmental time predisposes you for selection onto more elite teams, which in turn leads to more ice time and better coaching, which advances your abilities even further.

Sociologists call this phenomenon an "accumulative advantage." For the elite Canadian junior hockey leagues, the result of this advantage was that for many years, the distribution of birth dates for the top performing kids was heavily weighted toward "first-quarter" babies—kids born between January and March.

Whether we're talking birthdays in sports, or the fact that Bill Gates just happened to go to a high school that housed one of the most advanced computers of the time—a computer that most colleges didn't even have—we can easily see that being in the right place (physical, educational, societal, or otherwise) at the right time can influence our destinies as much as anything else.

Now, that doesn't mean our fates are written in the stars. We can wholly control our dedication to thousands of hours of study, training and work. And grasping opportunities is equally controllable. Sure, we may not be built for the NFL or Kentucky Derby, but we're surrounded by opportunities every day, everywhere we go. There is no shortage of problems to be solved, needs and desires to be fulfilled, and innovative ways to help others.

But there's a catch. Most opportunities never announce themselves with trumpets and confetti. They're easily missed, mistaken, or squandered. They can be scary. And they never come with a 110% money-back guarantee. They're often nothing more than chances to improve on something other people are already doing.

Opportunities are whispers, not foghorns.

If we can't hear their soft rhythms—if we are too busy rushing about, waiting for thunderclaps of revelation, inspiration, and certainty—or if we can hear them but can't nurture them into real advantages, then we might as well be deaf to them.

This realization points us to the real heart and mystery of greatness. Just knowing that great achievers work very hard and take advantage of opportunities isn't enough. Why do some people recognize, appreciate, and pursue opportunities with passion and determination, whereas others don't? Why are some people willing to push through hell and high water to win, whereas others quit early and easily? Are there practical answers to these questions, or are they unsolvable enigmas of human psychology?

Well, I believe there are very practical answers to what makes a genius tick. I believe there are principles that we can isolate and use to better our own lives. I believe that genius is a *path* that we can all take and derive much benefit, happiness, fulfillment, and success from…not a genetic windfall or divine gift. Ultimately, this is the *path* to greatness.

Not sure if you buy into that? Well, I wouldn't either if I didn't know about Dr. Alfred Barrios.

Psychologist Dr. Alfred Barrios conducted research on the nature of genius in the seventies. He set out to answer the same basic question I posed just a page ago: why do some people rise to greatness whereas others don't?

To look for an answer, he decided to analyze the lives of many of history's greatest geniuses. Were there patterns of circumstances, events, behaviors, attitudes, or ideas that could account for their success? Did the chronicles of their lives collectively hold the secrets to their greatness? He was going to find out.

He first noted and categorized a long list of factors outside of the geniuses' control. Things like lineage, birthright, geography, genetics, education, familial ties, upbringing, and unexpected windfalls. The more data he accumulated and analyzed along this line, however, the more it looked like a dead end. The backgrounds of our species' greatest thinkers and achievers appeared infinitely varied. If there were patterns among the data, he couldn't see them.

Barrios was undeterred and continued to study. Eventually, a different kind of common denominator emerged, one that he found *within* each of the people he studied. Barrios discovered that his subjects had each developed and routinely displayed a combination of very specific characteristics throughout their lives, and not just mildly but conspicuously.

This character-driven idea fascinated Barrios. It suggested that genius is much more than high intelligence, innate talent, extraordinary work ethic, or uncanny luck, but rather a composite manifestation: a synthesis of very specific types of worldviews and behaviors. The more he looked at data through this lens, the more things started to make sense.

Barrios then wondered if anyone could operate at a genius level—and achieve genius-level greatness—simply by learning and adopting the same educated views and disciplined behaviors that so repeatedly characterized history's greatest achievers.

By the end of his research, Barrios had pieced together his "genius code"— a profound insight into what really spawns greatness. He also concluded that we could all indeed use his genius code as a roadmap to walk in the footsteps of history's brightest and boldest, thereby learning to operate at a genius level.

An attractive concept, no doubt, but is it true?

This book seeks that answer. In each chapter, we will delve into a single characteristic of Barrios' code. We will look at how these traits have defined many of history's greatest geniuses, and how we can further develop them in ourselves. My proclamation for this book is that while Barrios' research may not be the end-all on the subject, it certainly illuminates the path to greatness via a unique, accessible, and practical decoding of genius. By the end of this book, I think you'll agree.

This immediately involves us in a bigger picture question, too—one that's deeply penetrating and personal: why do we desire to heighten our genius and pursue the path of greatness?

We all face a fundamental choice in our lives. Do we take the path prescribed by our "now you're supposed to" society, or do we take our own path toward the life we feel we ought to be living? Do we choose our life's work based on the U.S. Department of Labor's list of highest-paying jobs, or do we follow our bliss? Do we heed the call to conformity, or the call to adventure?

Every day we see how people have answered these questions, whether consciously or otherwise. We're constantly confronted with the lazy, the apathetic, the immoral, the indifferent, the irresponsible, and the disconnected—the signs of a decaying culture.

"What does it all mean?" many wonder while chasing purposes they're told are worthwhile, but which feel empty. "What is the purpose of this life?" humans have wondered for millennia, contemplating how insignificant we are in the great cosmic symphony.

Well, as the preeminent mythologist Joseph Campbell said, deep down inside, we don't seek the meaning of life, but the experience of being alive. And that's what this book is ultimately about.

It's about how we can empower ourselves to bring true meaning to our lives and the lives of others in ways most people would consider impossible. It's about rising above a life of, as Thoreau said, "quiet desperation" that ends with our songs still in our hearts, and experience the rapture of truly living. It's about saying yes to our adventures.

We rely on geniuses to entertain us, educate us, lead us, and show us all what our species is capable of. We rely on geniuses to give us smart phones, electric cars, cures for diseases, social networking sites, sublime art, world-class food, and, indeed, the very fabric of our culture.

If you've ever dreamed of playing a hand in the development of humankind, or if you just have a burning desire to improve one small aspect of it, then you have an adventure waiting.

Will you take it?

This book is your invitation.

2

CURIOSITY AND THE GREATEST GENIUS WHO EVER LIVED

"The important thing is not to stop questioning. Curiosity has its own reason for existing. One cannot help but be in awe when he contemplates the mysteries of eternity, of life, of the marvelous structure of reality."

-Albert Einstein

A bored Alice sits by the riverbank, contemplating the daisies. A White Rabbit scurries by, fretting about being late, and pulls a watch from its pocket. Alice is intrigued. *A rabbit with a waistcoat and pocket watch?* She races off after it.

Filippo Brunelleschi is commissioned by the powerful Medici family to complete a construction project previously abandoned as impossible. His challenge: to complete the largest dome in the world, and thus finish what is to be the greatest cathedral in Florence, the heart of the Renaissance. Nobody has a clue how to do it, but Brunelleschi buries himself in Classical teachings and devises ingenious solutions that the world has never seen before.

"The truth is out there, Neo," Trinity whispers into his ear. "It's looking for you and it will find you, if you want it to."

Adventures are quirky, indeed.

Sometimes they flash by, giving you only a moment to jump in or forever lose their trail, as Alice experienced. Sometimes they hide in plain sight, calmly waiting for someone to try them on for size, as Brunelleschi did. Sometimes they play hard to get, forcing you to prove you're worthy, as Neo discovered.

Perhaps the most interesting quirk about adventures, however, is their reflection of the universe itself—their *indifference*.

They care nothing of morality or tradition, of what's deserved or fair. They won't judge your race, sex, age, or customs. They won't beg for attention or force your hand. And they make no promises.

They must be willfully discovered and pursued. One must be able to find their clues—their invitations—hidden throughout a world that many people consider mundane, predetermined, or hopeless. This is a rare talent, one that relies solely on *curiosity*.

Curiosity is a lens through which you view everything around you. Without it, there are no adventures to be had. With it, there are enough for a million lifetimes.

At least that's how one man looked at it, a man widely considered the greatest genius of all time...

In the first century BC, at the dawn of the Roman imperial age, the architect Marcus Vitruvius published one of the most important sources of modern knowledge of Roman building methods, planning, and design. It covers almost every aspect of Roman architecture, from town planning, to building materials, to the construction of temples, civil and domestic buildings, pavements, aqueducts, and more.

Vitruvius' publication also describes what he felt were the ideal human proportions, and that sacred temples should conform to these proportions. In fact, he believed that the human body was imbued with the hidden geometry of the universe itself, and thus was a microcosmic representation of the physical realm.

Sound a bit far-fetched to you? Probably so to most average intellectuals, but not to Leonardo da Vinci.

Over fifteen hundred years later, sometime around 1487, da Vinci drew the human figure in accordance with Vitruvius' observations, and named it the *Vitruvian Man*. He had the same particular fascination with human anatomy as Vitruvius: he believed that, in his own words, "man is a model of the world."

The answer to that enigmatic statement lies in what's known as the *divine proportion* or *golden ratio*. For over two thousand years, esteemed mathematicians and scientists have studied, pondered, and debated this ratio and its ubiquity in nature, mathematics, architecture, and art.

So, what is this ratio? Euclid first defined it in his tour de force *Elements*, published in 300 BC. The concept is simple: two quantities are in the Golden Ratio if the ratio of the sum of the quantities to the larger quantity is equal to the ratio of the larger quantity to the smaller one.

Visually, it looks like this:

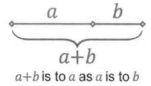

a+b is to *a* as *a* is to *b*

Now, the fascinating thing about the Golden Ratio is its plausibility as a natural law. Scientists have found its expression in the arrangement of branches along the stems of plants and in the veins of leaves, in the skeletons of animals and the disposition of their veins and nerves, and in the composition of chemical compounds and the geometry of crystals. Researchers have recently reported the ratio present even at the atomic level.

Nowhere is the Golden Ratio more exemplified than in the human body, however, as da Vinci knew so long ago. In fact, he found that the more the body reflected this proportion, the more beautiful it was.

The human face, for instance, abounds with examples of the Golden Ratio. The head forms a golden rectangle with the eyes at its midpoint. The mouth and nose are each placed at golden distances between the eyes and the bottom of the chin. The spatial relationship of the teeth and the construction of the ear each reflect the ratio too.

Further, the Golden Ratio is found in the overall proportions of the human body: the different lengths of the finger bones, the makeup of the feet and toes, and even the structure of DNA.

When da Vinci drew his masterful depiction of the ideal human body, he enclosed his man in a circle and a square, age-old symbols that represent the cosmic and the divine, and the earthly and the secular, respectively. Thus, the *Vitruvian Man* is far more than a pretty sketch—it's a statement on the fantastic order and harmony of the metaphysical and physical.

This iconic drawing was just one of da Vinci's many creations that still, centuries later, inspire awe, mystery, analysis, and debate, and that earn him wide recognition as the greatest genius to have ever lived.

Every masterpiece that da Vinci is known for has humble origins, though.

He didn't dream of fame or riches. He didn't chase approval or admiration. His motives were far nobler. Sir Kenneth Clark, one of the most accomplished art historians of the twentieth century, called da Vinci "the most relentlessly curious man in history." Da Vinci's life and greatness is best summarized by his own statement that "the noblest pleasure is the joy of understanding." He did what he did because he loved peeling back the skin of the universe to catch a glimpse of its vast inner workings. Pay or no pay, recognition or no recognition, this is just who he was.

If we are to awaken our inner genius, we must first learn da Vinci's lesson of curiosity. Let's take a closer look at him, then, and how his love of understanding weaved together the rivalrous fields of art and science with ingenuity and grace, and a flourish of the spiritual and divine.

The illegitimate son of a twenty-five-year-old gentleman, Ser Piero, and a peasant girl, Caterina, da Vinci was born on April 15, 1452 in the Tuscan hills of Vinci, in the Medici-ruled Republic of Florence.

He received an informal education in Latin and mathematics, and was exposed to Vinci's longstanding painting tradition. When he was fifteen, his father apprenticed him to the renowned Florentine workshop of Andrea del Verrochio. Here da Vinci received intensive theoretical training in the arts, and also learned a vast range of technical skills, including drafting, chemistry, metallurgy, metal working, plaster casting, leather working, mechanics, and carpentry, as well as techniques for drawing, painting, sculpting, and modeling.

Verrochio was struck by da Vinci's preternatural aptitude and focus. Thus, he chose the teenager to depict an angel in his painting, *Baptism of Christ*. According to the historian Vasari, Verrochio was so wonderstruck by the quality of da Vinci's work that he vowed to never touch a brush again. By the age of twenty, da Vinci qualified as a master in the Guild of St. Luke, a popular trade association for painters and other artists.

In 1477, da Vinci completed his tutelage under Verrochio and set out to make his mark in the world. He quickly received his first two commissions, but completed neither before leaving to work in Milan under the patronage of its duke, Ludovico il Moro.

The duke kept da Vinci busy painting, sculpting, and designing elaborate court festivals and weapons, and while his creations during this time are each lauded as masterpieces, his passion was his private studies. Driven by an unquenchable curiosity, da Vinci studied a wide variety of subjects including anatomy, zoology, geology, botany, optics, aerodynamics, civil and mechanical engineering, geometry, and architecture.

He believed that "all our knowledge has its origins in our perceptions," and thus preferred to approach science observationally, experiencing truth for himself, rather than theoretically. This philosophy led to thousands of experiments, which he would meticulously record the results of in a notebook that he would carry at all times.

There's a profound lesson here. Da Vinci wasn't content with reviewing and regurgitating the work of others. He was bold enough to view the teachings of his time—no matter how dogmatic—as springboards, not boundaries. His curiosity wasn't a robotic desire to stockpile and categorize foregone conclusions, but a dynamic energy capable of absorbing, transforming, and purifying anything it touched.

Da Vinci's anatomy studies of 1510 and 1511 are a perfect example of his uncanny ability to observe and record nature with precision, and his unwavering determination to unravel the secrets of life. Anatomy texts of his day featured long-winded, confusing descriptions of the body. Da Vinci knew that pages of puzzling text could be replaced by a mere handful of accurate drawings.

Da Vinci could think of only one way to produce the quality of drawings he envisioned: dissecting the rotting cadavers of criminals. He spent countless nights in charnel houses, surrounded by the hot, choking stench of death, "living through the night hours in the company of quartered and flayed corpses fearful to behold." He examined every bone, joint, muscle, sinew, and organ of the body in minute detail, even paying attention to nerves and capillaries. He also dissected, studied, and drew the anatomy of many animals—including cows, birds, monkeys, bears, frogs, and horses—in order to compare their structures with that of humans.

Da Vinci's anatomical drawings were nothing short of dazzling and revolutionary. They were unprecedented in scope, accuracy, and detail, and they revealed aspects of the human body that were completely unknown at the time, including the intricate inner workings of the female body and the formation of the fetus in the womb. The latter discoveries earned him the informal title of the father of embryology.

His gift to mankind was more profound than the collection of drawings, however. His work heralded the birth of a new method of scientific study that relied on close observation, repeated testing, and systematic, descriptive illustrations with brief explanatory notes. "Science is the observation of things possible, whether present or past; prescience is the knowledge of things which may come to pass, though but slowly," he wrote.

His dissections even led him to discover the relationship between the buildup of cholesterol and the onset of heart disease, but the academia refused to recognize his findings as he wasn't a formally trained physician. "I cannot quote from eminent authors as they can, these trumpeters and reciters of the works of others," he said. "I know that all knowledge is vain and full of error when it is not born of experience, and so experience will be my mistress." Da Vinci knew that the pursuit of questions is far more important in the journey to greatness than the memorization of others' answers.

The true testament to the transcendent perfection of his anatomical drawings is the fact that they're still used in medical textbooks today. Yet, incredibly, this was only a slice of his life's work and legacy.

Da Vinci believed that painting was a universal language. His curiosity and desire to paint things realistically was bold and fresh, and eventually became the standard for all Renaissance painters who followed. In his studies of light and shadow, da Vinci realized that objects are three-dimensional bodies defined by their illumination and shadowing, and from this insight he developed a highly refined technique for painting soft, detailed, lifelike figures. His curiosity also led him to discover that an object's detail and color changed as it became more distant, which helped him pioneer techniques that allowed a new level of realism in atmosphere and depth.

"A picture or representation of human figures, ought to be done in such a way as that the spectator may easily recognize, by means of their attitudes, the purpose in their minds," he wrote.

These advancements began as lighthearted curiosities, but they became much more. True to form, da Vinci's enthusiastic pursuit of his calls to adventure in painting changed the discipline forever. His works are some of the most imitated, analyzed, and discussed works of all time, and for good reason. Not only was his technique flawless and unparalleled, his paintings were rich in symbolism, and structured with mathematical precision.

The *Virgin of the Rocks* depicts a popular story of Mary and Jesus meeting an infant John the Baptist in the care of the angel Uriel, who pays homage to the Christ. The background is dominated by phallic rocks and womb-like imagery. Even the plants da Vinci chose to paint had layers of meaning: the stained St. John's wort suggested a martyr's blood, heart-shaped leaves represented love and virtue, sword-shaped leaves represented the sorrow that was to pierce Mary's heart, and palm leaves signified victory.

The Last Supper, which represents Jesus' last meal with his disciples and revelation of a traitor, was acclaimed as a masterpiece of design and characterization and is one of the most reproduced works of art in history. Historians recently discovered that the painting's proportions and layout are mathematical in nature, echoing the musical equation of 12:6:4:3, which is an octave, fifth, and fourth, respectively. Da Vinci left clues to this when he spoke of the "resonance between visual and aural harmonies" and intended to "offer praise to the harmonies of the universe."

The iconic painting is also the subject of ongoing debates regarding the meaning behind various mysterious elements, widely popularized by *The Da Vinci Code*, such as the apparent femininity of John, the disembodied hand holding a knife, the repetition of the "V" symbol representing the feminine, and others.

The Mona Lisa is arguably the most famous painting in the world. The portrait is so finely painted that, even up close, it's nearly impossible to see any brushstrokes on the canvas. For centuries, admirers have been guessing the real identity of the woman and the meaning behind her oblique smile. Scientists have recently discovered various tiny letters and numbers hidden throughout the painting, such as the letters *LV* in the right eye, the letters *CE* or *B* in the left eye, *72* or *L2* in the arch of the bridge in the background, and more. What are the meanings of these hidden codes?

Da Vinci's boundless curiosity, love of mastery, and need for patronage also led him to the worthy challenge of engineering. From his imagination poured forth scores of diagrams of "new machines" for a "new world"—machines hundreds of years ahead of their time. He drew the first ever airplane design, recently proven as capable of flight, now known as the "Da Vinci Glider"; the first concept of a helicopter; the first "automobile" in the form of a self-propelled wagon; the first system of concentrated solar power, which used concave mirrors to amplify the sun's energy and heat water—a method used in today's solar power plants; the first feasible parachute design; the first self-contained underwater breathing equipment; the first mechanical calculator; various novel musical instruments; the first concept of the hydraulic pump; and more.

His engineering curiosity didn't stop at civilian challenges. Although da Vinci detested war as "beastly," Renaissance Italy had been embroiled in it since he was a child. He won his first patronage with Ludovico by claiming that he was a military engineer capable of building all manner of fearsome weapons. He delivered on his promise by producing designs for innovative war machines and devices such as the military tank, missiles, multi-barreled guns for rapid fire, grenades, and finned mortar shells. Ironically, he withheld his underwater breathing device, believing that it would be used for "evil in war." "It vexes me greatly that having to earn my living has forced me to interrupt the work and to attend to small matters," he later wrote of such work.

As electricity was centuries away, water was seen as the ultimate source of power during the Renaissance. Da Vinci studied all forms of water—liquid, steam, and ice—and diagrammed a cornucopia of radical inventions, including a device to measure humidity, a steam-powered cannon, many varieties of waterwheels, myriad industrial machines powered by flowing water, webbed gloves to explore underwater, a life preserver to remain afloat, a form of floating snowshoes for walking on water, vessels that could travel underwater and attack and sink other ships, an "unsinkable" double-hull design for ships, and dredges for clearing harbors and channels. He even devised an intricate system of canals to revitalize Milan, which would require innovative construction machines also of his design.

Another brilliant product of his engineering curiosity was a life-sized automaton, which he built in 1495 to showcase during parties at his patron Ludovico's home. The robot, dressed in a knight's armor, could walk, stand, sit, open and close its mouth, move its head side to side, and raise its arms, and was powered by a crank. Like many of his pursuits, da Vinci built the robot to test a theory of his that the human body is, in essence, a machine whose structure and movements could be imitated with levers, pulleys, and gears (implements which, incidentally, he also pioneered the development of).

As if all of the innovations above weren't enough, da Vinci found another field to master: cartography. In 1502, at age fifty, da Vinci undertook the incredibly difficult task of mapping the town of Imola, the stronghold of the notorious son of the Pope, Cesare Borgia. There were no devices for simplifying this work—da Vinci had to personally walk the distances of every street, field, and hill, to draw his map. The result was an astonishingly precise, proportionate layout of the city, and when he presented it to Borgia to win his patronage, the powerful leader was in awe. Maps were extremely rare, and the unprecedented accuracy of da Vinci's compelled Borgia to hire him on the spot as his chief military engineer and architect.

From 1514 to 1516, da Vinci worked in Rome, undertaking various projects for the Pope. Following the death of his patron Giuliano de' Medici in March 1516, da Vinci was commissioned by Francis I, King of France, to create a mechanical lion that would walk forward and open its chest to reveal a cluster of lilies. The king was so impressed with da Vinci's work that he offered him the title of Premier Painter and Engineer and Architect of the King.

Francis was his last and most generous patron, providing him with an ample stipend, and a manor house near the royal chateau at Amboise.

Although his right hand was now paralyzed for reasons still unknown (a stroke is assumed), da Vinci spent his final years drawing and teaching. He produced studies of paintings, cats, horses, dragons, Saint Washington, the nature of water, the Deluge, and various machines.

Da Vinci died on May 2, 1519 in Clos Luce, France. In addition to his acclaimed art pieces, he left behind over thirteen thousand pages of notes and drawings, which were his daily observations, thoughts, findings, inventions, and even doodles that beautifully integrated art and natural philosophy in a way that has never been duplicated. His work was the precursor to science as we know it today, and his writings are still scoured by scientists for new discoveries and possibilities.

Hippolyte Taine, an influential French critic and historian, wrote of da Vinci, "There may not be in the world an example of another genius so universal, so incapable of fulfillment, so full of yearning for the infinite, so naturally refined, so far ahead of his own century and the following centuries."

A burning curiosity helped da Vinci become a giant of the High Renaissance, and a pioneer in just about every field of study he undertook. Such a desire to investigate the unknown is the starting point for every great undertaking in history. Your adventurous journey to genius requires a direction too. As with da Vinci, curiosity is how you'll discover it. And be open to directions you've never considered before. Paths of greatness aren't usually obvious. Da Vinci's weren't. In fact, most of history's remarkable minds followed their curiosity into uncharted waters.

The Wright Brothers started with a printing business, but a few years later, found themselves more interested in bicycles. They soon applied their fascination for engineering to the study of flight, leveraging the work of da Vinci and others. From the back room of their bicycle store in Ohio, they took on the best engineering and scientific minds in America and won the race to the skies.

Akio Morita was supposed to take over the four-hundred-year-old family sake business, but he was more interested in tinkering with electronics around the house. Morita nurtured a love for mathematics and physics, and after college, was going to pack his bags and join the faculty of the Tokyo Institute of Technology. Before he could leave, however, he read about an electronics research laboratory founded by a man named Masaru Ibuka. Morita met with

Ibuka, and they formed a company together, Tokyo Tsushin Kogyo K.K. The duo decided to rename the company for marketing purposes, and settled on a combination of the Latin word for sound—*sonus*—and a popular 1950s term for a boy, *sonny*. TTK is now known as Sony.

Don't be surprised if—or should I say *when*, really—your journey takes you in unforeseen directions and into places you never thought you'd find yourself. You never know what opportunity might beckon and, if you're interested enough in pursuing it, what it might mean for your life.

Regardless of what opportunities are out there, however, it takes *individual* interest to make anything of them. And real success requires much more than a flash of curiosity in the brainpan—it requires an enduring interest that must be renewed daily despite the long, hard work that it takes to make something of significance, and the sometimes crushing blows of setbacks, adversity, outright attacks, and many other reasons to quit.

But how does someone harness such individual interest for the long haul?

Da Vinci's most prominent trait was an overwhelming interest in the people and world around him. When studying physiognomy, the dubious art of determining personality based on facial structure and traits, he would often cruise piazzas looking for people with interesting faces. When someone caught his eye, he would follow them around for hours, sketching their face from every angle, observing their behavior and how they interacted with others.

"There are three classes of people," he wrote. "Those who see. Those who see when they are shown. Those who do not see."

Geniuses are, one for one, people who see things that others don't, and the first reason why is they're making the effort to *actually* look. They're *interested* in something outside themselves. They're so *curious* about the world around them that they just can't leave it alone. There is an opposite, however—a trait that is far more prevalent, and one that baits the trap of uninspired mediocrity.

As writer and philosopher L. Ron Hubbard once put it, "And when a person becomes terribly interesting, he has lots of problems, believe me." Of this essential difference, Hubbard further writes, "That is the chasm which is crossed by all of your celebrities, anybody who is foolish enough to become famous. He crosses over from being interested in life to being interesting. And people who are interesting are really no longer interested in life."

When you take interest and flip its polarity—when a person no longer creates and flows it outward, but only craves its warming rays from others, the adventures that come are grotesque mutations that lead to nothing but petty hostilities, jealousies, and contests of one-upmanship.

The *interesting* person goes on a date with a girl and talks about his expensive car, his Salesman of the Year Award and all his money. The *interested* person compliments his date and asks about her family, her hobbies, and her interests.

The *interesting* person goes to your brother's wedding and feels compelled to tell you how her wedding was held at a four-star resort, had three hundred guests, and one hundred doves. The *interested* person is thrilled to see family and wants to get an update of how everyone's doing.

The *interesting* person doesn't really listen to what you think or how you feel and can't wait to jump in and give his point of view. The *interested* person finds your opinion, though different from his, important and allows you to express it.

The *interesting* person hears that your business is finally making a profit and immediately tells you about how incredible his first year in business was. The *interested* person congratulates you and asks how you did it.

This problem has much larger ramifications, of course. Without curiosity and interest in something *meaningful,* no important goals can be formed. No matter our potentials, if they aren't willingly channeled to the pursuit of one knowable, worthwhile end, they diffuse. As Alexander Graham Bell said, "the sun's rays do not burn until brought to a focus."

Oscar Wilde once wrote that people have an "insatiable curiosity to know everything, except what is worth knowing." This couldn't be truer today. If you doubt me, look no further than the meteoric rise of ultimately meaningless entertainment like reality TV and commercialization of sports. A curiosity in who's going to win the next season of *Survivor*, whom Kim Kardashian is going to marry and divorce next, or who's going to lead the league in rushing is hardly the type of interest that will help you grow or improve.

We must be discerning with our interest out of necessity, as da Vinci was. We only have so much time in this life, and if we squander it on consuming and analyzing meaningless facts and baubles, we are squandering our potentialities and ultimately our destinies. Lao Tzu warned us of this when he said, "Watch your thoughts; they become words. Watch your words; they become actions. Watch your actions; they become habit. Watch your habits; they become character. Watch your character; it becomes your destiny."

There's something else to consider about curiosity and interest. The legendary composer Tchaikovsky said that "inspiration will come to those who can master their disinclination." That is, it must come from within you. Curiosity, the invitation to inspiration, can never be gifted by teachers, parents, mentors, bosses, or friends. You can be pointed, prodded, and persuaded, but in the end, you need to be willing to *create* it, *embrace* it, and *live* it every day of your life. Your adventures can only sweep you to far-flung places if you care to go.

Unsurprisingly, the ability to harness your curiosity and discover your own "White Rabbit" adventures is closely tied into another defining trait of da Vinci's: the power to observe.

"Anyone who conducts an argument by appealing to authority is not using his intelligence," da Vinci wrote. "He is just using his memory."

Unlike many of his contemporaries, da Vinci believed that the writings of the Bible and ancient Greece and Rome could only bring one so far in the pursuit of truth. While he was greatly influenced by the wisdom of his ancestors, through his work and writings, he introduced a brand new way of thinking.

Da Vinci believed that knowledge and understanding could only be advanced through actual observation, the asking of simple questions, and the systematic testing and recording of what was observed. This mindset and methodology was revolutionary in his time, and was an important milestone in our emergence from the superstition and ignorance of the Dark Ages into the rational empiricism of the scientific method.

While it might seem simplistic, the power of observation has a profound meaning and application in everyday life. What made da Vinci's brand of curiosity so unique was his insistence on accepting only what he could actually observe and experience himself, regardless of whether his findings were in line with the beliefs of his peers or not.

For example, his geometric observations and work, which included the first illustration of the highly complicated rhombicuboctahedron and other geometric shapes of significance that were later used in the development of the printing press, were shunned by academics because he lacked a formal education. Additionally, much of the intelligentsia scoffed at his description of a theory of evolution not unlike Charles Darwin's, which was developed over four centuries later, and his discovery of cholesterol and its connection to heart disease.

While the illogical rebuffs of da Vinci's work frustrated him, he never let them stifle neither his drive to know nor his drive to continue observing for himself and reporting factually what he saw. When his observations and conclusions were in contradiction with sacred cows of his time, or were even considered impossible, he didn't care. He simply continued to observe, deduce, test, and record. He knew that his enemy was not his naysayers, but time itself.

Da Vinci never set out to "fit in"—his goal was to join the small group of people in history that stretched the bounds of human knowledge entirely by the strength of their curiosity. "He who is fixed to a star does not change his mind," he wrote.

In this worldview, da Vinci teaches us a simple lesson: don't be afraid to play with the world in your head and wonder "what if?" Don't assume that there's no reason to look because everything is already known. Don't assume that there's nothing left for you to discover or add.

There's an old Christian proverb that goes like this:

Two men looked through prison bars; one saw mud and the other saw stars.

When the genius looks out to the world, she sees a vast playground of possibility and wonder, not unlike a child. This is an *exercised* ability and conscious choice, not a gift, and perhaps the genius' greatest virtue.

Sadly, in today's society, it's all too easy to spend the majority of our lives immobile in front of screens, vicariously living through pictures and sounds fed to our inert minds. The average American watches four hours of television per day. The average American youth spends more time watching television than in school, and plays about two hours of video games per day (on top of the average of four hours of television).

Our culture is making it easier and easier to disassociate from the natural itches of the mind and the real adventures of life. We're left as degenerates, little more than purposeless, visionless drones that punch buttons for paychecks and punch remotes for instant gratifications that remind us we're still alive.

"Iron rusts from disuse; stagnant water loses its purity and in cold weather becomes frozen; even so does inaction sap the vigor of the mind," da Vinci wrote.

Thankfully, no matter how far people fall from participation in life's great opportunities, no matter how miserable and uninterested they become, they can rise out of it. The human spirit is remarkably resilient. The human curiosity is fantastically eternal. With the most minor steps in the right direction, if repeated and reinforced, people can bring themselves back from the deepest depths of listlessness, desperation, and depression.

So, the first step in your journey to genius is to find the direction. Curiosity will unveil your adventure, and that requires a genuine interest in life and its many mysteries, wonders, emotions, experiences, rewards, tribulations, injustices, beauties, and imperfections.

Finding your direction is only the beginning, of course. You will then face the first test of a genius, and your choice will either bring you forward in your quest, or end it before it can even begin.

3

COURAGE AND THE CRIPPLE OF LEPANTO

"Whatever you do, you need courage. Whatever course you decide upon, there is always someone to tell you that you are wrong. There are always difficulties arising that tempt you to believe your critics are right."

-Ralph Waldo Emerson

Every great adventure begins with a call to leave the ordinary world and enter the unknown and strange.

A young Amelia Earhart visits a flying exhibition put on by a World War I ace. When he spots Earhart and her friend, looking on in a nearby field, he dives at them to give a scare. Earhart doesn't even flinch. "I did not understand it at the time," she later says, "but I believe that little red airplane said something to me as it swished by."

In junior high, Steve Jobs' friend introduces him to a computer junky named Stephen Wozniak, who shows Jobs a little computer board he's building. Jobs is fascinated, and years later, the duo forms the Apple Computer Company in Jobs' parents' garage.

Luke Skywalker snaps a metal fragment off a little droid and activates a hologram message of distress from a beautiful princess. "Help me Obi-Wan Kenobi, you're my only hope!"

Gandalf pulls a gold ring from the fire, drops it into Frodo's hand, and it begins to glow with Elvish markings that read, "One ring to rule them all, One ring to find them, One ring to bring them all, and in the darkness bind them."

The call can be accepted or refused. This is the first test in the path toward greatness.

Do you have the guts to follow, or will you shun it?

It takes courage—sometimes incredible courage—to take that first step, just as Miguel de Cervantes did.

The Spanish galley *Marquesa* was in the thick of the bloodiest front of what was known as the Battle of Lepanto, fought on October 7, 1571, in the Gulf of Patras, Greece. As far as the eye could see, smoke billowed and fires raged while over four hundred Christian and Ottoman galleys blasted, boarded, and burned each other into oblivion.

Below the *Marquesa's* decks, a young man named Miguel de Cervantes, nearly delirious with fever, rose from his bed to fight beside his countrymen, insisting that he would rather die for his God and king than hide with illness.

Cervantes was assigned with twelve men under him to a boat alongside the galley. He fought valiantly and was shot three times—twice in the chest and once in the left arm, which paralyzed his left hand. The Ottomans at large, however, suffered a devastating defeat, one that prevented them from invading Italy and moving farther into Europe.

After his wounds healed, Cervantes rejoined the Spanish navy. Three years later, in June 1575, Cervantes was granted leave to return to Spain, and had high hopes for promotion thanks to letters of commendation from Don John of Austria and the Duke of Sesa. Ironically, these auspicious letters were a double-edged sword in what was to come.

In September 1575, Cervantes set sail for Spain aboard the galley *Sol*. After two weeks of travel, the journey was nearly complete as the *Sol* approached the Spanish coast of Catalonia. It was there that a fleet of Algerian pirates ambushed the *Sol* and its two companion ships. The captain of the *Sol* and many of its crew members were killed. Cervantes evaded death again and was captured along with his brother Rodrigo and the surviving Spaniards.

The captives were taken as prisoners to Algiers and sold as slaves, with Cervantes becoming the property of a Greek pirate named Dali Mami. The letters Cervantes carried on him proved he was a man of importance and therefore worth a high ransom and deserving of special surveillance.

Undaunted, Cervantes immediately made plans for his escape. In 1576, Cervantes persuaded a Moor to guide him and other Christian captives through two hundred miles of treacherous desert to a Spanish fortress in the port of Oran.

The guide abandoned Cervantes and his friends on the road, however, leaving the fugitives stranded with no food, water, or idea of how to reach their destination. They had no choice but to return to Algiers. Cervantes was recaptured and severely beaten, but his life was spared because of his ransom value. His companions, however, weren't so fortunate: every day one of them was hung, impaled, or disfigured until all had been killed.

In the spring of 1577, two priests arrived in Algiers with three hundred crowns entrusted to them by Cervantes' parents, to be used in buying his freedom. The ransom was rejected as too low, however, and Cervantes used the money to bargain for his brother's freedom instead. The brothers had already carefully planned a second escape attempt, and Rodrigo's now imminent freedom would be instrumental in Cervantes' escape.

Later that year, in the fall, a Christian gardener helped Cervantes and fourteen other captives slip away while their master was privateering, and took them to caves on the outskirts of the city. They were to hide in these caves until a rescue party arrived, which was to be organized by Rodrigo.

Cervantes and his fellow captives hid in these caves for nearly two months before their rescue ship arrived, but, as fate would have it, nobody dared to disembark and notify the hidden men. The sailors returned the next night to an empty beach, and again nobody attempted to get Cervantes from the caves. They wouldn't return again, and wouldn't escape the treacherous waters—they were captured by the Algerians.

Things would get worse for Cervantes. A Spanish renegade who had been supplying him and the others betrayed them to the new viceroy of Algiers, Hasan Pasha—a man infamous for his cruelty to slaves. Hasan sent thirty heavily armed men to retrieve the Spaniards in hiding, and when they arrived at the caves, Cervantes insisted that he was to blame for the scheme, and that he had persuaded the others to join him.

Cervantes was taken before Hasan. Cervantes declared that he was the only culprit in the escape attempt, hoping that the other fugitives would be spared. Despite many threats of grueling torture and certain death, Cervantes wouldn't give up any names of accomplices, insisting that he alone be punished for the crime. Hasan, struck by Cervantes' courage, not only spared him torture but also bought him from his master for a tidy sum.

Hasan demanded an impossibly exorbitant ransom for Cervantes, effectively condemning the maimed Spaniard to indefinite detention. Unsurprisingly, Cervantes had other plans because, in his own words, "the hope of obtaining my freedom never deserted me."

In March 1578, Cervantes arranged for a secret letter to be delivered to the Governor of Oran, Don Martin de Cordoba, and other important people he counted among his friends. In the letter, Cervantes asked them to send spies and other trustworthy, resourceful men to help him and three other important captives escape. Don Martin was sure to listen to Cervantes' plea, as he was once a captive himself along with his father, who lost his life in the ordeal.

The Moor entrusted with the letter made it to the gates of Oran, but the letter never reached the hands of Martin. Hasan's spies stopped the messenger, found the letter suspicious, captured him, and brought him before the viceroy. Hasan had the Moor impaled and sentenced Cervantes to *two thousand strokes* across his stomach and the soles of his feet—a slow, tormenting death.

Amazingly, for reasons still not completely understood, Cervantes received no punishment for his third foiled escape attempt. And it wasn't long before he starting working on his fourth—and final—plan to break free and return home.

In September 1579, Cervantes persuaded a Spanish corsair named Giron to buy an armed frigate from a trusted Valencian merchant in Algiers. Another merchant sympathetic to Cervantes' cause advanced the money used for the purchase. Cervantes secretly spread word of the upcoming breakout to sixty other Christian captives in Algiers, inviting them to flee with him.

One month before his departure, Cervantes was betrayed yet again—this time by a Spanish monk, Juan Blanco de Paz, who was bitter at being excluded from the plan, and who hoped to gain favor with Hasan Pasha. Hasan kept his knowledge of the getaway hidden, hoping to catch the whole lot at once and appropriate them all to himself, as slaves condemned to death.

News of Paz's betrayal spread, however, and the merchant that lent the money for the frigate was sure that Hasan would extort all the particulars out of Cervantes through torture if he were caught. Fearful of losing his property, liberty, and likely his life, the merchant offered to pay Cervantes' ransom at any price and put him on a ship leaving for Spain.

Cervantes felt it would be too dishonorable to abandon his companions. He declined the offer, but promised that he would implicate nobody in the scheme, regardless of the suffering inflicted upon him—he would take the blame alone to save everyone else involved.

As the day of the escape approached, it became clear that Hasan was fully aware of the scheme. A few days after Cervantes sneaked out of his master's home, a formal proclamation was issued that anyone who harbored or helped Cervantes would be put to death. Displaying his indomitable courage once again, Cervantes turned himself in to Hasan voluntarily. Hasan was outraged; he had a noose fastened around Cervantes' neck, and threatened torment and the gallows if he didn't reveal who else was involved in the aborted escape. Cervantes remained resolute, accusing nobody but himself and declaring that he had no accomplices but four Spanish gentlemen who had recently obtained their liberty and were to sail to Spain as free men.

Hasan knew Cervantes was lying but, overcome again by Cervantes' extraordinary courage in the face of torture and death, spared his life for a second time. Although he didn't know it yet, Cervantes' magnificent generosity and grit had won him great honor among the twenty-five thousand fellow Christian captives in Algiers. Two Spaniards were foiled in an attempt to induce an insurrection on his behalf, and this intensified Hasan's fear that as long as he held Cervantes in captivity, he risked a Christian uprising that would destroy one of the most important asylums of the pirates of the Mediterranean.

In the spring of 1580, Philip II of Spain had become aware of Cervantes' meritorious military service and heroic deeds, and he dispatched two priests with instructions to ransom for captives, including Cervantes. The priests had two hundred and fifty ducats from Cervantes' family—the most they could muster—to apply toward his freedom. Hasan demanded one thousand crowns for Cervantes—an extravagant sum that was double what he had paid. Further, he would soon be leaving for Constantinople, and if he were not paid promptly, he would take Cervantes with him.

Negotiations continued to no avail and Hasan prepared to leave, placing Cervantes aboard his ship, loaded with chains. One of the priests, father Juan Gil, pitied Cervantes' plight and begged for Cervantes' freedom so earnestly that Hasan finally agreed to five hundred crowns. To raise the additional money needed, Juan borrowed it from several Christian merchants who admired Cervantes for his now-famous exploits, and drew on his church's general redemption fund.

The funds were delivered just as Hasan was casting off to sail. Cervantes paid nine doubloons to the officers of the galley as a compliment, and was permitted to go ashore as a free man—something he had so passionately pursued for five years, and that he described as "one of the greatest joys a human being can taste in this world: that of returning, after a long period of slavery, safe and sound to his native land."

And what did Cervantes do with his newfound freedom? His true love was adventure, travel, and duty to his country, so he re-enlisted in the Spanish navy. He participated in several campaigns, and used the long voyages to study diligently, driven to learn the art of poetry and prose by a deep love for a young lady from a noble Spanish family. He wrote a poem in her honor, *La Galatea*, which was his first major work, published in 1585.

For the next twenty years, Cervantes led a nomadic life as a sailor in the navy, a purchasing agent for the Spanish Armada, and a tax collector. He published the first volume of *Don Quixote* in 1605, and the second in 1615. Cervantes' literary legacy would ultimately include over twenty-five novels, short stories, plays, and poems. *Don Quixote* is one of the most influential works of fiction ever written, and Cervantes is widely considered one of the greatest writers of Western literature.

The story of Cervantes' rise to literary prominence pales in comparison to the story of the perils and hardships he overcame to even get a chance to put a pen to paper, and forever change the literary culture of the West.

There's a good reason Barrios included courage in his genius code.

Without courage, the adventure to genius and greatness can never even begin.

It takes a special strength to be willing to scrap the life that others have planned for us—safe, beaten trails walked by millions—and embrace one fraught with uncertainty, danger, and the unknown. While we may hope for paths that are clear and predictable, we quickly learn that like a night drive through the deep, dark country, our headlights can only help us see so far.

Courage is the primary catalyst in the genius code; it begins your transformation into something more.

WD-40, ANGRY BIRDS, AND THE DIRTY LITTLE SECRET OF OVERNIGHT SUCCESS

Do you know why WD-40 is called "WD-40"?

The abbreviation stands for "Water Displacement—40th Attempt."

"Who cares?" I hear you wondering.

Well, the formula that accounted for over $300 million in sales last year was successfully created only after 39 failed attempts.

Similarly, the incredibly popular game *Angry Birds* was software maker Rovio's 52nd attempt at creating a product that would make money. They eked out a living for eight years and nearly went bankrupt before creating a game that has now been downloaded over one billion times.

James Dyson endured a staggering 5,126 failed prototypes before creating his revolutionary vacuum cleaner. It took another ten years of dogged persistence before he had enough money to start the Dyson Company, which grossed over $200 million in sales last year.

Groupon almost died early on for lack of funds and interest. At the time of this writing, it's valued at $6.3 billion.

Captains of industry didn't have the undying support and encouragement of their peers when they began. At one point, most considered just about any fantastically successful person you can name an impractical, naive dreamer.

No great council decreed that Gates' vision of Microsoft was going to change the world of software forever. Nobody believed that Oprah Winfrey would amount to anything after running away from home at thirteen, following years of sexual abuse by family.

No, every great organization or cause that is around today exists because someone had the courage to unleash who they truly were, to refuse to believe they couldn't complete their journey, and to refuse to let setbacks defeat them. They tapped into their inner genius to unlock their full potential for greatness.

"Success seems to be connected with action," wrote hotelier Conrad Hilton, founder of the Hilton Hotels chain. "Successful men keep moving. They make mistakes, but they don't quit."

Maybe you'll fail ten times in your adventure. Maybe you'll fail one hundred times. But after months or years of hard work, you might just be that next story of "overnight" success that people marvel at, so long as you possess the courage to take the first step and not look back.

Without courage, the adventure to genius and greatness can never be completed.

Once the adventure begins, the stakes only get higher and higher, and more and more courage is needed to weather the storms of doubt, disbelief, and dismay. Cervantes' uncanny displays of bravery not only saved his life against all odds, they provided him with a rich, larger-than-life experience that later served as the basis of *Don Quixote*. If he had chosen a different path—if he had escaped captivity early, perhaps at the expense of his brothers in captivity—it's very possible he would've never written of the gentleman from La Mancha, and Western literature would've been robbed of one of its most influential landmarks.

Many of history's extraordinary geniuses had to overcome overwhelming obstacles and hardships to achieve greatness. They had to retain their strength of heart and faith in their convictions, proclaiming "yes!" when the world yelled "no!" They didn't care if they were criticized for their beliefs or plans. They spoke the truth as they knew it, even if it meant ostracism or worse. They weren't afraid of responsibility; rather, they embraced it. Our society advances because of their courage.

Like any hero on a great quest, as you strive to accomplish great things in life, you will face trials to test your resolve. People will try to stop you. Circumstances won't always be favorable. Sometimes all might look hopeless, and you'll really know fear. In each case, you'll have two simple choices: give up or get tough.

You will be faced with this predicament many times in your voyage, and your choices will depend solely on your guts. Are you willing to carry forward into the belly of the whale, or will you turn back?

Courage is your compass. It illuminates your path.

FROM CARTOONIST TO CULTURAL ICON

Walt Disney dropped out of high school at sixteen to enlist in the army. He was rejected due to age, of course, but decided to join the Red Cross instead of returning to school. He was sent to France to drive an ambulance and chauffeur Red Cross officials.

When he returned to Kansas City in 1919, Walt decided to pursue his dream of an artistic career. As he was a talented cartoonist, he tried to get work as a newspaper artist, but nobody would hire him. His brother Roy got him a temporary job at a local studio. When that expired, Walt decided to start his own studio with friend and fellow cartoonist Ubbe Iwerks, a venture that never got off the ground.

The Kansas City Film Ad Company hired both Walt and Iwerks to work on cutout animations. Walt fell in love with animation while working there, his head full of ideas for shorts. He soon decided that he would become an animator and opened his second company shortly after, in 1922.

Walt's cartoons quickly became popular in the Kansas City area. He used the money to hire a large number of animators and expand his business into a proper studio. Walt paid his employees handsomely, but profits couldn't cover the salaries. Financial burdens mounted. To ease the financial pressure, Walt chose to live at the office and take a bath once a week at the Kansas City Union

Station.

The Laugh-O-Gram Studio, as it was known, collapsed under debt in 1923. Walt was only twenty-one years old. Instead of resigning his dreams, he sold his movie camera to buy a one-way train ticket to join his brother Roy in Hollywood, and together open a cartoon studio. In his suitcase were Walt's only possessions: a few changes of clothes, an unfinished reel of a film for a project he was working on, and twenty dollars. But he never lost confidence in the value of his ability to create characters and stories that brought laughter and pleasure to others. This, he knew, would carry him through even the roughest times.

Walt and Roy began the Disney Brothers Studio. Iwerks and his family relocated to the area to join the duo. As their first order of business, they set out to finish Walt's series of cartoons known as the "Alice Comedies," and hired a young woman named Lillian Bounds to ink and paint the celluloid. Walt and Lillian's immediate chemistry turned to love, and they married within a year.

The Alice Comedies were completed and became a modest success, allowing Walt, Roy, and Lillian to move from Walt's uncle's garage to the back of a real estate office. In 1927, Universal Studios decided to get into the cartoon business, and they contracted Walt's studio to create a character and series that would become known as "Oswald the Lucky Rabbit."

The new cartoon was a runaway hit for Universal. People loved Walt's lighthearted, engaging style as well as Iwerks' endearing illustrations. The windfall allowed Walt to re-hire some of the talented animators that were with him at Laugh-O-Gram, and together they continued to build Oswald's popularity.

In 1928, Walt traveled to New York to negotiate a higher fee per animation for his team. Charles Mintz, Walt's distributor, not only dismissed the request, but told Walt that he would either accept a reduced fee, or lose the entire project and all of his main animators, who were secretly under contract with Mintz to form a new studio that would continue the work. Universal owned the Oswald trademark, not Walt, and the show would go on, with or without him.

Walt wouldn't give in to Mintz's bullying. Instead, Walt had a simple solution to the predicament: he would create a new character to replace and outshine Oswald. On his train ride back from New York, when his business fortunes were "at lowest ebb and disaster seemed right around the corner," an idea struck Walt. He got out his sketch pad and drew a cute, small character that would change his life, and the world of animation, forever. It was a mouse inspired by a particularly tame pet he kept at the Laugh-O-Gram Studio.

The sketches of "Mortimer Mouse," as Walt called him, were brought to Iwerks, who redesigned the character using circles to make him easier to animate. Lillian insisted that the name was too "sissified," and suggested "Mickey Mouse" instead.

Walt and Iwerks secretly began work on animating a Mickey Mouse cartoon while still under contract with Universal. The first screening of the brand new character in 1928 received a lukewarm response from the audience. Consequently, Walt couldn't find a distributor interested in picking up the cartoon. He was disappointed, but not defeated. He and Iwerks immediately began the production of the second Mickey Mouse cartoon, which also languished for lack of distribution. But then, in true fairy tale form, their third attempt at Mickey's debut was a charm.

Walt and Iwerks created a cartoon with synchronized sound called *Steamboat Willie*, and it was an instant success. *Steamboat Willie* catapulted Walt, Iwerks, and Mickey Mouse to international fame, with wide praises of cartoon ingenuity and laughs galore.

"Born of necessity, the little fellow literally freed us of immediate worry," Walt said of Mickey. "He provided the means for expanding our organization to its present dimensions and for extending the medium of cartoon animation toward new entertainment levels. He spelled production liberation for us."

Walt won an Academy Award for Mickey Mouse in 1932. His success launched what became known as the Golden Age of Animation, which included the creation of iconic characters such as Donald Duck, Goofy, and Pluto plus groundbreaking full-length animations such as *Snow White and the Seven Dwarves*—for which he won one large Oscar and seven miniatures—*Pinocchio*, *Fantasia*, *Bambi*, and *Dumbo*.

"Somehow I can't believe there are any heights that can't be scaled by a man who knows the secret of making dreams come true," Walt wrote. "This special secret, it seems to me, can be summarized in four Cs. They are Curiosity, Confidence, Courage, and Constancy and the greatest of these is Confidence. When you believe a thing, believe it all the way, implicitly and unquestionably."

Walt lost nearly everything multiple times in his life, but he never lost that which matters most: confidence in himself and in his ideas, and the courage to follow his adventure. He never gave in to the fears that lurked inside or loomed outside—fear of failure, of destitution, of the realization that his dreams were just not meant to be. He knew that fear is merely a byproduct of any courageous adventure. The word itself actually has this connotation built in.

"Fear" can be traced back to the Germanic *per*, which meant "to try, risk, come over, go through," and the Greek *piera*, which meant "trial, attempt, experience." Mark Twain said that courage is the resistance to and mastery of fear, not the absence of it. Aristotle said that courage is the mean between fear and recklessness.

Hence, you could fairly conclude that fear is a good thing. It's an indicator that tells us what we have to do. The more scared we are of what blocks our path, the more important it is that we face it, the more we can be sure that we must overcome it, and the more we can expect out of its defeat.

The only thing to really be afraid of is not trying. Wilting in the presence of fear guarantees misery. That brings the death of dreams, which is, in many ways, the death of the individual.

"A person should set his goals as early as he can and devote all his energy and talent to getting there," Walt wrote. "With enough effort, he may achieve it. Or he may find something that is even more rewarding. But in the end, no matter what the outcome, he will know he has been alive."

Spoken like a true genius.

The first act of courage taken by every genius in history was the whole-hearted acceptance of the calls to their adventure. They had the courage to rise above their fears, insecurities, and boredom to recognize who they really were and what they must do. Like Theseus' daring offer to slay the fearsome Minotaur, they voluntarily marched into the labyrinths of the world to face and conquer the unknown.

Cervantes could've ignored his call and remained below the *Marquesa's* decks. His fellow sailors even pleaded for him to do so. To join the fray, they said, would mean certain death in his condition. But he didn't care. Some part of him recognized the moment for what it was: the call to his greatness.

Likewise, Disney could've dismissed the silly cartoons he drew on his Red Cross ambulance as childish and worked on a farm or railroad instead, like his father. He easily could've given in to Charles Mintz's oppressive negotiations. But, no matter how little others believed in him, he refused to sell his desire to bring cheer to the world for an easy paycheck and a life of comfortable, anonymous mediocrity.

Looking back, Cervantes' and Walt's calls to adventure were obvious.

That's the clarity of hindsight. Foresight is far less clear. What will the invitations to *our* adventures look like? How might they manifest in our lives? Will they reveal themselves under normal circumstances?

Discovering your calls to adventure gets easier when you know their other name: *opportunities*. They're problems that need solving, challenges that need conquering, gaps that need filling. Such opportunities exist wherever you look, waiting for people to adopt and nurture them into the products, services, and art that change the world. They're flashes of insight and hints of possibility that stir in people's minds when they connect two dots in a way that nobody else did before.

You're not looking for just any problems, challenges, insights, or possibilities, though. You're looking for the ones that speak to you, even if nobody else gets it. They're the ones that you just can't resist. Invariably, those are the ones that produce the greatest rewards, both material and spiritual.

Don't be surprised if your calls to adventure scare you a bit. They should. I snuffed my call to write multiple times before I finally had the courage to accept it and face the big, bad world of publishing. But once I did, I discovered that writing and publishing is easier and more rewarding and fulfilling than I could've ever imagined.

That's me. What about you? Are you ready for *your* adventure? Have you already begun looking and listening for its call? Deep down inside, do you already know what it is?

Lao Tzu said that a journey of a thousand miles begins with a single step. Your journey begins the moment you take that first step. And as for the thousand miles ahead, who knows where it will take you or what the outcome will be? But in the end, you'll know one thing: that you've been alive.

4

IMAGINATION AND THE MAN WHO INVENTED THE 20TH CENTURY

"Facts and ideas are dead in themselves and it is the imagination that gives life to them."

-W. I. B. Beveridge

Many calls to adventure are puzzles waiting to be solved. Anyone can apply, but the price of admission is paid in imagination. As journeys unfold, new challenges arise and pressures mount. These successive tolls must too be paid in creativity and ingenuity, as they were by history's most imaginative minds.

The only way that Jason can claim his rightful place as ruler of Iolcus, Greece is by retrieving the fabled Golden Fleece from distant lands. The problem? Everyone considers the task impossible, fraught with terrifying perils certain to kill any man. Jason isn't so sure. He assembles a mighty team of warriors—the Argonauts—and builds the largest ship ever constructed. He then figures out how to successfully navigate the legendary maze of crushing rocks known as the Symplegades, yoke fire-breathing, bronze-hoofed oxen, trick a mighty army guarding the Fleece into ravaging itself to pieces, and drug a sleepless dragon into its first slumber. Four months after departing, Jason returns with the Fleece to take his throne.

It's the late 1800s. Anesthesia has just been introduced. Surgeries are on the rise, but a disturbing number of patients are dying due to infection. Joseph Lister is determined to figure out why and what can be done about it. After much research and thought, he concludes that Pasteur's controversial germ theory holds the key to the mystery. Killing germs in wounds with heat isn't an option, however—a completely new method is required. Lister surmises that there may be a chemical solution, and later that year, he reads in a newspaper that the treatment of sewage with a chemical called carbolic acid reduced the incidence of disease among the people and cattle of a nearby small English town. Lister follows the lead and, in 1865, develops a successful method of applying carbolic acid to wounds to prevent infection. He continues to work along this line and establishes antisepsis as a basic principle of surgery. Thanks to his discoveries and innovations, amputations become less frequent, deaths due to infection plummet, and new surgeries previously considered impossible are being routinely planned and executed.

Andrew Carnegie is thirteen years old and changing spools of thread in a cotton mill twelve hours per day, six days per week. Two years later, he gets a job as a telegraph messenger for $2.50 per week, and he's determined to advance through the company's ranks despite his age. He quickly learns to distinguish the different sounds of incoming telegraph signals, and then learns to translate them by ear. Within a year, he's promoted as an operator. By the time he's in his mid-twenties, he's made a small fortune through shrewd investments in railroad-related industries, and he's working to repair and re-open rail and telegraph lines vital to the Union's war efforts against the Confederacy. The war impresses upon him the importance of manufacturing to the overall success of the American economy, which informs his shift of capital and interest to ironworking. Over the next thirty years, Carnegie's innovations set the standard for cheap, efficient, and profitable mass production of steel, achievements that forge the most extensive iron and steel operations ever owned by an individual in the United States.

The philosopher Edmund Burke said "there is a boundary to men's passions when they act from feelings; but none when they are under the influence of imagination." Imagination is the life force of the genius code. This force amplifies and colors every other piece of the code, and unlocks our potential for understanding and ability. It's no coincidence that geniuses not only dare to dream of the impossible for their work, but do the same for their lives. They're audacious enough to think that they're not just an ordinary player.

Few stories better illustrate this better than the life of the father of the modern world, a man of legendary imaginative power and wonder.

Nikola Tesla strolled through the Varosliget city park of Budapest with a friend, reciting Goethe's *Faust*, unaware that he was about to change the course of history.

The year was 1882. Only two years earlier, Edison had patented a system for electricity distribution using direct current generators, which produced a flow of electricity in one direction. Edison's breakthrough was a modern miracle despite having serious limitations. Namely, the generators had no efficient way to change the voltage of direct current circuits, so generation plants could only serve customers within a two-mile radius. Thus, it was unlikely that this form of electricity would ever be available in non-metropolitan areas.

Telsa was admiring the prismatic rays of the Hungarian sunset when a vision struck him. Following a blinding flash of light, he saw the complete workings of a motor that used a rotating magnetic field to produce an electric current that alternated its direction many times per second. He grabbed a stick and diagrammed the motor in the sand while his friend watched, unsure of what to think. After all, such a machine was theoretically impossible. In fact, seven years earlier, his professor at a college in Austria ridiculed him for suggesting that direct current generators could be modified to produce an efficient alternating current. Telsa dropped out of college a year later, but his imagination never quit.

Shortly after his Varosliget park revelation, Tesla took the first step to make it a reality: he relocated to Paris to work for the *Continental Edison Company* installing lighting systems in commercial properties. His passion, however, was designing improvements to the equipment brought overseas from Edison's ideas. If he could catch the attention of his superiors with his work, there was a chance he could present his revolutionary motor and win funding and support. Tesla's aptitude for electrical engineering was quickly noticed, and several ideas of his were implemented to improve Edison's direct current dynamos.

A year later, Tesla was in Strasbourg, France to repair a railway lighting system. He made the necessary repairs, but that wasn't all he did. He built the first prototype of his visionary alternating current motor, which worked exactly as he had conceived it in his mind. His own miracle in-hand, Tesla immediately courted investors for his radical device. One by one, wealthy businessmen that couldn't understand the device and didn't see the commercial value in it rejected him. Tesla was undaunted. He concluded that the only way he could realize his motor was to meet the world's greatest electrical engineer, Thomas Edison, directly.

There's a lesson here. In every field of human endeavor, the more visionary the work, the less likely it is to be quickly understood and embraced by lesser minds. For one reason or another, many people just "don't get it." Tesla took this in stride. As he saw it, he was offering an opportunity not only make an untold fortune, but to change the world forever. Instead of wasting time trying to convince ignorant naysayers to see the forest for the trees, Tesla chose to take his work to another extraordinary mind who would, he assumed, immediately recognize it for what it was.

Later that month, Tesla arrived at the Strasbourg railway station to travel to the harbor and board the ocean liner *Saturnia*, which would take him to New York City—to Edison. His uncles had given him some money, and his boss had given him a letter of recommendation that read, "I know two great men and you are one of them; the other is this young man."

After almost missing his train, losing all his money along with his ticket, passport, and luggage, Tesla still managed to make it aboard the steamship. A mutiny broke out during the voyage, and he got caught in the middle of a battle royale between crewmates. Tesla was arrested, pleaded innocence, and was released, and finally arrived at New York City on June 6, 1884. He had nothing but a few cents in his pocket, a few poems, calculations for a flying machine he dreamed of building one day, and the letter of recommendation. He went straight to meet his hero, Edison, and was starstruck. He briefly described the engineering work he had done for Edison's company, and talked about his plans for an alternating current motor.

Direct current was barely a decade old when Tesla shook hands with Edison. His distribution network in Manhattan was not only immensely profitable, but it was the only option if you wanted electricity. So, when Tesla explained that alternating current would be the future of electricity, Edison dismissed it as fanciful and unnecessary. Direct current was getting the job done, people liked it, and it was making Edison and his financier, J.P. Morgan, exorbitant sums of money. In Edison's eyes, anything that challenged it was seen not as a praiseworthy advancement of science and industry, but a threat.

Despite his monopolistic perspective, Edison liked Tesla and hired him on the spot to work with his electrical engineers. Tesla's work began with simple tasks such as repairing lighting systems, but within several months, he was one of Edison's most valuable engineers, and was solving some of the company's most difficult problems. Edison referred to him as a "damn good man."

In 1885, Tesla informed Edison that he could greatly improve his direct current generators by redesigning key elements. Edison thought it impossible and promised Tesla $50,000 if he could deliver on his claims. Tesla worked tirelessly for the better part of a year to improve the generators, installing parts of his own design. Once completed, his generators were a vast improvement over Edison's. They were far more efficient and durable, and thus far more profitable. Edison was thoroughly impressed, but when Tesla asked to be paid, Edison laughed and claimed he was only joking about the reward.

"Tesla, you don't understand our American humor," he said. Instead, Edison offered Tesla a raise of $10 more per week, to be added to his current salary of $18 per week. Tesla was disgusted and immediately resigned. This was the beginning of a lifelong feud between these two great inventors—one that Edison would later lament as his "greatest mistake."

Betrayed by men he trusted, Tesla found himself unemployed and in desperate need of work to survive. Ironically, he took a job as a ditch digger for an Edison company, and was paid $2 per day. He described this time as one of "terrible headaches and bitter tears," a dark period so grim that he began to question the value of his education and knowledge. Despite his heartbreak, he continued to expand on his designs for an alternating current system of generators, motors, and transformers, but lacked the money to build prototypes and apply for patents.

Word slowly spread among Manhattan's elite that a man of incomparable genius was digging ditches to survive. Sensing an opportunity, a band of wealthy investors eventually approached Tesla to develop an improved system of arc lighting. Although it wasn't the ideal opportunity for Telsa, it beat shoveling dirt. Plus, the group was willing to finance the Tesla Electric Company, so Tesla agreed. As the proud owner of a new company, he immersed himself in the venture and developed a unique arc lamp of beautiful design and efficiency.

Once the company became profitable, Tesla realized that he had been swindled. The vast majority of the earnings were going to the investors, and when he tried to interest them in financing his alternating current motor, they not only rejected his ideas but also ejected him from the company. Tesla was again dejected, unemployed, and broke. But his luck was about to change.

Two men approached Tesla—Alfred Brown, director of Western Union, and Charles Peck, a New York City attorney—in 1887 to learn more about his alternating current theories and designs. Tesla passionately described how the entire system would work, from generation to transmission. The men were impressed and agreed to invest in the project. They set up Telsa with a small laboratory close to Edison's office, where he quickly developed all the necessary components for the system.

"The motors I built there," Tesla later said, "were exactly as I imagined them. I made no attempt to improve the design, but merely reproduced the pictures as they appeared to my vision and the operation was always as expected."

In November 1887, Tesla filed for seven U.S. patents for his inventions, which were so original that they were issued without challenge. These patents comprised a complete system of generators, transformers, transmission lines, motors, and lighting. They would become the most valuable patents since the telephone. In accordance with their agreement, Tesla split the ownership of the patents on a fifty-fifty basis with his investors.

Tesla had won the battle to produce his revolutionary alternating current motors, but the war was far from over.

Word of the extraordinary patents reached the academic world. Tesla was soon invited to lecture before the American Institute of Electrical Engineers. His presentations were lauded as visionary, breakthrough, and incredibly practical. Engineers around the world were abuzz, and this caught the attention of business magnate George Westinghouse, the inventor of railroad air brakes. He had a dream of providing electricity throughout the entire United States, and he believed that alternating current was the future of electrical generation and long-distance transmission.

Westinghouse visited Tesla's lab and made an offer for his patents: $25,000 in cash, $50,000 in stock in his company, and a royalty of $2.50 per horsepower of alternating current motors sold. The terms were more than acceptable—if his motors were going to be as successful as he and Westinghouse envisioned, the royalties alone would make him one of the richest men in the world.

Tesla happily accepted, spent half of his cash payment to construct a new lab, and oversaw the building and installation of alternating current systems across the country. He also immediately began research into what he termed "radiant energy." His studies led him to discover what we now know as X-rays, and how to use them to produce radiographs. He didn't make his discoveries widely known, however, which is why they would later be attributed to German physicist Wilhelm Röntgen. X-rays were the first of several groundbreaking discoveries of Tesla's that would wind up misattributed to others.

Tesla was never one to chase recognition—he was after the pure thrill of discovery and creation. His imagination was a factory with unlimited resources, and the world an exciting playground with unlimited possibilities. He was excited to see men like Röntgen pioneer new fields of understanding, and was happy that his work contributed to the rise of other great men.

With Tesla's electrical revolution poised to redefine the world of industrial development, Edison and Morgan launched a full-scale propaganda assault against alternating current. Edison knew that direct current would have to stamp out alternating current to survive. More personally, he was heavily invested both financially and emotionally in his direct current network of generators and distribution lines.

Edison declared publicly that alternating current delivered to a home would kill a customer within six months. Leaflets about the dangers of alternating current were distributed. Lobbying efforts were made in New York to limit levels of electricity to 800 volts "as a matter of public safety," which would conveniently make long-distance alternating current transmission impossible.

Edison's efforts then took a turn for the grisly. He began holding weekend demonstrations of the hazards of Tesla's work by electrocuting animals found roaming the streets. He directed two technicians to do the same, including the execution of cattle and horses. The morbid campaign climaxed in 1890 with Edison's involvement in the use of a Westinghouse generator to execute a convicted ax-murderer. The voltage to kill had been misjudged, leaving the criminal badly injured, and the process had to be repeated. A journalist described the event as an "awful spectacle, far worse than hanging." The torturous method of execution was dubbed "Westinghousing," and Morgan and Edison tried to popularize the term in the media.

Disgusted by Edison's shameless cruelty and dishonesty, Tesla began performing regular exhibitions of his technology in his laboratory in which he lighted lamps by allowing alternating current electricity to flow through his body. Public opinion swung to and fro, unsure of whom to believe.

In this we can see the necessity of being willing to fight for your creations. Morgan and Edison weren't satisfied with trying to ruin Tesla through capitalistic competition—they were resorting to outright depravity and dishonesty. Imagine the pressure Tesla faced: both the world's most powerful financier—one of the last enemies you'd want—and the world's greatest inventor were trying to draw a bead on him and pull the trigger. Most men would've quietly resigned, or begged for scraps, but not Tesla.

Ultimately, no amount of opposition could stifle Tesla's creative powers. Enthused by his discoveries with X-rays, he devoted his energies to the realm of high-frequency electricity. Two decades earlier, James Clerk Maxwell had proven mathematically that light was electromagnetic radiation—electricity that was vibrating at an extremely high frequency. In 1888, Heinrich Hertz had confirmed that an electric spark emits electromagnetic waves. Tesla knew that this unexplored territory would yield astounding inventions—lights could glow brighter, energy could be transmitted more efficiently and even pass through the body harmlessly.

The first milestone in this new research was Tesla's invention of what became known as the "Tesla coil." It was a device that took normal sixty-cycle-per-second alternating current electricity and stepped it up to an ultra-high frequency of hundreds-of-thousands of cycles per second, and extremely high voltages. Tesla used his coil to invent the first high-efficiency, high-frequency fluorescent lamp. This discovery pales in comparison to what he uncovered next, however.

In 1891, in his New York City lab, Tesla proved that energy could be transmitted through the air by wirelessly lighting lamps. This discovery fascinated Tesla, sparking his lifelong obsession with wireless energy. He immediately envisioned a network of transmission stations that would provide free, wireless energy to not only the United States, but the world.

His coils helped him discover yet another phenomenon that would change the world: radio waves. When Tesla tuned two coils to resonate at the same frequency, he found that he could send and receive signals. He had accidentally built the first radio transmitter and made the first transmissions, methods he would patent within two years.

Tesla's continued research in the field of ultra-high-frequency energy led him to conclude that it was only a matter of time until science would discover a veritable source of inexhaustible, free energy—a way to attach machinery to "the very wheelwork of nature."

While Tesla had begun envisioning the dawn of an electrical era of unimaginable sophistication, he and Westinghouse still had to prove that alternating current was a worthy heir to direct current's throne. The "War of the Currents" was at a fever pitch. Edison's gruesome stunts and vigorous propaganda campaign were driving wave after wave of negative press, but alternating current won an opportunity to once and for all prove its value.

The Westinghouse Corporation won a bid for illuminating the 1893 Chicago World's Fair, which was to be the first all-electric fair in history. The fair was also to be a celebration of the 400-year anniversary of Columbus' discovery of America. Because of the efficiency of Tesla's inventions, Westinghouse's proposal was half of what Edison's newly formed General Electric company required for the job. Edison was furious that he lost the bid, and forbade the use of his light bulbs in the fair. Westinghouse would use Tesla's fluorescent bulbs instead, and Tesla even had the idea to bend the glass tubes and thus spell the names of famous scientists. Thus, the world's first neon signs.

On the evening of May 1, 1893, over 27 million people anxiously awaited to see the future of electricity. When President Grover Cleveland pushed a button, over 100,000 lamps, wired to 12 new thousand-horsepower alternating current generators, turned night to day. Attendees looked on in awe, dubbing the wonder the "City of Light."

During the fair, Tesla amazed the millions of fairgoers by allowing electricity to flow through his body to illuminate light bulbs. He also used his coils to shoot large, harmless lightning bolts into the crowd, frightening and delighting the audience. He even demonstrated wireless energy by lighting lamps that had no wires.

Within a week, the entire nation was raving about alternating current as the future of electricity. The fair was a debilitating blow to Edison's direct current, and foreshadowed the coup de grâce in the War of the Currents.

Westinghouse was contacted late in 1893 by the Niagara Falls Commission, which had been charged with developing a power plant that would harness the force of the falls. The commission had solicited and rejected proposals from around the world, reviewing schemes that ranged from using pneumatic pressure to constructing bizarre devices of ropes, springs, and pulleys. Lord Kelvin, the famous British physicist, headed the commission and, after inspecting Tesla's work, was certain that the falls needed to produce alternating current electricity.

It was a dream project for Tesla, and Westinghouse was awarded the contract. Construction began immediately, and Tesla would oversee it. Progress was slow. The project was perilous and fraught with setbacks, doubts, and financial crises, despite having the backing of opulent financiers like J.P. Morgan, Lord Rothschild, John Jacob Astor, and W.K. Vanderbilt. After five years, the venture approached completion, but the investors were less than optimistic that the unproven and expensive machines would work. Tesla, however, assured them that they would work just as they did in his mind.

A year later, the Niagara power plant was ready for operation. When the switch was thrown, all worries and anxieties melted. The first power reached Buffalo at midnight November 16, 1896, nearly 22 miles away. Plans were immediately set in motion to power all of New York City with the station. Tesla was praised worldwide as a hero, and was referred to as the "Wizard of the West."

Morgan, who controlled Edison's direct current patents, was now fully convinced that alternating current had defeated Edison's work. He approached

Westinghouse to strike a deal. Morgan didn't care what kind of electricity was used in the world, as long as he controlled it.

One of Morgan's managers, Charles Coffin, gloated to Westinghouse about how easily Morgan had established Edison's monopoly by bribing local politicians and installing systems that are too expensive to change. The same could be done for Westinghouse and alternating current, Coffin claimed. Westinghouse rebuffed Morgan's offers and made it clear that their styles of business weren't compatible.

Morgan retaliated with a strategy that would become one of his hallmarks. He spread rumors to Wall Street that Westinghouse's company was financially unstable, which dissuaded investors from giving Westinghouse the capital that he needed to expand the production and installation of his alternating current generators. Morgan then began an attack through stock manipulation, and moved to gain control of The Westinghouse Corporation, and thus Tesla's patents.

By the end of 1897, Westinghouse was nearly bankrupt, and it looked as though Morgan would usurp everything that Tesla and Westinghouse had built together. Westinghouse owed Tesla over $1 million in royalties, an amount that grew daily. When Westinghouse described to Tesla the desperate situation, Tesla replied with the following:

"Mr. Westinghouse, you have been my friend, you believed in me when others had no faith; you were brave enough to go ahead when others lacked courage; you supported me when even your own engineers lacked vision. … Here is your contract, and here is my contract. I will tear them both to pieces, and you will no longer have any troubles from my royalties."

In time, these royalties would've made Tesla the world's first billionaire. Instead, they enabled Westinghouse to save his company. Tesla's selflessness was a testament not only to his generosity and goodwill, but his belief in his ability to continue to create his future. He was certain that his best work still lay ahead of him, and that he would soon invent machines that would dwarf everything that he had accomplished thus far.

This is the beauty of imagination. An unexpected dead end in one journey is merely an opportunity to set a new course for another. Losing what we have can only do us real harm when we feel we can't create it, or something equally valuable or compelling, again, and that ability resides squarely in our imagination.

"There is something within me that might be illusion as it is often case with young delighted people, but if I would be fortunate to achieve some of my ideals, it would be on the behalf of the whole of humanity," Tesla wrote.

Tesla's imagination inspired him to focus a large portion of his efforts on radio, high-frequency electricity, and radiation. He formulated principles that led to the discovery of cosmic rays, and invented an "electric igniter," or spark plug, for internal combustion engines.

In 1898, Tesla announced his latest invention: a way to remotely control machines with radio technology. Skepticism was widely expressed and quickly diffused thanks to his Madison Square Garden demonstration of remotely driving a small metal boat through an indoor pond. Many spectators believed that he was somehow controlling the boat with his mind.

The brand new use of radio technology could be used for many things, Tesla said. He envisioned one or several operators directing scores of vessels or machines through radio transmitters and receivers tuned to different frequencies. When a *New York Times* writer suggested that Tesla's discovery could be used in war to create a remote-controlled torpedo, Tesla quickly refuted him, "You do not see there a wireless torpedo, you see there the first of a race of robots, mechanical men which will do the laborious work of the human race."

In his new Manhattan lab, funded meagerly by friends, Tesla's wondrous imagination led him to research the resonant frequencies of the earth. He mistakenly caused an earthquake that engulfed the surrounding city blocks, breaking windows and shaking the plaster off of the walls. He announced that he had discovered how to turn the earth into a giant tuning fork, and that, in theory, the principles could shatter the Empire State Building or even possibly cause the earth to "split open like an apple."

Tesla then suspected that the upper atmosphere of the planet could be used to transmit electrical power great distances due to thinner, more conductive air. He decided that to fully explore these possibilities, he would need to establish a lab in relative seclusion so as to not endanger neighboring buildings and people.

With money from his friend and patent lawyer, Leonard Curtis, and magnate John Jacob Astor, Tesla and several assistants moved to Colorado Springs and began building a new experimental research station. He told local reporters that he intended to send a radio signal to Paris, but provided no details.

While his lab was under construction, Tesla studied the phenomenon of lightning, and made what he considered his most important discovery to date. He found that the earth was "literally alive with electrical vibrations," and that the entire planet can be "thrown into vibration like a tuning fork." Tesla was absolutely certain that this phenomenon could be used to transmit unlimited electrical power and telecommunication signals anywhere in the world with virtually no signal loss or degradation.

"When the great truth accidentally revealed and experimentally confirmed is fully recognized, that this planet, with all its appalling immensity, is to electric currents virtually no more than a small metal ball and that by this fact many possibilities, each baffling imagination and of incalculable consequence, are rendered absolutely sure of accomplishment," he wrote.

Once completed, his new lab's most prominent feature was a wooden tower that stood over 80 feet tall and supported a 142-foot metal mast that was capped by a large copper ball. Inside the tower was the world's largest Tesla Coil, which was to be used to send powerful electrical surges into the earth.

To further test his theory of the conductivity of the earth, Tesla needed to create electrical effects on the scale of lightning. The result was the creation of the world's largest man-made lightning bolts, which shot out from his tower over 100 feet into the air, and which blew out the generator of the local power company. The experiment was a resounding success for Tesla; his lightning "flashed a current around the globe," proving that he could indeed deliver power to any point on the surface of the planet.

For the next nine months, Tesla conducted a wide variety of experiments at Colorado Springs. He wirelessly lit over 200 lamps from a distance of over 25 miles, proving that electricity could be transmitted great distances through the air. Through the transmission of ultra-low-frequency signals through the space between the surface of the earth and the ionosphere, he calculated that the resonant frequency of this area was approximately eight hertz—a discovery that was dismissed in his time but confirmed nearly 50 years later. His research indicated that if he could send a charged beam of electricity about 50 miles into the sky—into the ionosphere—that it could be carried around the world and drawn upon for power.

While working late one night, Tesla noticed that his powerful radio receiver was picking up a strange, rhythmic signal for which he had no explanation. One thing was certain: the pulses were not of natural origin. He concluded that they must be communications from the stars. When he revealed this incident, he was widely ridiculed for suggesting such "nonsense."

After Tesla left Colorado Springs in January 1900 to return to New York City, he wrote a sensational article for *Century Magazine* in which he eagerly described his plans for a future where we could tap the sun's energy, control the weather with electricity, end war with machines that would make it an impossibility, wirelessly transmit power and radio signals around the entire globe, engage in interplanetary communications, and even construct robotic "automatons" that would conduct themselves independent of operators. To many readers, this vision was almost incomprehensible, but Tesla was fully convinced that it all—and more—could be accomplished, and that he knew how.

The article caught the attention of J.P. Morgan, who called on Tesla. Tesla met with Morgan and explained that he could build a "world system" of wireless communications to relay telephone signals, news, private messages, secure military communications, and even pictures to any point in the world. "When wireless is fully applied the earth will be converted into a huge brain, capable of response in every one of its parts," Tesla promised.

Morgan offered to fund the construction of the power plant and transmission tower necessary to pursue Tesla's fantastical claims. One would think that Tesla would balk at any offerings of Morgan's as he clearly couldn't be trusted—he was one of the driving forces behind the propaganda used against Tesla in the War of the Currents. And just three years earlier, Morgan maneuvered to steal Westinghouse's company, costing Tesla his lucrative royalty agreement. Nevertheless, Tesla chose to partner with Morgan, a decision that would prove to be the biggest mistake of his life.

Tesla calculated that he would need about $1 million to construct the power station and transmission equipment. Morgan offered $150,000 instead and, in exchange, wanted 51% ownership in all of Tesla's existing and future patents and inventions relating to both electric lighting and wireless telegraphy or telephony. Tesla accepted Morgan's hard-fisted terms and went to work immediately.

Tesla acquired 200 acres on the cliffs of Long Island Sound and, in December 1901, began construction on the project. The most prominent feature of the installation would be a 187-foot tower capped by a 55-ton steel sphere housing a massive Tesla Coil. Beneath the tower was to be a shaft that would plunge 120 feet into the ground. Sixteen iron rods would be driven over 300 feet deeper for sending electrical currents deep into the earth. "It is necessary for the machine to get a grip of the earth, otherwise it cannot shake the earth," Tesla said. "It has to have a grip ... so that the whole of this globe can quiver."

Construction of the Wardenclyffe Tower, as it became known, was slow and expensive. Delays in receiving equipment plagued Tesla due to the complicated and unusual nature of his designs. In 1903, the tower structure was nearly complete, and the transmitter was operational. As testing began, residents in the area reported seeing "all sorts of lightning" flashing from the tower's poles, filling the air with "blinding streaks of electricity which seemed to shoot off into the darkness on some mysterious errand."

"As soon as it is completed, it will be possible for a business man in New York to dictate instructions, and have them instantly appear in type at his office in London or elsewhere," Tesla explained in an interview. "He will be able to call up, from his desk, and talk to any telephone subscriber on the globe, without any change whatever in the existing equipment. An inexpensive instrument, not bigger than a watch, will enable its bearer to hear anywhere, on sea or land, music or song, the speech of a political leader, the address of an eminent man of science, or the sermon of an eloquent clergyman, delivered in some other place, however distant. In the same manner any picture, character, drawing, or print can be transferred from one to another place. Millions of such instruments can be operated from but one plant of this kind. More important than all of this, however, will be the transmission of power, without wires, which will be shown on a scale large enough to carry conviction."

Last-minute design changes were required, however, necessitating more money. Tesla had already obtained a second loan from Morgan, and when those funds ran out, he again approached the financier for additional capital. In an attempt to convince the powerful Morgan to invest another large sum, Tesla explained that the tower could be used for more than transmitting radio signals—it could be used to saturate the entire globe with electricity harmless to living things so that everyone could obtain usable power by simply sticking wires in the soil.

Morgan considered Tesla's words carefully and coldly replied, "If anyone can draw on the power, where do we put the meter?" He refused Tesla's pleadings for more money, forcing Tesla to use his own funds, which he knew to be insufficient to complete the project. Undaunted, Tesla approached other potential investors, including John Jacob Astor, but nobody was interested in picking up a project abandoned, and now condemned, by the most powerful man in America. Despite his continued efforts, Tesla watched in horror as his Wardenclyffe dream began to fade.

Only months later, in 1904, the U.S. Patent Office stripped Tesla of his radio patents and awarded them to the Italian inventor Guglielmo Marconi, instead. Marconi had used radio technology pioneered by Tesla 11 years earlier to transmit the letter "s" in morse code over 2,000 miles, which gave him no claim to the patents, of course. What did give him claim, though? He had the financial backing of Morgan, Edison, and steel baron Andrew Carnegie, all of whom held sway in every level of government.

By 1905, Tesla ran out of money and was forced to lay off the Wardenclyffe workers and shut down the facility. Newspapers decried it as his "million dollar folly," to which Tesla responded, "It is a simple feat of scientific electrical engineering, only expensive ... blind, faint-hearted doubting world."

His malaise couldn't snuff his imagination and love of his work, however. He refocused his efforts on commercially viable machinery and—in 1906, on his 50th birthday—presented a 200-horsepower bladeless turbine engine to the world. He was also contracted by the Waltham Watch Company to build the world's first and only air-friction speedometer, which he patented.

Marconi was awarded a Nobel Prize in 1911 for his "achievements" in radio, and was hailed as the "father of radio." Tesla was infuriated and, in 1915, sued Marconi for infringement on his patents. He didn't have the money to take on the flush Marconi, however, and the suit was dismissed. In the same year, it was announced that Tesla and Edison were potential laureates to share the Nobel Prize of 1915. Both men refused to accept the award together, or separately if the other were to receive it first.

A year later, Tesla was forced to declare bankruptcy due to back taxes owed, inciting the media to disparage him as a penniless wizard. Humiliated and defeated, Tesla began to spend more time visiting the New York City parks, rescuing injured pigeons and nursing them back to health in his hotel room at the Hotel New Yorker, where he lived. This fueled rumors that he had lost his mind, and that nothing more would come from his extraordinary genius. They were wrong.

The *New York Herald Tribune* ran a story on October 15, 1911 called "Tesla's New Monarch of Machines." In it, Tesla proclaimed that he was working on a flying machine that "will have neither wings or propellers" or any on-board source of fuel, and that would resemble a gas stove in shape. Using the gyroscopic action of an engine that Tesla had built, and assisted by devices that he was "not prepared to talk about," the machine would be able to "move through the air in any direction with perfect safety, higher speeds than have yet been reached, regardless of weather and oblivious of 'holes' in the air." Further, it would be able to "remain absolutely stationary in the air, even in a wind, for great length of time."

Allis Chalmers, an American manufacturing company, and the railway and lighting division of the Westinghouse Company contracted Tesla to build his flying machine, but the project never began for unknown reasons.

After the outbreak of World War I, in 1917, the U.S. government was looking for a way to detect German U-boats and put Edison in charge of finding a workable method. It was Tesla, however, that proposed the use of radio waves to detect the ships—the first description of radar. Edison rejected the idea as ludicrous, and the world had to wait nearly two decades before Emile Girardeau would develop an obstacle-locating radio device "conceived according to the principles stated by Tesla," as he put it.

Tesla spent the 1920s working as an engineering consultant, regularly finding himself at odds with his employers due to the "impractical nature" of his plans and designs. In 1928, at the age of 72, he received his last patent, "Apparatus For Aerial Transportation." This was an ingeniously designed flying machine that was a hybrid of a helicopter and airplane. The vehicle would weigh 800 pounds, ascend vertically, and then rotate its engines to fly like an airplane. This was the predecessor of what we now know as the tiltrotor, or VS-TOL (Vertical Short Takeoff and Landing) plane. Unfortunately, Tesla lacked the funds to build a prototype.

TIME Magazine featured Tesla on its cover for his 75th birthday, in 1931, and Einstein praised him as "an eminent pioneer in the realm of high frequency currents." Later that year, Tesla announced that he was on the verge of discovering an entirely new source of energy, and when the press asked him to describe it, his reply was, "The idea first came upon me as a tremendous shock... I can only say at this time that it will come from an entirely new and unsuspected source."

The following year, the Pierce-Arrow automobile manufacturer and George Westinghouse commissioned Tesla to develop an electric motor to power a car. The motor he built measured a mere 40 inches long and 30 inches across, and produced about 80 horsepower. Under the hood was the engine: a small, 12-volt storage battery and two thick wires that went from the motor to the dashboard.

Tesla connected the wires to a small black box, which he had built the week before with components he bought from a local radio shop. "We now have power," he said. This mysterious device was used to rigorously test the car for eight days, reaching speeds of 90 mph. He let nobody inspect the box, and cryptically said that it taps into a "mysterious radiation which comes out of the aether," and that the energy is available in "limitless quantities." The public responded superstitiously with charges of "black magic" and alliances with sinister forces of the universe. Affronted, he took his black box back with him to New York City and spoke nothing further of it.

Meanwhile, Europe was again marching toward war. Tesla had long dreamed of a way to make war technologically impossible. On July, 11 1934, the *New York Times* ran a front-page headline that read, "TESLA, AT 78, BARES NEW 'DEATH BEAM,'" and described a new "teleforce" invention that would send "concentrated beams of particles through the free air, of such tremendous energy that they will bring down a fleet of 10,000 enemy airplanes at a distance of 250 miles…" Tesla said that war would be unfeasible when every country had his "invisible Chinese wall."

The announcement generated considerable controversy, and Tesla was widely criticized as a "mad scientist" whose sanity was slipping. Undaunted, he approached J.P. Morgan Jr. in search of funding for a prototype, but unsurprisingly, Morgan Jr. wasn't interested. Rumors spread that Tesla had interested the Prime Minister of Great Britain, Neville Chamberlain, but this prospect evaporated when Chamberlain resigned from his position.

Frustrated by the lack of interest in his "super weapon to end all war," Tesla sent detailed schematics to a number of Allied nations, including the United States, Canada, England, France, and the Soviet Union. None were willing to make the investment required to build the device, but two years later, one stage of the plan was tested by the USSR. They sent Tesla a check for $25,000, gave little details of their experiment, and communicated nothing further.

Tesla continued to work diligently, and in 1937, stated to the press that he had completed a "dynamic theory of gravity," and that he would hope to soon give it to the world. It would never be published. He also criticized Einstein's theory of relativity, calling it a "magnificent mathematical garb which fascinates, dazzles, and makes people blind to the underlying errors."

On January 5, 1943, Tesla placed a small "do not disturb" sign on his door in the New Yorker Hotel. Two days later, the sign remained. The maid entered to find him dead in his bed. He was 86 years old. Despite receiving over 800 patents in his lifetime, and quite literally inventing the twentieth century, he died penniless and alone. A medical examination determined a blood clot in his heart was responsible for the death, and that there were no suspicious circumstances.

When his cousin, Sava Kosanovic, arrived at his room the next morning, Tesla's body was already gone as were his effects. Papers and notebooks were missing, including a treasured black notebook that contained hundreds of pages of technical research notes. Two days later, the U.S. Office of Alien Property seized all of Tesla's possessions, and his papers were declared top secret by the War Department due to the nature of the inventions and patents.

One year later, nearly three decades after Tesla began the fight, the U.S. Supreme Court confirmed that Marconi's radio patents indeed infringed on

Tesla's and therefore declared Tesla as the true "father of radio."

Einstein said that "imagination is more important than knowledge," because "knowledge is limited to all we now know and understand, while imagination embraces the entire world, and all there ever will be to know and understand."

All great geniuses are incredibly creative in their own ways. They're able to take what is known, dream of new possibilities, and bring them into the world. Every mathematical enigma solved, every masterful symphony composed, every revolutionary machine invented, every brilliant philosophy penned, every great corporation built…they all sprang from a person with an extraordinary imagination.

Marcus Aurelius once said that a person's life is "dyed with the color of his imagination." Your journey to greatness certainly will be too. Stop and think for a second the frontiers that lie ahead for our species. The Earth has been thoroughly conquered. The once radical philosophies of equality, tolerance, and individualism are embraced by much of the civilized world. The secrets of the atom have given us the ability to extinguish every living thing on the planet. What is next? We look to the imagination of geniuses for the answers.

What is imagination, though? Michelangelo said he saw angels in the marble and carved until he set them free. Most of us regard creativity in the same way we regard that statement—as a mysterious gift that can't be explained or cultivated. But we're wrong. Like genius itself, creativity is a process, not a providence.

THE SECRET TO CREATIVITY

Dylan's *Like a Rolling Stone*. Shakespeare's *Hamlet*. Bell's telephone. Pythagoras' theorem.

How did they come up with such unique, profound ideas? Well, there's an answer, and it's probably not what you think.

Steve Jobs said creativity is "just connecting things."

Salvador Dali said "those who do not want to imitate anything, produce nothing."

Picasso said "good artists copy but great artists steal."

Mark Twain said "all ideas are second-hand, consciously and unconsciously drawn from a million outside sources."

No magnificent product of the imagination—whether a machine, painting, or philosophy—was created in a complete vacuum. The invention of the telegraph took the efforts of a thousand, but the last man, who added that final inspired touch, got the credit.

When you start viewing creativity as a process of combination, and imagination as the ability to connect, stretch, and merge things in new ways, creative brilliance becomes less mystifying. A creative genius is just better at connecting the dots than others are.

That's why the coffee house in the Age of Enlightenment and the Parisian salons of modernism were such engines of creativity; they were spaces where many people from many different backgrounds and areas of expertise came to swap, join, and borrow many different ideas.

Don't confuse creativity and imagination with "thinking" either. Ray Bradbury said that thinking is the enemy of creativity because it's self-conscious. When you think, you sit calmly and try to reason through something in a structured, logical way. Creativity dances to a different tune. Once you flip that switch, things get a bit chaotic. Ideas start buzzing. Images start popping into your head. Fragments of all kinds of data find their way into orbit. We're pulled in one direction, then suddenly our instincts send us flying in another. Material collides and fuses, disappears and reappears. This chaos is essential to the creative process. A breakthrough occurs when pieces happen to come together in unique and harmonic ways.

"Our first endeavors are purely instinctive prompting of an imagination vivid and undisciplined," Tesla wrote. "As we grow older reason asserts itself and we become more and more systematic and designing. But those early impulses, though not immediately productive, are of the greatest moment and may shape our very destinies."

There's a catch to "combinatorial creativity," though. Before you can connect dots, you need to have dots to connect. The more material you're exposed to in the world, the more grist you'll have for your imagination mill. Tesla fully immersed himself in the world of electricity. He read hundreds of books. He conducted thousands of experiments and took copious notes. The more varied your knowledge and experiences are, the more likely you are to be able to create new associations and fresh ideas.

Your mind has an incredible ability to cross-pollinate—that is, to connect disparate things to solve problems in unique ways or envision new creations. Einstein attributed many of his physics breakthroughs to his violin breaks, which he believed helped him connect ideas in very different ways.

This brings us back to the beginning of the genius code: curiosity. It's an essential part of becoming more creative. Expand your interests in life. Seek out new, interesting experiences, no matter how mundane or inconsequential they might seem to others. Read books, watch documentaries, and discuss your ideas with others. No subject, no matter how specialized or esoteric, is off limits. You never know where your imagination will find pieces for its puzzles.

"The air is full of ideas," Henry Ford said. "They are knocking you in the head all the time. You only have to know what you want, then forget it, and go about your business. Suddenly, the idea will come through. It was there all the time."

By exposing yourself to an abundant variety of ideas, facts, art, and stories, and by pulling from your vast collection in many different ways—by entertaining any idea no matter how seemingly absurd—you can bring your imagination to life. And when you do, there's no telling what new things you can bring into the world and how it will change. Or, as Tesla put it, "A single ray of light from a distant star falling upon the eye of a tyrant in bygone times may have altered the course of his life, may have changed the destiny of nations, may have transformed the surface of the globe; so intricate, so inconceivably complex are the processes in Nature."

It takes curiosity to find your call to adventure, it takes courage to venture into the unknown, and it takes imagination to create your path. And to, like Tesla did, create it exactly as you envision it, no matter how much work it takes, or how many people try to stop you.

What ends will you work toward on your journey, and why? Where will you diverge from the trails laid by people before you, and where will you go instead? How will you tackle problems faced by your predecessors, and what will you do that they didn't? When will your eureka moments strike?

A genius answers those questions audaciously and lavishly. She dares to imagine everything and anything as possible, and carries our culture to worlds that never were. You can do the same.

5

DEVOTION TO GOALS AND THE WIZARD OF MENLO PARK

"When it is obvious that the goals cannot be reached, don't adjust the goals, adjust the actions."

-Confucius

Every adventure has a point of no return, where there's no turning back. If the hero is to carry on, he must abandon life as he knew it and give himself fully to what lies ahead.

Dorothy lives in a one-room house on a treeless prairie scorched by the sun. She shares the home with an equally bleak aunt and uncle. Her only source of happiness is her dog Toto. A twister rips through the plains one day and carries her to the lush Munchkin Country in the Land of Oz. To return home, she must venture to the City of Emeralds and meet the mysterious Wizard of Oz.

Rome breaches its land treaty with Carthage. Hannibal retaliates by laying siege to the Roman protectorate of Saguntum. Rome demands justice from Carthage, but instead, war is declared and the Second Punic War begins. Hannibal's numbers are far inferior to the mighty Roman Empire, but his military brilliance and daring bring it to the edge of collapse.

Siddhartha Gautama is born into a royal Hindu family, destined to enjoy a life of privilege and luxury. One day, he leaves his palace to meet his subjects and witnesses human suffering and the decay of old age for the first time. His utopia-shattering experience motivates further trips beyond the palace walls. Eventually, his conscience drives him to escape his sheltered, princely life and unite his people in pursuit of a spiritual solution to misery.

Each of these adventurers had goals: the goal of returning home, the goal of vanquishing a mighty oppressor, the goal of rejuvenating an entire people. Goals fuel action because goals give your adventure *purpose*. Only in purpose can you find the strength to cross the Rubicon and march toward greatness. Goals are the milestones you create for your journey. They determine how far you go and why as well as how you know you've accomplished something worthwhile. They are vessels into which you pour your curiosity, imagination, passion, and sweat. In turn, they fill you with drive, enthusiasm, and joy.

Einstein said that if you want to live a happy life, tie it to a goal, not to people or things. This was also the philosophy of one of the greatest inventors of all time: the Wizard of Menlo Park.

A passenger train rattled down the tracks that stretched from Port Huron to Detroit, and in the corner of the cluttered baggage car, a 12-year-old Thomas Edison huddled over a rickety table that was his makeshift laboratory. He was experimenting with dangerous chemicals labeled "poison" that he had sneaked onto the train.

The cramped space also housed a printing press, which he had built from parts scavenged from a local newspaper and which he used to print his own newspaper—the *Grand Trunk Herald*. He sold his paper to the daily commuters along with produce and other wares.

Edison had finished selling his goods to passengers for the day and, as he did every day, was using the remaining four hours of travel to study and conduct rudimentary experiments inspired by the writings of Sir Isaac Newton and others. The ride was rough and vibrating, and derailments were frequent and dangerous; but this didn't dissuade Edison from toying with hazardous substances for his scientific investigations.

As the train rounded a bend, the baggage car lurched suddenly and bottles of chemicals flew off a shelf, breaking on the floor. Edison watched helplessly as they mixed, quickly caught fire, and threatened to engulf the surrounding passenger luggage. He flew into a panic, scrambling to find something with which to extinguish the flames. The conductor burst in before he could put out the fire. He walloped Edison across the side of his head—the beginning of his hearing problems—snuffed out the fire, and threw Edison off the train along with all of his equipment.

It was déjà vu for Edison. When he was six years old, he had set fire to his parents' barn to "see what would happen," which earned him a public whipping with a birch branch by his father. That branch was used so often that the bark eventually wore off.

Undeterred, Edison moved his laboratory back into his parents' basement and continued to sell his newspapers and other wares on the railroad. His voracious reading had inspired in him a fascination with electricity, mechanics, chemistry, manufacturing, and technology. The recent invention of the telegraph particularly enthralled him. He spent hours each day loitering in the depot just to listen to the incoming transmissions.

One day, the stationmaster's child wandered onto the tracks of an oncoming train, unaware of the mortal consequences hurtling his way. Edison heroically rescued the toddler, and, as a token of his gratitude, the stationmaster taught Edison how to use a telegraph machine. Soon after, Edison built his own telegraph out of scrap metal and used it to practice morse code. His relentless practice paid off when he landed a job at the local Western Union telegraph office. In the evenings, Edison practiced receiving press reports about the Civil War.

Over the next several years, Edison traveled the country, working his way from a telegrapher's assistant to a first-class operator. His days and nights were spent practicing transcribing and sending transmissions, and studying a wide variety of engineering texts and experimenting. Then, after reading Michael Faraday's seminal works on chemistry, electricity, and magnetism, Edison's overarching goal came into focus: a life dedicated to finding ways to make living better, not just dissecting how it works.

At 20 years old, Edison found himself working in Western Union's Boston bureau. Despite heavy workloads, he was filling notebooks with ideas for inventions, some more practical than others. It was here, in 1869, that Edison received his first U.S. patent for an electronic vote recorder. The device was a commercial failure, but Edison was undaunted and announced to the world via a national newspaper that he would be resigning from Western Union to focus on "bringing out his inventions." Despite having little money, he moved to New York City in the same year. His friend let him sleep in a basement office below Wall Street.

Edison turned his inquisitive mind to the stock ticker, and spent much time studying how it worked and how it could be improved. His diligence paid off when he happened to overhear that the ticker machine owned by The

Gold Indicator Company was out of order. He offered to fix it and did. The company was so impressed with his work that they hired him as a superintendent with a salary of $300 a month. This windfall was short-lived, however—a change of ownership in the company saw him removed from their employment.

Soon after he was fired, he released his first successful commercial invention: an improved stock ticker, known as the Universal Stock Ticker. He was hoping for $3,000 – 5,000 for his invention, but was stunned when the Gold and Stock Telegraph Company paid him $40,000 for it—a sum equal to over $1 million today.

Ecstatic at his unexpected success, Edison immediately moved to Newark, New Jersey and started a business that built stock tickers and high-speed printing telegraphs. He focused his time on new inventions, which included a new type of automatic telegraph machine that sent pre-made messages much quicker than manual Morse messaging; submarine telegraph cables that could do the work of multiple existing cables, which he sold to the Atlantic and Pacific Telegraph Company for $30,000; a microphone that used carbon granules to help transmit sound over wires, which he sold to Western Union for $100,000; and an early type of telephone receiver device known as the electromotograph.

At 27, Edison arguably had already achieved his goal of improving life thanks to his impressive early inventions. But Edison's thirst for achievement pushed him further. So, in 1876, Edison moved to a new laboratory in Menlo Park, New Jersey, where he promised to launch a minor invention every 10 days, and a major one every six months. He devoted himself to improving the telephone and telegraph; he worked on a machine that would transcribe telegraphic messages using indentations on paper tape, which could then be sent by a telegraph repeatedly. This tinkering led Edison to speculate that he could record a telephone message and replay it in the same way. In 1877, Edison accomplished this vision using a telephone receiver, two needles, and a tinfoil cylinder. He received $10,000 for the manufacturing and sales rights, plus twenty percent of the commercial profits.

In the following years, Edison continued to work on phonographs but became increasingly absorbed by the many other projects vying for his attention. With over 60 employees—his devoted "insomnia squads"—they worked day and night on new inventions, applying for nearly 400 patents in a single year.

Edison's endless pursuit of life-changing creations led him to his next famous endeavor: electric light. Electric lighting had been around since the beginning of the 19th century, but the light bulbs invented up to 1878 were either too expensive, required too much power, or burned out too quickly to be commercially practical. Thus, the majority of people were still using candles and smoky, smelly gaslights.

In the face of the long odds, Edison boldly told the world that he would invent a safe, odor-free, inexpensive electric light that would put electric light-bulbs in every home in America. The mystery that he had to solve, however, was regarding the filament of the device. What material would burn brightly, cleanly, and lengthily without demanding too much power?

Driven by the opportunity to profoundly and permanently change the course of human life, Edison sent people to the jungles of the Amazon and forests of Japan in his quest for the perfect filament material. He analyzed thousands of plants and vegetables and finally, after a year of grueling experiments, his hard work paid off. In 1879, after spending over $40,000 on the project and conducting over 1,200 experiments, Edison had his first major breakthrough. Using carbonized cotton thread as a filament, his lightbulb burned for nearly 14 hours.

Invigorated by this success, Edison was certain that he could do better. He continued his filament research and, several months later, discovered that a carbonized bamboo filament would last over 1,000 hours—a miraculous development. A year later, he patented a system for electricity distribution, which was essential to capitalize on his lightbulb. A new company was formed for the venture—the Edison Illuminating Company—and it established the first investor-owned utility in 1882, which provided 59 homes in lower Manhattan with direct current electricity. Earlier in the year, Edison had flipped the switch on the first steam-generating power station in London, England, which provided direct current to street lamps and homes.

By now, Edison was a household name of nearly mythical proportions, widely known as the "Wizard of Menlo Park." In just over a decade since establishing his Menlo Park laboratory, the lab had expanded to occupy two city blocks and carried a stock of, as he put, "almost every conceivable material." This translated to over 8,000 kinds of chemicals; every kind of screw available at the time; every size of needle; every kind of cord or wire; the hair of humans, horses, hogs, cows, rabbits, goats, minx, camels, and other mammals; every type of silk you could find; a plethora of materials from animals such as hoofs, shark's teeth, deer horns, tortoise shell, ostrich feathers, and peacock tail; all metal ores; and so much more.

In 1887, Edison built a massive laboratory complex of 14 buildings in

West Orange, New Jersey, known as Edison Laboratory. The main building alone was the size of three football fields and included machine shops, glass-blowing projects, electrical testing rooms, stockrooms, electrical power generation, and more.

Edison employed over 5,000 people at this location and continued to produce breakthrough inventions. One was the fluoroscope, which is a machine that uses X-rays to produce an image of the human body. Edison's experiments with X-rays nearly cost him his eyesight and gave his assistant, Clarence Daily, radiation poisoning that would ultimately lead to his death. Shaken by Daily's demise, Edison said in 1903, "Don't talk to me about X-rays. I am afraid of them."

The first motion picture camera was produced in Edison Laboratory, which produced silent moving pictures. Edison then invented the concept of film reels and figured out how to connect the motion picture camera to a phonograph, leading to the first moving pictures with sound, which debuted in 1913. Ironically, Edison later disliked "talkies" and lamented that the quality of acting had degraded because of the novelty of dialog.

In 1915, Edison was appointed president of the U.S. Navy Consulting Board, and in 1920, he urged Congress to establish the Naval Research Laboratory—the first military research lab.

Inventions poured forth from Edison Laboratory for more than 40 years, impacting the lives of millions of people around the world. Edison remained active in the pursuit of greater innovation right up to his death. Just months before he died of diabetes complications in 1931, he completed an electric train project and was at the throttle of the very first such train to depart from Lackawanna Terminal in Hoboken, New Jersey, driving it to Dover, Delaware.

Edison's legendary odyssey of imagination and invention spanned six decades and won him over 1,000 patents—a record he still holds today. Over his Menlo Park desk—the location of his most fruitful work—he displayed a placard with Sir Joshua Reynolds' famous quotation:

"There is no expedient to which a man will not resort to avoid the real labor of thinking."

"Show me a thoroughly satisfied man and I will show you a failure," Edison once said. He didn't just talk the talk, though. Edison had an overabundance of goals to fuel his adventures. In 1888, his list of "things doing and to be done" was five pages long and included, but was not limited to, the following:

- Cotton picker
- New standard phonograph
- Hand turning phonograph
- Deaf apparatus
- Electrical piano
- New expansion pyromagnetic dynamo
- Artificial silk
- Phonographic clock
- Marine telegraphy
- Chalk battery
- Ink for blind

Edison always knew where he was going, but rarely how he would get there. When he set out to perfect the light bulb, he had a vision of what he wanted to accomplish, but nothing that even remotely resembled a clean, clear plan of how it could be done. After going through thousands of unworkable filaments, he was challenged about his "lack of results."

"Results? Why, man, I have gotten lots of results!" he replied. "If I find ten thousand ways something won't work, I haven't failed. I am not discouraged, because every wrong attempt discarded is often a step forward."

By formulating goals, your adventure will begin to take shape in both direction and substance. A singular winding path will open in the hazy landscape of life—one that you and only you can walk, because while many other people have had and will have similar goals, they aren't you.

Dr. Gail Matthews of Dominican University conducted a study to see how formulating, stating, and being accountable to goals ultimately affects one's success or failure.

The study was conducted over a one-month period and included 149 participants split into five groups: one which simply thought about goals; one which wrote goals down; one which wrote goals down and formulated action steps to reach them; one which wrote goals down, formulated action steps, and sent these steps to a friend; and finally, one which wrote goals down, formulated action steps, sent them to a friend, and created weekly reports on their progress, which they also sent to the friend.

The fifth group—those that wrote goals down, formulated action steps, sent them to a friend, and reported weekly on their progress—were *77%* more successful in accomplishing their goals than the first group—the people who just thought about their goals. The group of people who simply wrote their goals was *44%* more successful in accomplishing them than those in the first group.

The findings of the study were clear: writing down specific goals, working out specific steps to achieve them, and creating accountability for achieving them, and thus commitment, are very conducive to success.

These phenomena were known thousands of years ago. We can look to Aristotle's elegant formula for success and happiness, for example.

"First," he wrote, "have a definite, clear practical ideal; a goal, an objective. Second, have the necessary means to achieve your ends; wisdom, money, materials, and methods. Third, adjust all your means to that end."

You would be hard pressed to find an eminent genius in any field that didn't or doesn't approach life in this way. They don't "have goals"—they're *defined* by them.

Edison's lifelong, defining goal was to bring out the secrets of nature and apply them for the happiness of man. Every lesser goal—every invention of his—was merely an offshoot of that one, perennial, unquenchable ambition that embraced the entire world and human race.

Like Edison, Marie Curie's goals also forged her identity. She was once a young governess with a burning passion to leave Poland and study science in Paris, as women weren't permitted an advanced education in her home country. This was beyond the means of her family, however, so she arranged a deal with her sister, Bronya, whereby Marie would tutor children to help pay for Bronya's education, and once Bronya had graduated, the favor would be repaid.

For nearly three years, Marie spent her days working to cover her sister's costs and spent her nights alone, at her desk, reading outdated volumes on sociology, physics, and mathematics without guidance or advice—studies that she later said were "encompassed with difficulty." But her perseverance paid off and at 24 years old, after her sister had graduated from Sorbonne and married, Marie was able to pursue her dream.

Marie's university studies were incredibly challenging due to a deficient secondary education in Warsaw. She overcame her academic shortcomings, however, in glorious fashion by winning a Nobel Prize, the first woman to do so, for her doctoral thesis on radioactivity, which was an immensely difficult subject only recently discovered. Eight years later, she won a second Nobel Prize, the first man or woman to do so, this time for her research into radium and polonium.

When you survey the goals of great achievers like Edison and Curie, you'll quickly notice something else in common. Their goals have a simple, defining characteristic: *they can't be easily achieved*. The goals of geniuses are always *big*—the type that fill you with a peculiar mixture of excitement, intimidation, and restlessness. As Einstein said, you must "develop an instinct for what one can just barely achieve through one's greatest efforts."

While big goals create big landmarks for you to strive toward in your journey, they also require a big commitment if you're to bring them into reality. Comedian Steve Martin beautifully described that commitment paradox.

THE STEVE MARTIN METHOD FOR DOMINATING YOUR FIELD

Steve Martin is one of the most famous comedians of the 20th century. Many "modern" devices that young people think are so novel actually have their roots in Martin's work. Martin is a highly accomplished stand-up comedian, writer, actor, and musician…

…but how did he do it?

In his memoirs, *Born Standing Up*, Martin wanted to share his insights on how he achieved his success, not just what he achieved. His key secret to success in the entertainment industry, however, usually disappoints. It's just one simple, unsexy line:

"Be so good they can't ignore you."

Before you dismiss Martin's insight as clichéd, let it sink in, because it captures the essence of success in any area of your life, and it has everything to do with using the genius code to achieve greatness. While his "secret" might seem daunting, it can actually be invigorating. It simplifies the quest for success, which is often made to look very complex and overwhelming.

What Martin is saying is forget the secret backdoors, the gimmicks and tricks and let go of the frustration of feeling like you're missing some mystical element. Instead, focus on just one thing: become really, really good at something. Become extraordinary at it. Better than everyone you know. So good that people can't help but be amazed.

Martin had two other powerful pieces of advice to go with his philosophy.

First, you should always strive to *innovate*, not just "work." Going through the motions to "put in your time" isn't enough to become outstanding. You need a restless desire to figure out new, better ways to do things. You can't be afraid to experiment and learn from the successes and failures.

In other words, don't be content with just following the crowd. Take the time to understand the principles and laws of the activity. Look to others to see what they do well and what they don't, and then dream up new ways to mix, match, stretch, and augment these things into something new and better.

Second, focus on one primary goal at a time. Martin said he owes his success to his unwavering perseverance in one field until he had mastered it. He resisted the urge to branch off into other, newer types of work or projects until he was truly ready to move on to something else.

In today's age of never-ending distractions and possibilities, it can feel a bit counter-intuitive to sharpen your ambitions to a razor's edge, but it's actually the most effective way to dominate in any activity. Martin was right when he said that if you don't align your entire life with one, singular quest for greatness, you'll dilute your focus and drive to a point where becoming extraordinary is not possible.

So, as you forge your path to greatness, forget about comparing yourself to others for consolation or justification. One for one, geniuses became so good at something that people simply couldn't ignore them. You're going to have to do the same.

In 1926, an anonymous millionaire known only as "RHJ" published a short book titled *It Works*. The mysterious RHJ attributed all that he had accomplished in his life—from amassing wealth, to overcoming great hardships, to winning loyal friends—to the three principles taught in his book. And they are:

1. Write down your goals in as much detail as you can. He stressed the importance of *writing* the goals—not just thinking about them.

2. Think about the goals as much as you can. Don't be distracted off onto other goals or forget about the ones you've set. Learn to focus on exactly what you want and remain so until you've accomplished it.

3. Don't talk about your goals until you can show objective results. The reason for this is twofold: it prevents the fear of what others might think if you fail, and it prevents you from feeling satisfied with yourself by merely talking about what you're "going to do" as opposed to actually doing it.

The latter is supported by multiple scientific studies that show that people who announce their goals to others and receive acknowledgment for them are less likely to actually work hard to achieve them, and ironically, are strangely optimistic about their (lack of) progress.

On the other hand, people that *didn't* announce their goals worked harder toward them, and were more realistic about their progress and the work still ahead to actually accomplish the goals. The group of people who didn't announce their goals, of course, accomplished them far more often than the group who did.

Being admired for *planning* on doing something great can often feel just as good as being admired for *doing* something great, but the two couldn't be more different. If someone is going to commend us, let it be for something we've achieved, not for something we're planning on or in the middle of achieving.

That's what geniuses do. Geniuses don't set vague goals that can't be measured, such as "to do my best" or "to work hard." They envision specific, challenging goals, like, "to win the XYZ award" or "to create product X by January 1." Hence, it should come as no surprise that hundreds of scientific experiments involving dozens of types of tasks and thousands of participants have proven conclusively that the more specific and challenging the goals are, the better the resulting performance.

You know you have it when a goal is stated in definite terms, when it can be tangibly seen or measured, when you can outline the specific steps that you need to take to fulfill it and feel you can actually do those things, and when it *excites* you.

Setting big, exciting goals is necessary to unlock another piece of the genius code.

But, as your adventure unfolds, your loyalty to your goals will be tested. You'll face many external and internal challenges. Some people will doubt and criticize you. Boulders will fall into your path that look shockingly insurmountable. You'll find yourself in situations that feel like quicksand, where any attempt at forward movement just buries you deeper in place. No matter the circumstances, there's only one way out, and that's *through*.

After ancient Greek armies landed on enemy shores, the first order commanders gave was "burn the boats." The Greeks knew that the body can endure almost anything, but the mind needs convincing. And nothing steels resolve better than *necessity*, as Edison proved time and again. When there's no option of retreat, humans are capable of incredible things.

At some point in their journeys, all great achievers burned their boats. Edison, you'll recall, moved to New York City to pursue his invention ideas with hardly any money and stable source of income. Such remarkable individuals don't just believe that quitting isn't an option—they actually put themselves into situations that wouldn't allow it. They committed to courses of action that couldn't be backed out of without throwing their dreams and, in a sense, their lives away.

In December 1955, after the arrest of Rosa Parks, Martin Luther King Jr. decided to help organize and lead the first great Negro nonviolent protest of social inequalities: the bus boycott. It lasted 382 days before the Supreme Court declared bus segregation laws unconstitutional. During the boycott, Dr. King was arrested and physically abused, and his house was bombed, but there was no turning back. Over the next 13 years, he traveled over six million miles, wrote five books, spoke over 2,500 times, and died not only the symbolic leader of the Blacks but also of nonviolent opposition to oppression.

Michelangelo claimed that his rivals Bramante and Raphael convinced the Pope to commission him to paint the sprawling ceiling of the Sistine Chapel as an underhanded attempt to undermine his position as a leader of the Renaissance. Fresco was an unfamiliar medium for Michelangelo; if his work failed to impress, his reputation would be tarnished, and nobody refused a Pope's request. What did Michelangelo do? He designed a special scaffold and spent the majority of four years suspended 60 feet in the air, staring upward, applying and painting plaster. The result was a dazzling array of Biblical scenes that was instantly heralded as a cornerstone of High Renaissance art, an achievement that cemented Michelangelo's position as a true equal of da Vinci's.

The legendary football coach Vince Lombardi said that once you learn to quit, it becomes a habit. Every genius' journey has brought discouragement, frustration, and distraction, but they just never used any of these things as an excuse to walk away. Their boats were burned.

How did they find the inner strength to do this, though? What did they tap into that gave them the certainty to push forward despite it all, and how can you do the same?

6

DRIVE AND THE MACEDONIAN WHO CONQUERED THE WORLD

"Don't ask what the world needs. Ask what makes you come alive, and go do it. Because what the world needs is people who have come alive."

-Howard Thurman

Any great adventure involves trials and tribulations that transform the hero into something greater than she was when she began it.

It's been seven years since J.K. Rowling graduated from university. She sees herself as the biggest failure she knows: she is recently divorced after only a year of marriage, jobless, and living off social security with a young daughter to support. She's diagnosed with depression and even considers killing herself. She has something, though—an unfinished manuscript of a story that occurred to her while riding a train several years ago. She walks her baby each day to lull her asleep and then settles into various cafes around Edinburgh, Scotland to hammer away on a manual typewriter, writing and re-writing chapters. She finishes *Harry Potter and the Philosopher's Stone* in 1995, which 12 publishing houses reject before Bloomsbury picks it up. She's paid an advance of £1,500 and told by her editor to get a day job because she has little chance of making money with children's books. The height of her ambition is for the book to just get reviewed, but within five months of its publication, she wins her first book award. Her story is already being compared to the vaunted work of C.S. Lewis and J.R.R. Tolkien. Rowling is in shock. This is it, she realizes. This is her chance to shed the grief of her past and create a beautiful new future. Five years later, she releases the fourth book in the series, which sells over 370,000 copies on the first day. Today, the books are the #1 best-selling series of all time with over *400 million* copies sold worldwide. For the first time in her life, Rowling doesn't have to worry if she'll have enough money to make it through the week, and she summarizes her journey of transcendence thus: "We do not need magic to transform our world. We carry all the power we need inside ourselves already. We have the power to imagine better."

Jesus travels through the Judean desert without food for 40 days and nights. The Devil plans on leading him astray in his mission, and appears in disguise with an offer of stones that Jesus can change to bread and eat. Jesus refuses to use his powers for selfish purposes. But the Devil has another trick ready. He leads Jesus to a great temple atop a summit overlooking Jerusalem and challenges him to test God by jumping off the peak to be caught by angels. Jesus sees no reason to prove himself, and declines. In desperation, the Devil takes Jesus to the pinnacle of a soaring mountain and shows him the world. "All this I will give you if you will bow down and worship me," he says. Jesus has had enough and finally dismisses Satan as a false god. Only then is he joined by angels and allowed to continue toward the final establishment of his divinity.

Some people like to think that geniuses are so inherently extraordinary that they navigate their journeys with clairvoyant ease. This simply isn't true. Greatness does not come lightly. It requires that you make sacrifices of time, interests, and—sometimes—possessions. The further you move toward greatness, the more greatness demands from you.

In whatever form your adventure takes, there will be obstacles to overcome. Your dedication to your cause will be tested. Your wits will be forced to their limits. People will try to exploit your weaknesses and negate your strengths. The journey toward greatness is not for the meek.

But all barriers yield to one mythical quality: *drive*. The will to persist and overcome. To never give up. To never accept defeat.

Writer and philosopher L. Ron Hubbard said that "there's no excuse for any failure that ever occurred any place in history, except this: there was just not quite enough carry-through and push-through." The annals of history offer many examples of this sentiment in action. However, there is perhaps no finer example of one person's capacity to persevere and prevail than the greatest military commander of all time, a man who accomplished in four years what his ancestors had failed to accomplish in the centuries prior, and what nobody has matched since.

When Alexander III of Macedon was ten years old, his father, King Philip II, saw him tame a fierce horse and thus prophesied that the kingdom of Macedon was too small for his ambitions. The king wouldn't live to see it, but his prediction would prove to be an understatement.

Alexander was only 16 when Philip led a military invasion into the neighboring lands of Thrace, which relinquished to him the power to rule all of Macedonia, the most powerful kingdom in ancient Greece. Macedonian dominance was new and precarious, however, and dissent mounted in the recently conquered lands.

With Philip and a large portion of the Macedonian army absent, a Thracian tribe saw an opportunity to start a revolt against their rulers. Their underestimation of the young Alexander, however, proved great and fatal when he quickly marshaled an army, marched them into battle against the rebels, crushed the resistance, and renamed their city to Alexandropolis.

Impressed with his son's achievement, Philip employed his teenage son's military prowess further by dispatching him to deal with other Thracian and Greek revolts. One by one, Alexander broke the mutinies and subdued the dissidents. He even saved his father's life in a battle against the Greek city of Perinthus, and repelled an invasion by the nearby kingdom of Illyria. Upon this momentum, Philip, Alexander, and their armies continued to march through Greece to cement Macedonian rule, taking city after city. Those that surrendered were spared bloodshed. Those that resisted fell to the Macedonian sword.

The last bastion of Greek resistance was the powerful city of Thebes, which had allied with Athens against Macedonia. The powerhouses collided in the village of Chaeronea, with Philip commanding the right wing of the army and Alexander the left. A protracted, ferocious battle ensued. Alexander faced the fearsome brotherhood of 300 elite warriors known as the Sacred Band of Thebes. Through ingenious infantry and cavalry maneuvering, Alexander secured an advantageous position and launched a charge that broke the Theban line. The Sacred Band held their ground until all 300 had fallen.

Alexander's military feats were so tremendous that rumors began to spread that he, now only 18, was in fact a descendant of Achilles or possibly the son of Zeus. The rumors were steeped in prophecy; Alexander would rise to incredible power. Two years later, he would take the next step in fulfilling the myth that was quickly forming around him.

In 336 BC, while attending the wedding of his daughter, Philip was assassinated by the captain of his bodyguards, Pausanias. The regicide's motive is unknown as he was chased down and killed on the spot, but whispers pointed to Alexander's mother, Olympias, and possibly Alexander himself as the instigators. Olympias desired revenge for Philip's divorce and glory for her son by taking the throne and surpassing his father's accomplishments. Alexander wasn't wanting of a motive either; he was bitter after being exiled for two years over a filial feud regarding Philip's desire to produce a full-blooded Macedonian heir with his new wife.

Involved or not in his father's assassination, Alexander was proclaimed king by the nobles and army at age 20. News of Philip's death caused an outbreak of revolts in Thebes, Athens, Thessaly, and the Thracian tribes to the north of Macedon. Alexander would have to act quickly and decisively as the new king, or his sovereignty would collapse before his crown could even settle.

He began by eliminating any potential rivals to his throne, including his cousin and two other Macedonian princes. And he executed his late father's trusted general Attalus, who was secretly being courted by Athens to wage war against the young king. Olympias also moved to protect Alexander's regency by having her two daughters by Philip burned alive—a barbarism that infuriated Alexander.

Once the home front threats were neutralized, Alexander turned his attention to the intrigues of his Greek neighbors. Advisers urged Alexander to deal with the rebellious cities diplomatically, but he had no interest in delicate, protracted negotiations. He mustered the entire Macedonian cavalry—a formidable force of over 3,000 experienced warriors—and rode south toward Thessaly. He ambushed a large Thessalian army while en route, and added to his forces.

Before Alexander reached Corinth, the Greek and Thracian insurgents reconsidered their position. Fearing the wrath of the fierce young king, they backed down and declared Alexander the leader of the "Hellenic Alliance"—a league formed by his father. Alexander pardoned the rebels, and announced that he would continue his father's plans for the conquest of Persia.

His stated motives were uncharacteristic of his position, however; they were greater than mere vengeance and imperialism. Alexander's purpose was to "combine barbarian things with things Hellenic, to traverse and civilize every continent, to search out the uttermost parts of land and sea, to push the bounds of Macedonia to the farthest Ocean, and to disseminate and shower the blessings of the Hellenic justice and peace over every nation." Such altruism seems ironic when you consider his hawkish plans. Was it empty rhetoric used to raise an army with which he could smash, usurp, and dominate, or would Alexander act in accordance with his professed intentions to unite and uplift the known world? What *really* drove him? We shall see.

Before Alexander could begin his Persian campaigns, however, Thracian tribes again revolted against his rule. He immediately gathered his army and advanced east into Thrace to quell the insurrections. The Thracians planned to ambush Alexander in a narrow mountain pass near the Thracian and Macedonian border, but he out-maneuvered the garrison and defeated it, gaining entry to the lands. Alexander then caught a tribe of barbarians lurking in his rear, and led an attack. The Thracians lost over 3,000 men in the battle, and Alexander lost less than 50.

The Macedonians continued on to the shores of the Danube, and faced off with 15,000 warriors of the Thracian Gatae tribe. Alexander knew that his enemies expected him to use boats to ferry his men over in waves, so instead, he organized a mass crossing of the river in the middle of the night using dugouts and other improvised rafts and floating devices. 1,500 cavalry and 4,000 troops swam nearly 1,000 feet through the powerful Danubian currents, and upon a surprise attack at sunrise, the Gatae soldiers disbanded and fled. Nearby tribes heard of Alexander's bold deeds and sent ambassadors to ask for the young king's friendship, which was gladly granted. The Thracian revolts were hushed.

Alexander's drive would be challenged next by an Illyrian revolt that threatened to cut off his passage back into Macedon. If Alexander's return to Greece was delayed for too long, his kingdom was vulnerable to another Athenian and Theban uprising, who were reported to be amassing forces.

The Illyrians held the pass of Pelium, and its nearby fortress, which was the only way back into Macedonia. The Macedonians bore down on the city but were repelled. Precious time was lost and, to make matters worse, King Glaukias of the Taulanti tribe marched in a massive army to reinforce the Illyrians. They spread out amongst the hills and forests surrounding the gap, ready to cut off any advance through the pass or retreat back into Illyria. Alexander was in dire straits: supplies and rations were scant; his enemies outnumbered him many times and held superior, fortified positions; and the Greek insurgency swelled in his absence. He couldn't retreat or wait for reinforcements—he had to take Pelium, and fast.

What Alexander did next was a brilliant display of his resourcefulness and cunning—two characteristics that flourish through extraordinary drive. Just as nothing produces paralyzing apathy like doubt and resignation, nothing produces cleverness like staring down a crisis with a lionhearted snarl.

Alexander marched a sizable portion of his army into plain sight in the fields in front of Pelium, surrounded by the enemy, and began a rehearsed military drill that his men had perfected. The Macedonian phalanx paraded in perfect synchrony, as if going through a rigorous inspection by their generals. The Illyrians looked on in bewilderment, wondering what their enemy was doing and how they should respond. Their amazement at the procession led to careless formations on Alexander's left flank. This was the opportunity he was looking for. He suddenly called for his infantry to aggressively charge the weakened ground, and the barbarians quickly realized their mistake and fled the hills. Simultaneously, Alexander led a cavalry charge to the hills on his right flank, which was also surrendered by Glaukias' men.

The dispersion of the enemy forces allowed Alexander to secure the entirety of the surrounding hills, winning him a place of safety. Before he could return to Macedonia, however, he needed to take the city to guard against any future Illyrian attempts at invasion through the pass.

Three days later, Alexander's scouts reported that Cleitus and Glaukias had become careless in their position in front of Pelium, and were vulnerable to attack. That night, Alexander led a body of infantry and archers to the flank of the barbarians' camp, and launched an assault. The Illyrians were caught by surprise, with many still in their beds. The resulting slaughter led to a quick rout. Pelium was again under Macedonian control, and the defeated Illyrian kings accepted Alexander's terms and swore fealty to the fearsome commander.

Alexander's ingenuity at Pelium offers another insight into the special nature of his drive, something that is often summarized as impatience but is actually quite more than that. Some historians criticize the young king's ruse as reckless and its success as lucky. But, as you'll see in the baffling successes of his later campaigns, Alexander was either the luckiest man in history, or there was some other force at work. I believe the latter, but what might that force be? His actions at Pelium offer an answer.

Alexander's position was desperate. His officers suggested retreat. Reinforcements could be sent, they said, but Alexander would hear nothing of it. Not only were their rations insufficient for it, it's very likely that his kingdom would fall to Athens and Thebes while they waited. No, he had to have Pelium, and quicker than any of his men believed was possible. But Alexander felt otherwise. While his men saw an impenetrable citadel, he saw frail bowling pins ready to be smashed by the right roll of his mighty forces. Behind Alexander's "impatience" was an incredible impetus and sense of forward motion that made nothing of anything or anyone that dared get in his way. He rarely paused because, frankly, nothing was intimidating enough to really give him pause. In analyzing the drive of men and women of Alexander's caliber, you find in every case a downright heroic concentration of confidence and flippancy that inspires others to believe that they, too, can do the impossible.

Within a few days of taking the pass, Alexander learned that the Persians were spreading money amongst the anti-Macedonian Greeks to encourage revolution, and that a rumor had spread that the Illyrians killed him. These influences spurred the Thebans to throw out Macedonian garrisons, declare independence from Alexander's rule, and recruit several other city-states to do the same.

Enraged, Alexander marched an army of over 30,000 men 300 miles south to Thebes at a breakneck pace, arriving in only two weeks. The sudden emergence of Alexander and his formidable army stunned the Theban allies, causing them to withdraw their support for the rebellion, leaving Thebes to stand alone against Alexander. Alexander camped north of the city and waited, giving the Thebans the chance to send an embassy and ask for pardon. The Theban generals responded by sending out a force of infantry and cavalry to attack Alexander's outposts, which was repelled.

Nevertheless, Alexander remained patient with the Thebans. He demanded the ringleaders of the resistance, and promised no harm to any others that surrendered. Theban leaders refused the demand despite the fact that the bulk of the citizens favored giving in.

Theban soldiers built fortifications outside of the city to prepare for the upcoming battle, and Alexander made plans for an invasion. He still refused to act, however, wishing to save the glorious city and prevent loss of his ranks. The delay was brought to an end not by Alexander, but by his general Perdiccas, who seized an opportunity to siege the city and break through the city wall. The breach was successful, and Alexander ordered thousands of his soldiers to reinforce the attack.

Thebes' warriors fought bravely, but their defenses fell and the city was overrun. Boetians, Phoeians, and Plataeans—fighting within Alexander's ranks–slaughtered thousands of Thebans, including women and children, out of revenge for years of Theban oppression. 30,000 survivors were captured and sold into slavery, and the city was razed to the ground.

The force and cruelty with which Alexander smashed the Theban rebellion sent shock waves throughout all of Greece. Athens wouldn't dare risk his wrath and immediately withdrew troops they had sent to fight with their now-vanquished allies. Sparta was amazed to see the powerful city, which had conquered them at Lenetra, shattered to pieces as if by the gods themselves. Athens and its allies again asked the king's forgiveness, which Alexander again granted. What happened at Thebes served as a warning, while at the same time a call for peace. Alexander had no desire to inflict any more suffering on his people.

In one year, Alexander secured himself against the barbarians of the north and subdued all of Greece. But that was only an overture to what was to be his life's work and ambition: Persia, the land of Xerxes, of Darius, of Cyrus—a land of untold resources and wealth, and full of brave men. The conquering and integration of Persia represented the truest test of his ambition for greatness, an adventure that would rival the exploits of his idol, Achilles, as well as transform the course of human history forever.

Invading Persia promised to be the most formidable of undertakings, challenging Alexander's genius and drive in every way. And yet, despite Persia's impressive wealth and might, the great kingdom had a key weakness: it was a disjointed mass 30 times the size of Macedonia's territories, comprised of many independent regions ruled by local governors. Many of these "satraps" were dissatisfied with the sovereign and with each other. Alexander knew this and counted on their discord to mean lax, uncoordinated defenses.

But Alexander wasn't one to take things for granted. His obsessive attention to detail and uncompromising work ethic drove him to spend the coming winter months relentlessly working to assemble his army, equip his ships, and devise a plan for the largest attack ever attempted by a man. In this we glimpse another chromosome of the DNA of drive. Alexander's adamantine will and belief in himself stemmed from the fact that he was willing to out-plan, out-work, and outlast anyone. He didn't chase dubious shortcuts, and in some cases, purposely avoided them just to experience the glory of overcoming a great challenge. He didn't beg for the favor of the gods; he strove to overawe them.

Alexander's thorough preparations accounted for what would be a long absence from his home kingdom. He appointed his trusted general Antipater as regent and left him with a sizable army to maintain the peace. He even gave away all of his personal possessions to be sold to help cover the tremendous costs of his ambitions, leaving himself, as he laughingly said, only with his hopes. Many of the rich men that served in his elite Companion cavalry unit were inspired to do the same. Regardless, Alexander had to borrow a sizable sum to fully ready his military.

In 335 BC, at 22 years of age, Alexander crossed the Hellespont strait into Asia Minor with over 35,000 Macedonian, Greek, and Thracian troops, a fleet of 120 ships with crews numbering nearly 40,000, and only a month's worth of supplies. Once his ship reached the coast of Asia Minor, Alexander threw a spear into the ground, stepped ashore, and declared that he would accept the whole of Asia as a gift from the gods.

Darius, the Persian king, ignored the crossing, unafraid of an army that his military outnumbered by many times. Consequently, the Macedonians moved through Asia Minor with little resistance, liberating several Greek towns from Persian rule. Darius still refused to take Alexander seriously despite these affronts against his empire and the warnings of his experienced generals that the young Macedonian was not to be underestimated.

Memnon, a competent general favored by Darius, knew that Alexander's provisions and funds were scant, and recommended a "scorched earth" strategy wherein the satrapies that lay before Alexander would be burned to the ground, denying him forage and resources. Persian officers wouldn't hear of it, however, and resolved to meet the Macedonian king in pitched battle. An army of 20,000 cavalry and an equal number of Greek mercenaries was assembled to drive back Alexander and his invaders.

Alerted by his scouts that the Persian forces were in his vicinity, Alexander forged ahead to the Grancius River. As the Macedonians approached the shore, the sun was setting and the Persian army could be seen in the plains on the horizon. Parmenio, Alexander's chief general, advised that the army camp for the night and persuade the enemy to do the same.

Alexander had other plans, though. He preferred the morale-boosting effect of a bold offensive, and didn't want the Persians to think that he would pause even for an instant at such a pitiful barrier, which may bolster their confidence to repel his advance.

Instead, he ordered his scouts to survey the Persian lines and report their findings. As he had suspected, the disposition of the Persian troops was faulty, and he was determined to force a fight at once. Alexander's commanders moved the Macedonian armies into position, and there was a moment of profound silence as they faced their neighbors across the river. Then, a Macedonian bugle sounded, followed by a deafening war cry, and spear-wielding infantry began to cross. The Persians rained javelins down upon them, and dispatched cavalry to drive them back.

A furious fight ensued. Alexander slew several notable Persians, including Darius' son- and brother-in-law. The latter almost took Alexander's life, slicing part of his helmet off before falling to his spear. This heroic charge enabled the entire right wing of the Macedonian army to cross the river and press the attack. The full might of Alexander's cavalry fell upon the Persians and broke their lines, but the Persians still had their Greek mercenaries, which had been merely spectators to the slaughter thus far. They would prove no match for the Macedonians. Over 18,000 were cut to pieces, and the remaining 2,000 were captured.

When the fighting finally stopped, the Persians had lost over 1,000 horsemen, many nobles, and 18,000 Greek mercenaries. Alexander lost less than 200 men.

Although the road to the heart of Persia was now open, it couldn't be taken until Alexander had the coastal cities under his control to protect his rear and flanks from the formidable Persian navy. All of the important coastal cities were Greek, and many welcomed Alexander with open arms. In each case, he threw out the Persian tyrants, established a democratic form of government, began some type of public improvement in commemoration of their freedom from the Persian yoke, and granted the inhabitants ancient privileges that had been denied to them for the last two hundred years of foreign rule.

Several cities that had been granted exceptional privileges by Darius resisted Alexander, but one by one, they fell to his superior tactics. As he conquered each, he continued his strategy of befriending the Greeks, pardoning surviving citizens, and granting the cities autonomy and freedom. There was no plundering to help pay for the campaign, as was customary in wartimes, only the collection of reasonable taxes to fund his war chest.

With the coast of Asia Minor now under his control, Alexander had effectively nullified Persia's most powerful military asset: its world-renowned navy. He was now prepared to move into the interior of the Persian Empire. But winter was approaching, and Alexander's men needed to rest and heal. So he granted a leave of absence to a considerable number of his newly married soldiers to be with their wives until spring, when they would move to bring down the entire Persian empire.

Alexander himself, however, would not rest. His unremitting drive wouldn't allow it. So he gathered a body of troops and set out to close any remaining ports on the mainland and further starve out the Persian navy. Over the next several months, he and his men marched through bitter weather and conquered all of western Asia minor—nearly 40 towns were subdued, with most surrendering without contest, knowing that they would be treated liberally by the conqueror. Those that rebuked his offer of a peaceful surrender, no matter how well fortified, fell.

When spring of the next year came, the wounded warriors had healed and the soldiers on leave returned, many bringing new recruits. It was time for Alexander to drive his spear through the heart of Persia, fulfilling his ambition to conquer and civilize the known world.

Darius believed that the defeats of his generals in Asia Minor were mere accidents and misfortunes. The territory lost was a sliver on the fringe of his vast empire, and while he didn't comprehend the significance of Alexander's progress, he did comprehend that Memnon's early advice should've been followed. He put the Greek rogue in supreme command of the Persian military with the orders to crush the Macedonian invader.

Memnon, an incredibly intelligent and able general, and probably the only man in the service of Darius who could pose a threat to Alexander, set plans in motion to bring the war to Macedonia and instigate a revolt amongst Alexander's enemies in Greece. To do this, he would muster a large fleet of warships and soldiers to take islands near Macedonian shores and use them as bases from which to launch an invasion. But, as fate would have it, Memnon died of fever after only the first successful siege of the island of Chios, and his successor was by no means up to the task he inherited. Alexander's good fortune shone once again.

Alexander reunited with the main body of his army at the city of Gordium, which contained the famous Gordian Knot. Legends held that the intricate knot was tied by King Midas, and the man who unraveled it would go on to become king of all of Asia. How Alexander solved the knot is disputed. According to certain historians, he thoughtfully disassembled the looped mass. According others, he promptly drew his sword, slashed the rope, and unraveled it. Either way, he made his intentions clear, which offers us another chance to understand the effectiveness of his uncanny drive.

Whether sieging an "impregnable" city, facing an "invincible" army, or solving an "impossible" knot, Alexander refused to believe he couldn't succeed. He was driven to win by any means necessary, and he rarely played by the "rules." One of his hallmarks was, through diligent analysis and planning, devising radically new strategies and tactics that his enemies had no preconceived defenses for. Sometimes circumstances called for a carefully orchestrated gambit, as you saw in Pelium. As you'll see in one of his greatest military victories, however, the most unexpected move is sometimes a direct assault so audacious that nobody would dare attempt it. Nobody but Alexander, that is.

The Macedonian forces moved on toward their goal, taking minor cities as they went and leaving garrisons to consolidate their position. They met little resistance as they moved deeper into the Persian lands, but finally, in 333 BC, Alexander met the full power of the Persian king at the city of Issus. Darius commanded the forces in person upon the advice of his courtiers and generals.

Macedonian scouts estimated the Persian army at no less than 200,000 men and possibly as many as 500,000. Alexander had just over 40,000 soldiers. He called his Companions and other commanding officers to ascertain their views about the proximity and enormity of the enemy's forces. They were eager to follow him into battle, and plans were outlined of where and how to stage the confrontation.

Darius and his hordes were expected to wait in nearby plains where his numbers could engulf and swallow the smaller Macedonian army. Instead, however, Darius impatiently marched his massive army to Alexander's rear, choosing a much narrower theater of engagement, as the flatlands in front of Issus were bound by the ocean on one side and the mountains on the other.

When the Macedonians learned that they wouldn't face the Persians in three days as anticipated but rather the next day, disconcert spread amongst their ranks. Alexander was himself startled at the maneuver, but he emboldened his men by delivering an impassioned speech:

"Our enemies are Medes and Persians, men who for centuries have lived soft and luxurious lives," he bellowed. "We of Macedon for generations past have been trained in the hard school of danger and war. Above all, we are free men, and they are slaves. There are Greek troops, to be sure, in Persian service—but how different is their cause from ours!

"They will be fighting for pay—and not much of that. We, on the contrary, shall fight for Greece, and our hearts will be in it. As for our foreign troops—Thracians, Paeonians, Illyrians, Agrianes—they are the best and stoutest soldiers in Europe, and they will find as their opponents the slackest and softest of the tribes of Asia. And what, finally, of the two men in supreme command? You have Alexander, they…Darius!"

The next morning, both armies faced off, looking for an opportunity to strike the first blow. Through skillful reconnaissance and positioning, Alexander gained an advantage on his right flank and launched the first successful attack on the Persian lines.

As the two commanders manipulated their armies into the battle, it was Alexander who systematically gained ground and position first, namely on the Persian left. At the same time, however, the Greek mercenaries under Darius' command attacked Alexander's center phalanx with a dangerous ferocity. The tide was turning against the Macedonian center, and the phalanx was in grave danger.

As usual, however, Alexander came to the rescue. His wing had completely driven back the Persian left and thus was free to rush to his center's aid. Alexander and his cavalry and brigades tore into the Greek flank and relieved the center, which reformed and thereafter held its own against the aggressors. Meanwhile, a veritable avalanche of Persian cavalry poured forth and imperiled Alexander's left flank. Despite being outnumbered and all but crushed, Alexander's Thessalian riders bravely stood their ground, rallying and returning again and again to the charge.

Darius, as was customary with Persian kings, occupied the absolute center position in a gleaming chariot, surrounded by his top officers and family. Having secured his own center and cut a path through the Persian line, Alexander headed straight for Darius and his nobles. Within minutes, the Companions came down upon Darius' royal guard with a godlike fury and slaughtered his men wholesale. When Darius saw that his left flank had collapsed and that his life was in danger, he chose to flee the battle, signaling defeat.

Persian cries of the king's flight crushed morale, and soon the entire army was fleeing for the hills. Vast numbers of Persians were slain by the end of the conflict, stated at over 100,000 including many generals. Darius even abandoned his wife, mother-in-law, and son. The Macedonian loss was 450 men.

After the victory at Issus, Alexander moved south into Phoenicia to secure its important coastal cities and neutralize all opposition as far as Egypt. He met little resistance as he moved from city to city, offering, as always, amenable terms for surrender.

While in Syria, he received a letter from Darius, in which he asked for his family back and proposed a friendship and alliance. To this letter, Alexander responded by reciting the injuries of Persia to Greece, the beginning of hostilities by Darius, and the instigation of his father's murder by the Persian court. He ended his letter in no uncertain terms:

"I am lord of Asia. Come to me, and you shall receive all that you can ask. But if you deny my right as your lord, stand and fight for your kingdom. I will seek you wherever you are."

Alexander's dauntless drive would next meet a much more formidable foe, however—one that would strain his resourcefulness to its limits.

Tyre remained as the last city of importance to take in Phoenicia, which was not only the chief naval station of the region but of the world. Once it was secured, Alexander could safely continue south into Egypt and Babylon. Tyrian ambassadors met with Alexander and offered submission and their fleet, but with the stipulation that he would not be allowed to enter the city. The Tyrian officials wanted to retain their independence in case Persia won, an unacceptable condition to Alexander. So the city shut its gates and prepared their defenses.

Alexander and his officers agreed that Tyre must be taken. But the question was how? The city was situated on an island two miles long, less wide, and separated from the coast by a channel a half-mile wide and some eighteen feet deep. High, sturdy walls surrounded it, and housed 30,000 men fit for battle, machines to resist a siege, and a number of warships.

The Macedonian generals thought their task impossible, to which Alexander replied, "There is nothing impossible to him who will try." As he had no ships, Alexander made up his mind to build a highway of stone, earth, and wood across the channel, two hundred feet wide.

Laborers were procured from every part of the neighboring country, and the highway progressed rapidly. As they approached the deeper waters, however, they came within missile range of the city, and the Tyrians were waiting. They attacked Alexander's causeway day and night from the walls with archers, ballistae, catapults, and other siege weapons, and from the sea with ships loaded with similar weapons. Alexander responded by building fortifications to protect his workers, and two large towers to lead the construction, manned with archers and siege engines of his own to keep the Tyrian ships at a distance.

Under this cover, the work progressed again. The Tyrians mounted a devastating counter-attack, however. They waited for a day when the winds were blowing directly into the highway, and loaded an old ship with a massive store of flammable material and hung cauldrons of combustible substances off the yard-arms and booms. They towed the fire ship to the Macedonians, set it ablaze, and smashed it into the towers, fortifications, and siege engines, engulfing everything in flames.

The strong winds fanned the fires, which proved too violent to be extinguished. The towers and breastworks were lost, and the end of the highway was cracked and weakened, and was being washed away by the waves. The work of months and multitudes had been destroyed in a short hour.

Several of Alexander's officers suggested that they offer a treaty with Tyre, but he was convinced that he couldn't move further into Persia so long as their navy could ferry troops into Tyre and thus gain access to his rear. No, Alexander said, Tyre must fall, and he already had plans to overcome the setback.

They would construct a wider highway in a better position; it would support more than two towers, which would shield his workers and soldiers from the city's defenses. And they would deploy warships of their own.

"Warships?" his officers asked. They had no ships. Not yet, at least.

After work began on the new highway, Alexander mustered a small army and marched to nearby cities that he didn't control. He quickly received their surrender and formed a fleet of 80 ships, which were outfitted with siege engines. When his fleet was ready and highway completed, he set sail for Tyre to launch his attack.

The siege proved tremendously difficult for the Macedonians. Under constant attack from the Tryian engines, they fought bitterly to secure positions from which they could work to reduce the walls of the city. This effort proved almost impossible, however. Alexander's siege weapons, which were on ground thanks to the highway, and mounted on ships, could make no impression on the city walls, which were widely renowned as the sturdiest in the world.

After long efforts and trials on every part of the city, the floating engines finally found what they were looking for: a section of wall that was of weaker masonry, as the Tyrians never expected siege engines to be mounted on ships and sailed to their walls.

The Macedonians succeeded in breaching the wall, but the first storming party was driven back by showers of missiles, fire-pots, and other devices. Three days later, however, when the sea was calm, Alexander arrayed his battering engines at the weakened position and ordered his vessels carrying missile-throwing engines and archers to skirmish around the island so as to confuse the garrisons. Once the siege engines crumbled a large section of the wall, bridges were thrown down, and Macedonian infantry poured in.

Alexander led the second wave of soldiers into the city, and although the Tyrians fought bravely, their men were no match for the highly skilled Macedonians. The city was swarmed and taken. Alexander's men wanted vengeance for their brothers who had been captured, tortured, executed on walls in full sight of the invaders, and tossed into the sea to prevent a proper burial. Thousands of Tyrians were slaughtered.

Thus fell Tyre, after a seven-month siege, and Alexander's reputation grew in the lands to that of an invincible god.

While Alexander was besieging Tyre, he received a second letter from Darius in which he offered a fantastic sum for the release of his family, his daughter's hand in marriage, and all the Persian territory west of the Euphrates. "If I were Alexander, I would accept," Parmenion told the king. "So would I, if I were Parmenion," he replied.

Alexander told Darius that the whole of Persia was his, that he would marry his daughter if he so wished, with or without Darius' consent, and that he had no need for the money. He would keep Darius' family hostage, albeit nobly cared for, to further distress the Great King and to interfere with his ability to defend his kingdom, or so Alexander hoped.

It's interesting to note that a great drive often produces a pride that can, at times, manifest as hubris. Darius wasn't half the man that Alexander was, and the Macedonian took offense at the mere implication that they were peers. No great men or women, no matter how outwardly humble and gracious, are self-deprecating, diffident weaklings. They possess a rare concentration of intelligence and ability, and they aren't ashamed to make it known, even if only by their actions. This self-confidence is often misinterpreted and denounced as shameless self-love, implying that the only way to be "acceptable" is to assume an air of tottering docility. The genius knows better, though.

September 331 BC soon arrived and saw Alexander marching toward Egypt. He reached the formidable city of Gaza, which refused to submit. Like Tyre, Gaza presented imposing problems for the siege parties, namely the height of the ground on which the city was built. But Alexander would consider no difficulty whatsoever.

He conferred with his engineers and devised a plan to build a massive mound around the city so that the siege engines could be rolled up to the walls and set to work. The scheme worked: Alexander's engines breached the walls within two months. The first three raiding parties were driven back by fierce Gazan warriors. The fourth broke through, however, opening the gates of the city and bringing the destruction of the Gaza garrisons.

Alexander continued through the region, setting up a strong government in Syria and Phoenicia, and headed for the country of the Nile. Egypt had no bond whatsoever with its Persian masters. They were a peaceful folk, and the arrival of a new conqueror mattered little to the population and rulers alike.

The Egyptians, who had lived under the Persian yoke for two centuries, welcomed Alexander and his Macedonians with open arms. Alexander returned to the Egyptians the freedom to exercise their religions and ancient customs, gave them political autonomy, and arranged for the taxes to flow to his coffers. At the mouth of the Nile, Alexander founded the city of Alexandria-by-Egypt, which would later become a major economic and cultural center in the Mediterranean world. Month by month, Alexander was making good on his promise to use his sword and the swords of his brethren to not just kill, but lift the known world to a new echelon of economic, social, and academic prosperity.

After receiving reinforcements from Europe, Alexander reorganized his forces and started for Babylon. He marched north up the Tigris River, deeper into the bowels of the Persian territory, and founded cities as he went to provide asylum for the wounded. Together, these cities formed a chain of military posts that served to provide communications, and to build up a knowledge of Hellenic culture throughout the country.

A year had passed since Darius' embarrassing defeat at Issus, which he spent amassing an unspeakably large army. Alexander's men had captured Persian scouts, who claimed that Darius' army stood at a million soldiers to Alexander's 41,000. Anxiety gnawed at the Macedonians. No obstacle thus far was insurmountable for Alexander, but a million men?

Alexander learned that Darius had positioned his hordes to intercept his planned crossing of the Tigris, which would spell certain disaster for his army. So the young king changed his point of crossing to well north of Darius, and the army forded the river without opposition. After days of marching, the Macedonians finally encountered the Persians at the plains of Gaugamela. Darius' army was a sight to behold: Infantry as far as the eye could see. Rolling waves of cavalry numbering close to 100,000. Companies of fearsome war elephants.

Alexander and his Companions conducted a careful survey of the enemy and grounds. He was slow to fight, knowing that his only chance to succeed against such odds was strategic and tactical perfection. General Parmenio suggested a surprise night attack, but Alexander rejected it. He wanted to defeat Darius in open battle and leave him with no excuse to use to rally another army.

The armies squared off the following morning. The large, open field had been leveled and cleared of obstacles to allow Darius' masses maximum mobility, which would be used to try to encircle the Macedonians. The Macedonians were heavily out-flanked, but Alexander had anticipated this and brilliantly arranged on each side of his army a "flying" column of highly maneuverable troops, which could spread out and guard against outflanking movements.

The battle began when a Persian chariot charged into Parmenio's left flank and center. Alexander countered by leading his Companions into battle on the right.

Parmenio and the men of the left repelled the chariots. By contrast, Alexander made headway into the overwhelming numbers that lay before him. Darius tried to out-flank Alexander on both sides, but the protective columns fanned out and held the edges admirably. Darius tried the maneuver again, this time ordering his center cavalry to try, and edged his center infantry in that direction too. Alexander's exceptional ability to retain complete battlefield awareness even while engaged in combat himself detected the ploy and, consequently, the gap in the Persian front.

Alexander seized on the opportunity by rapidly forming a deep wedge of infantry, headed it personally with his Companions, and drove it like a battering ram into the Persian center. Darius was positioned just beyond them.

The bravest Persians stood fast and contended the charge, but they were no match for Alexander and his Companions and phalanx, which had never yet found their match. The Macedonians hewed their way through the living masses. Darius watched in horror as Alexander broke his center and angled toward him. Instead of ordering reinforcements to retrieve what might have been a temporary disadvantage, Darius turned and fled.

Despite Darius' second cowardly retreat, his skilled and able generals knew that the battle could still be won, and pressed on with ferocity. Alexander's bold move had opened a gap in his own lines, which allowed Persian infantry and cavalry to pour in and envelop his left flank. This put incredible strain on Parmenio's lines, which were on the brink of being fatally compromised.

Sensing the threat, Alexander wheeled his Companions and galloped to Parmenio's aid. Simultaneously, vast columns of Persian troops heard that their king had abandoned them yet again. They melted into retreat, completely dissolving the Persian center.

Despite the carnage on the left, which left 60 of Alexander's elite Companions dead, demoralization spread quickly amongst the Persian ranks. Macedonian fervor rose in response, galvanizing them to regain their position and drive back the enemy until their ranks collapsed completely. Alexander wasn't done, however—he immediately set out to pursue and capture Darius. His men marched rapidly, covering 70 miles by the next day, but Darius kept well ahead.

Although he would live to see another day, Darius lost between 40,000 – 90,000 men at Gaugamala as well as any hope of retaining his throne. Alexander's losses were just over 1,000 men. Word of the unthinkable victory spread quickly. If a million men couldn't stop Alexander and his claim to Asia, what could?

This sentiment was the final, wheezing breaths of the Persian Empire, which illustrates an important lesson in overcoming incredible odds. No matter the journey, one will always face opposition, whether in the form of competitors, enemies, meddlers, saboteurs, incompetents, and the like. The simplest way to defeat them all is to *accomplish what you set out to accomplish.* Don't let them divert your efforts into undesirable directions. Don't let them convince you that compromises are advantageous or necessary. Be like Alexander in your drive: show them just how dauntless and relentless you really are, and just as the sprawling Persian Empire did, with its millions of able-bodied men, they'll lose their will to keep fighting and accept your ascendance.

Alexander's story isn't complete, however. There is more we can learn about drive—including its dangers—from his legendary exploits.

The wondrous wealth of the megalopolis Babylon and the treasure-laden Susa, the next cities to capitulate to Alexander and welcome him as their king, staggered even him. He used the riches to pay his troops handsomely. He also sent a sum home to Antipater six-times the annual income of Athens to put down a Spartan rebellion.

Alexander named Mazaeus, a Persian general who had fought bravely in Gaugamala, viceroy of Babylon, and appointed several other ranking Persians who had surrendered to other positions of political power. The military control, however, would remain with Macedonian soldiers. This was another stroke of Alexander's genius, as it fostered allegiance and respect among the conquered, and reinforced his standing offer to the remaining peoples that lay ahead: accept me and live well, or oppose me and perish. "I have not come to Asia to destroy nations," he explained to the defectors. "I have come here that those who are subdued by my arms shall have naught to complain of my victories."

The rugged Macedonians enjoyed a long rest and the many luxuries of Babylon before preparing for their final journey to take Persepolis, the primary capital of Persia, and thus the entire kingdom. To get there, however, would require the traversal of several rivers and a mountain range comparable to the Alps in size and altitude, which was occupied by hostile, hardy tribes. And it was the winter. Nevertheless, the Macedonian legions set out into the labyrinth of rocks, precipices, torrents, valleys, and passes at the end of 331 BC.

The Uxian mountaineers maintained a fortress deep in the mountains and controlled the lands. If Alexander was to pass, they said, he would have to pay them tribute just as the Persians did. Alexander laughed at their demands and found another road, albeit a very difficult one, onto the mountain. He soon located the Uxian villages and quickly swept over them. The Uxians were dumbfounded at the speed with which Alexander navigated the rugged terrain, and mounted a last stand at their stronghold. Despite a staunch defense, Alexander led a siege that only lasted a few hours before the Uxians offered surrender, which Alexander accepted.

Onward Alexander went, moving ever closer to the treacherous mountain pass known as the Persian Gates. The Gates marked one of two routes that lead to Persepolis, through the lands controlled by the satrap Ariobarzanes, who remained loyal to the Persian cause. While Alexander could have avoided the pass by taking the safer road to Persepolis, he decided not to—quite literally choosing the road less traveled. He did so for a good reason, though: to prevent Ariobarzanes and his force of 40,000 men from having a clear view of his rear as well as a direct path to Susa, Babylon, and other freshly conquered lands.

Thus, Alexander split his army, sending Parmenio with the baggage and siege train along the secure road through the foothills to the south, and leading himself the Companion cavalry, the lancers and horse-bowmen, and the archers to the dangerous canyon. He arrived at the Gates to find it walled off. Alexander prepared a direct assault, as was his custom. Once the offensive began, however, he was dismayed to learn that he had led his men into a devastating ambush.

Ariobarzanes had anticipated the Macedonians and allowed them to march deep into the pass with no resistance whatsoever. When the head of their column reached the narrowest section, the Persians unleashed a terrifying attack from above, raining down arrows, stones, and boulders. Whole files of Macedonians were crushed, but they pressed on. They tried to scale the granite walls of the pass, helping each other up and defending each other with their shields. But the onslaught continued to decimate the Macedonian ranks, forcing Alexander to withdraw his forces from the seemingly unassailable defense. He had to find another way to the Persians.

As if sent by the gods themselves, a shepherd came forth who had been sold into Persian slavery and who knew the region intimately. He showed Alexander several unknown, difficult paths through the foothills that would take him to Ariobarzanes' rear. Alexander promised the shepherd incredible wealth if he led his army honestly, and a quick death if he betrayed them.

The plan was simple: Alexander would take a large contingent of his best soldiers with the shepherd while Craterus, his commander of the phalanx, would keep the rest of the men looking busy in front of the wall so as to maintain pretenses of another frontal assault. When Alexander was in position to strike from the rear, he would sound trumpets, and Craterus would lead a charge in the front.

The shepherd, Alexander, and his men set out that night, into a violent storm. They had 12 miles to cover and time was of the essence. If Ariobarzanes suspected the maneuver and caught Alexander in the wilds with a force of his own, Alexander's saga would likely come to a bloody end. But Alexander took such calculated risks with carefree ease, as if the sheer force of his intention would bend the universe to his favor. A reflection of his accomplishments makes one wonder if such is possible.

The group marched through the night in hushed silence and, by the morning, reached a path that led directly to the Persian camp. Alexander waited through the day until the following night, and then split up his men. A detachment would head to the nearby Araxes River and build a bridge over it to occupy the only escape route available to the Persians. The second detachment, led by Alexander, would descend directly into the Persian camp.

Alexander's vanguard soon came upon their enemy's outposts and, through surprise attacks, eliminated each, allowing him and his men to reach the edge of the camp unperceived. Meanwhile, Craterus had done well maintaining his pretense with numerous campfires representative of Alexander's full army. When Alexander's trumpets blared, the entire camp froze. Mayhem immediately followed when thousands of Macedonians poured in from all sides. Craterus and his brigades simultaneously charged the wall, scaled it, and overran the dumbfounded garrisons.

The ambush was a resounding success. The enemy was cut to pieces. Ariobarzanes and his bodyguard tried to escape through the rear, only to meet the Macedonians that had bridged the river. The Persians chose to die with their swords in hand. Afterward, Alexander gathered his Companions and set out to Persepolis at once, traveling over 40 miles in one night, through the snow, and reached the magnificent capital before word had even arrived of what happened in the mountains. The city opened its gates and welcomed its new king.

Great feasts were held in Persepolis, and against his usual habit of preserving whatever he conquered, Alexander gave in to his men's demands of retaliation. Athens had been burned and desecrated by the Persian king in times past, and the Macedonians wanted to inflict the same wounds upon Persepolis. Thus, the great city was given up to plunder and the magnificent palace of the Persian kings was burned to the ground after a drunken celebration. Women and their jewels were to be left untouched, however, as ordered by Alexander.

Alexander lavished his men as usual, who spent their days and nights in revelry. He was never one to rest for long, though. Within a month of taking Persepolis, he made various excursions to neighboring tribes to complete the Hellenic subjugation once and for all. This included a clan of fierce mountaineers not unlike the Uxians who controlled roads from Persis to the sea, which Alexander intended to use. To reach the tribe, icy rain had to be endured and snow-clad hills traversed; steps had to be cut into frozen slopes; and roads had to be hewn through the woods. Every difficulty was overcome with the king leading the way. The mountain people were reached and agreements were struck, thus accomplishing Alexander's great vision. In a mere four years, the Macedonians had vanquished the mighty Persian army and claimed its lavish empire, reversing the conquest accomplished by King Xerxes over a century before.

By 324 BC, 11 years after his ascension to the Macedonian throne, Alexander had led his army 22,000 miles, was undefeated in battle, and founded some 70 cities in the lands he conquered, 22 of which he named after himself. These epic achievements pay homage to his simple philosophy on life. "I would rather live a short life of glory than a long one of obscurity," he wrote. Thanks to his unparalleled ambition, drive, and willpower, few figures in the pages of history embody a spirit of carpe diem—seize the day—like Alexander did.

In June of 323 BC, at age 32, Alexander contracted a mysterious fever. Within a week, he was dead. Whispers of conspiracy and murder filled the air, but nothing definitive was brought to light.

Alexander had written a lengthy will in case of his death, which called for his successors to conduct military expansion into the southern and western Mediterranean, build monumental constructions, and further unify Eastern and Western populations. After he was gone, his generals dismissed the plans as impractical and extravagant. Instead, they carved up the conquered territories for themselves and went to war with each other and the rest of Greece. This feud lasted 40 years and culminated in the blood-soaked collapse of the entire kingdom of Macedonia.

Alexander's legendary apotheosis is a testament to the transformational power of drive, and of the will to physically, mentally, and spiritually push oneself beyond the impossible. Although his method was war, and some choose to remember him as a ruthless savage, there's no denying that his compassion for the vanquished and diplomacy represented something much greater in him, and that his legacy was far more profound than meaningless carnage.

Geniuses don't work long and hard from a begrudging sense of duty—they do it because they have a strong desire to give everything they've got to a project and see it through to the best of their abilities. Ambition shows you the path to success, but drive is what gets you through it.

"I do not think there is any other quality so essential to success of any kind as the quality of perseverance," wrote John D. Rockefeller. "It overcomes almost everything, even nature."

Many people now recognized for their stellar achievements were once listless and purposeless. Stephen Hawking was once a young college student who felt "bored with life" without "anything worth doing." When he was diagnosed with Amyotrophic Lateral Sclerosis at age 21, the doctors gave him two-and-a-half years to live. While many people would have sunk into a depression and accepted that death was on the horizon, Hawking decided that there were still many things he wanted to do in his life. Stephen turned 70 this year, baffling scientists with his extraordinary longevity, and he has become one of the most celebrated scientists of our times.

Alexander's drive was nothing short of godlike. "Sex and sleep alone make me conscious that I am mortal," he said. When he landed on the shores of Asia Minor, he looked at the vast expanses ahead of him—the invincible cities, the millions of Persian soldiers—and simply saw heaps of mud and stone to take and hordes of men that will soon call him king.

Our journeys to greatness will probably never require the sheer power of will that Alexander's did. I don't know if there's any modern experience quite comparable to charging headlong into a few hundred thousand roaring soldiers. But if we could capture just a fraction of Alexander's spirit and world-view, we would be unstoppable in our adventures.

"A passionate desire and an unwearied will can perform impossibilities or what may seem to be such to the cold, timid, and feeble," wrote the famous English doctor Sir James Simpson.

So what lies behind drive? How do geniuses find the energy and confidence to believe in their goals and their abilities, as well as the audacity to continue so believing until their wills are reality?

THE POWER OF PURPOSE

Purpose is the primary fuel of ambition. Purpose creates a destination. We can only become fully engaged in life when we feel that we are doing something that really matters. Purpose is what inspires us, lights us up, and floats our boats.

Washington Irving—the famous author, historian and essayist—said, "Great minds have purposes, others have wishes. Little minds are tamed and subdued by misfortune, but great minds rise above it."

The search for purpose and meaning is one of the most powerful and lasting themes in every culture since the dawn of time. You'll find it in Homer's Odyssey, and it has inspired some of the greatest spiritual figures in history: Jesus, Buddha, Moses, Mohammad. You'll even find it in modern culture in movies like *Indiana Jones and the Last Crusade*, which re-tells the story of Perceval's search for the Holy Grail through the daring character of Indiana Jones, as well as the famous Star Wars trilogy, in which Luke Skywalker confronts his deepest fears by confronting and vanquishing Darth Vader and the Empire. It's no coincidence that these movies—which modernize the legendary virtues of the hero's journey, the search for meaning and the triumph of good over evil—are among the most popular and successful of all time.

"There is one quality we must possess to win," said Napoleon Hill, author of one of the best-selling books of all time, *Think and Grow Rich*, "and that is definiteness of purpose, the knowledge of what one wants, and a burning desire to possess it."

For a time, Alexander was an almost inhuman force, alive with unbridled and unmatched purpose. While many in his position would've been content with a life of kingly hedonism, Alexander was cut from a different cloth. He pawned off everything he owned to finance what he truly cared about: his vision of a glorious destiny and immortality. But perhaps more impressively, he conducted himself with extreme equilibrium, sanity, and benevolence startlingly uncharacteristic of a conqueror. He lived in a time where men of his ilk were expected to indulge in mindless slaughter and degradation of the people they subdued, but he not only discouraged it, he forbade it.

One year before his death, however, his quest required an advance from Persia to India to conquer what was left of the known world. When Alexander announced this to his soldiers, they mutinied. They were exhausted and longed to return to their families. Despite inspired, moving speeches, Alexander couldn't convince them to continue, so he released them from duty and relegated himself to the role of administrator of his empire—a post he loathed. Months later, Plutarch wrote that the king "lost his spirits, and grew diffident of the protection and assistance of the gods, and suspicious of his friends."

Ironically, during this time of ennui, Alexander suffered his worst losses.

Intrigues led to the execution of his great friends and loyal generals Philotas and Parmenio. He killed his brave and loyal officer, Cleitus, over drunken slurs. Alexander sank into a deep depression, almost driving him to suicide, and sowed much discontent amongst his people that had come to love him dearly.

Alexander's plight didn't stop there. His best friend and general Hephaestion died a mysterious death, rumored to be from poisoning. The loss sent Alexander into an irrevocable rage that cost thousands of Persians their lives and led to his further self-deification as well as his increased adoption of Persian customs, which many Greeks despised.

Finally, Alexander—a man who had defied death so regularly and against such odds that his enemies had declared him invincible—lost his life to an unexplainable fever that began after a night of heavy drinking. The morality of Alexander's ambitious purpose notwithstanding, it's very clear that once he had lost it, he rapidly lost everything. If we are to succeed in our endeavors toward greatness, we must learn and apply this final lesson of Alexander's to our journeys. Simply put: If purpose dies, the entire adventure quickly follows suit.

But what is a purpose, exactly? The dictionary defines it as follows:

The reason why something is done or why something exists. It is something set up as an object or an end to be attained; an intention.

Where the goal is the what, the purpose is the all-important why. Purpose gives goals meaning. When the intention to make something happen is weak—when you're just not feeling the "fire"—it's not going to happen. People that ignore purpose don't go very far in life. Nobody can love what they don't feel in their hearts. The will to go on expires, soon or later.

How excited are you to get to work in the morning? How much do you enjoy what you do for its own sake rather than what it gets you? And how accountable do you hold yourself to a deeply held set of goals?

These are the questions of purpose all adventurous souls must ask themselves. If your answers to these questions are enthusiastic, then chances are you're bringing a strong sense of purpose to your pursuits. If your answers to these questions are anything less, chances are you're just going through the motions. The former path breeds persistence and grit, which lead to opportunities and successes thereafter. The latter breeds indifference and lethargy, which can't handle even the pettiest of pressures.

Imagine that you're out at sea on a boat, voyaging to a far-off destination.

Your boat springs a leak, which immediately becomes your priority. You jump down and start bailing water to prevent going under, but forget that nobody is left to navigate the ship. One day, after doing nothing but bailing water for who knows how long, you poke your head over the bow and wonder where the heck you are and how you got there. This is the purposeless life. People can become so preoccupied with just staying afloat that they fail to realize that nobody is at the helm.

Unfortunately, clarifying purpose takes time—quiet, uninterrupted time—which is something many of us feel we don't have. We rush from one obligation to another without a "50,000 foot" view of where we're going. It may seem self-indulgent to stop and reflect on questions of meaning and purpose, but your journey will demand it.

When Steven Spielberg, Jeffrey Katzenberg, and David Geffen started DreamWorks, their purpose was to entertain and delight people. Profits were second to that. They went through some tough times, coming close to bankruptcy twice. But they persevered in large part due to their dedication to the studio's vision and reason for being. Today, DreamWorks is one of the largest film studios in the world.

Nobody can force a purpose on you—you must choose it of your own free will. There are so many ways to help people in the world, but you need to find your way—the way that makes you want to put this book down right now and get into action. As Howard Thurman said, you must find what makes you come alive.

So, before beginning any adventure—before choosing any particular path—don't forget to ask yourself *why*: Why are you doing this? Why is it exciting? Why does it really matter? When you've addressed these questions with true convictions, you know you've unlocked your purpose. This is the wellspring of any strong drive to succeed.

There's more to this story, though. By awakening purpose, you've created an ember, not a fire. You've begun something, but must quickly pile on the kindling to complete the transformation that all geniuses undergo. You're ready to fight the first battle in your journey to greatness, the battle between the Work and the Resistance.

———

Some people will do anything to avoid the work. They have pretty spreadsheets, fancy proposals, slick PowerPoint presentations, and sparkling visions of champagne baths and keynote speeches.

They'll rattle off a long list of industry bloggers that love their ideas, the interviews they have lined up to woo top talent, and the play-by-play of their ten-year plans and distribution models. But ask them about the *real* work—the hard work that's required to materialize ideas into something usable, valuable, and viable—and they're likely to fall into an awkward silence.

These self-styled visionaries just don't get it. Or they don't want to get it. They aren't doing the work, and they won't succeed regardless of how busy they keep themselves with not doing it. So what is the work, anyway?

The work consists of the actions that directly create something with tangible, exchangeable, enduring value. Once that's complete, the work includes the actions that move the creation out into the hands of users and consumers, in exchange for something of equal value. The drive of a genius is always in the direction of *doing the work*.

If you have a brilliant idea that will change the way some part of the world works, tweeting and blogging about it isn't the work. Coding a proof of concept that you can use to raise funding with is, however. If you have a story stirring inside you that the world needs to read, spending another 50 hours searching for inspiration or bouncing your ideas off others isn't the work. Finishing the outline and starting the first draft is.

Alexander was renowned for his unequalled dedication to the work. Once he locked his sights on the next milestone in his journey, whether it be the next city to subdue or next region to assimilate, he spent every waking minute in action, making it so. In his own words, the most slavish thing was to "luxuriate," whereas the most royal thing was to "labor."

He also understood the power of *momentum*. Once you're in motion, it's much easier to stay so, which allows for greater and greater acceleration. And the closer Alexander approached the accomplishment of a goal, the harder he pushed. Look at his actions after his brilliant, but harrowing, breakthrough at the Persian Gates. He hadn't slept in over a day and had just completed another perilous assault, and his officers suggested that he join his men in celebration of what was sure to be the last of the Persian defenses. After a well-deserved rest, Persepolis would be theirs. Instead, Alexander did what just came naturally to him. A man of such impetuous drive couldn't stop when the finish line was just over the horizon.

If doing the work is the key to victory in our journeys to greatness, what has the power to stop us? The answer takes us inward, and if we are to advance in our quests, it must be conquered with the same vigor and determination of Alexander.

THE INVISIBLE, INSIDIOUS, AND IMPERSONAL ENEMY THAT HATES THE WORK

Resistance is invisible, insidious, and impersonal. It can't be seen, but it's in you right now, and it can be felt. Resistance tells you anything to keep you from doing the Work. It will lie, argue, bluster, seduce, and bully you to get its way. It will say anything to strike a deal and then stab you in the back. It doesn't care who you are or what you want to do. It has no conscience. While the genius code awakens our potentials, Resistance obscures them.

What kinds of things does Resistance hate most?

Any creative artistic action. Any type of entrepreneurial venture. Any new diet or fitness regimen. Any method of spiritual advancement. Any type of education. Anything courageous. In short, anything that requires us to forego immediate gratification in search of long-term growth or fulfillment.

Resistance loves excuses, justifications, and compromises. Start tomorrow, it says. Wait until you're a bit smarter, stronger, wealthier, happier, motivated, or prepared. Don't rock the boat, it advises. Who are you to challenge the status quo? Do you really think you can bear the cross that comes with it? Resistance's stock in trade is diversions, follies, and dead ends, and it's a *remarkable* salesperson.

In his last year, Alexander lost the only work that mattered to him—the heroic pursuit of glory for himself and for Greece—and with it, the only defense against Resistance. This malevolent force relished the chance to conquer the man that conquered the world, and proved more than capable of the task. If it can undermine someone of Alexander's strength, it can do at least the same to us.

Resistance has a fatal weakness, though. We can turn the tables on it. It can be defeated.

In his brilliant book, *The War of Art*, Stephen Pressfield reveals that Resistance's Achilles' heel lies in the fact that it will only fight that which is truly important in your life. It wants to kill your deepest purposes and desires, your true calling and gifts. Yes, *kill* them. In this way, however, it shows you what work you must do—your very personal path to profound fulfillment, happiness, and success. Resistance dares you to meet it in pitched battle.

When you do anything but the Work, Resistance sneers at you. It's playing you like a marionette. You're feeding it, making it stronger. But when you do the Work, it shrieks in horror. "Anything but the Work!" it cries. It invades your mind and flashes shiny distractions. Facebook! Twitter! Television! Phone! ANYTHING BUT THE WORK!

Make no mistake. The fight against Resistance is a war to the death. It will tell you you're too weak to kill it. Too stupid. Too lazy. But you're not. Ironically, it depends on your obedience for its strength.

Defiantly do the Work instead and Resistance withers. Every bit of Work done strikes at it. Do enough Work and its armor crumbles, its power fades, and all that's left is a whispering ghost. Do more Work and it even stops whispering.

If you're trying to create a business, a career, a relationship, or anything else in your life, you're a warrior.

Your primary enemy is Resistance, and as we saw in Alexander's story, it's ultimately more dangerous—and powerful—than barbarian hordes, impenetrable castles, and sweeping empires.

The journey to greatness requires that you fight the battle against Resistance anew every day by doing the Work. Drive compels you forward. If we are to learn from Alexander's brilliance, you strengthen your will by clarifying purpose, getting into motion, and never relenting. And if we are to learn from Alexander's greatest mistake, you retain your strength by never accepting anything less than the adventure you yearn for—your call to greatness.

7

KNOWLEDGE AND THE GADFLY OF ATHENS

"I am but a small child wandering upon the vast shores of knowledge, every now and then finding a small bright pebble to content myself with."

-Plato

All quests toward greatness require that the hero become wiser, stronger, and better suited to face the challenges that lie ahead. Oftentimes, the knowledge and wisdom required to complete the journey is attained through unassuming and unconventional means.

Mr. Miyagi trains Daniel—the young "karate kid"—for his upcoming showdown in a most unusual way: household chores. Daniel waxes cars, sands wood, fixes a fence, and paints a house. How could these menial tasks possibly teach him anything about karate? Miyagi reveals the answer just as Daniel's patience cracks. To his great surprise and pleasure, Daniel hadn't been spinning his hands for nothing; he's been learning defensive blocks through muscle memory.

In his mid-twenties, Vincent van Gogh is sure he's found his true calling: a Protestant pastor. He prepares for his entrance exam, but fails. He then enrolls into a three-month course in a missionary school near Brussels, and fails. Discouraged but not defeated, he takes a job as a missionary in a dreary mining village and empathizes deeply with the poverty-stricken people under his care. The church fires him within six months for fanaticism, but he finds consolation in a new hobby of his: sketching with charcoal. Van Gogh's father encourages him to pursue his artistic interests, and arranges for van Gogh to study with the prominent Dutch artist Willem Roelofs. Roelofs cultivates van Gogh's talents and persuades him to attend the Academie Royale des Beaux-Arts in Brussels. It's here that van Gogh learns anatomy and the basic rules of modeling and perspective—things which "...you have to know just to be able to draw the least thing." With a new understanding and appreciation of the arts, van Gogh decides to fully commit himself to a new calling: to give happiness to others by creating beauty.

At age fifteen, young Arthur receives the British crown and becomes legendary King Arthur when Saxon barbarians assassinate his father. Arthur turns to the magician Merlin for help in restoring order to the realm. Together, they devise a plan for pacifying the kingdom, and Arthur sets out to make it so. He quickly makes a name for himself by defeating the barbarian hordes, and—under Merlin's close guidance—continues on to expand his empire to include Scotland, Ireland, and Iceland.

These legendary tales of history and fiction illustrate how vital knowledge is to the genius code. The genius is, in the end, someone that knows how to do things better than most. Knowledge is much more than mere information, though. Just as imagination puts facts into motion and gives them life, true knowledge is the result of another process altogether, one that can be best understood through the teachings of the enigmatic founder of Western philosophy.

Socrates could no longer feel his legs.

A tingling numbness was creeping up his body, and soon it would reach his heart. When it did, one of history's greatest thinkers would die.

The people of Athens had charged him with disrespecting the gods and corrupting the youth, for which he was given two choices: exile, or execution. He refused exile and declared that he was unafraid of death, and that he would uphold his civic duty to abide by the laws to which he had agreed to conduct himself, and accept his punishment of death.

Socrates would eventually become known as one of history's most insightful and influential philosophers—indeed, one of the founders of Western philosophy itself—despite not writing a single word.

His students embraced his teachings and used them to change the world in ever-widening spheres: Plato founded the famous Academy, where he guided the likes of Aristotle, Heraclides Ponticus, Eudoxus of Cnidus, and others, to prominence; Xenophon led 10,000 soldiers into the heart of Persia, and his book detailing the exploits proved invaluable to Alexander the Great in his conquest of the entire Persian empire; and Antisthenes adopted and developed the ethical side of Socrates' teachings, and is recognized as the founder of Cynic philosophy.

But Socrates was once a young boy more interested in fighting in the gymnasium than intellectual pursuits. When he was eighteen, he enlisted in the Athenian army and began his rigorous military training. But just a year later, he had begun cultivating his love of knowledge and truth. When he wasn't training for war, Socrates spent copious time in study and discussion with the famous educators of his day, such as Protagoras, Prodicus, and Hippias. And thanks to Athens' rich culture of festivals, competitions, and celebrations, Socrates would spend hours talking with great philosophers visiting from neighboring lands.

The more Socrates learned, the more he realized he didn't know, and the more he came to resent the common superstitions and pretensions of his fellow countrymen. These views mounted and, in part, led to his belief that he was destined to become "a sort of gadfly" to the Athenian state. Undeterred by this revelation—in fact, further inspired by it—Socrates decided that he would devote his life to the moral and intellectual reform of its citizens.

The war between Athens and Sparta was intensifying, however, and many feared that it would engulf all of Greece. Socrates was soon deployed as a hoplite (a foot soldier) to help end a revolt in Potidaea, which turned into a protracted siege that drove the population to cannibalism.

While on their way home, Socrates and his fellow soldiers were met by a large enemy force near Spartolus. The Athenians suffered heavy losses in the fierce skirmish that followed. Socrates distinguished himself, however, by saving the life and armor of the wounded Athenian general Alcibiades, who would later become an admirer of his works.

Socrates' military active duty continued and intensified when, after the battle of Delium, the famous Athenian general Laches commended him for the heroic courage he displayed despite his army's defeat and retreat. Such stories of Socrates' bravery made him a hero in the eyes of many Athenian youths.

Once back in Athens after his final battle in Amphipolis, Socrates immersed himself in philosophy and epistemology. He strongly disagreed with the popular Sophists of his day that claimed that there was no objective standard to what's true or false, right or wrong. Socrates set out to prove that universally valid knowledge existed through a not-yet-formalized science of human conduct on universally valid moral principles.

One of the first lessons that Socrates taught was the importance of self-knowledge. He believed that the primary source of confusion in any intellectual or practical pursuit, no matter how small or large, was the failure of people to realize how little they actually knew about anything, and that the "beginning of wisdom is the definition of terms."

To teach this concept practically, Socrates developed a unique method of instruction that included two stages: the negative and the positive. This became known as the "Socratic method" of investigating truths, which is arguably his most important contribution to Western thought.

In the first (negative) stage, Socrates would adopt an attitude of ignorance and begin to question a person for clarifications in some subject. The questioning would continue until the person would finally realize and admit his ignorance of the subject. This became known as the "Socratic Irony" due to Socrates' pretended deference to the "superior knowledge" of the questioned.

In the second (positive) stage, Socrates employed another series of questions that were designed to distill the answer the person sought, which was the true meaning or definition of the matter at hand.

The principal aim of the Socratic method was to establish knowledge through clearly defined and understood concepts. Socrates believed that reaching such a conceptual level of understanding applied not only to theoretical knowledge, but to moral principles. In point of fact, he maintained that all right conduct depended first upon clear knowledge and definitions of what is right, wrong, virtuous, and evil. Without such a foundation, knowing anything further about morality was impossible.

Socrates loved experimenting with his method and, thus, spent much of his time in the marketplace and other public places speaking with anyone and everyone that would join into discussion with him—slave or free, rich or poor. He would employ his question-and-answer method to probe the many aspects of life that he considered important, such as courage, love, reverence, moderation, and spirituality, driven by the belief that "the unexamined life is not worth living."

When his friend Chaerephon asked the oracle at Delphi if anyone was wiser than Socrates, the oracle declared that nobody was wiser. Socrates wasn't celebratory upon hearing the news, however. In fact, he set out to disprove the oracle by approaching the men considered as the wisest in Athens—poets, statesmen, and artisans—to question them and judge their wisdom as greater than his. Upon completing this experiment, however, Socrates concluded that while each person was certain of their ingenuity and wisdom, they actually knew very little. Thus, Socrates concluded that he must be the wisest in Athens because he was the only man of prominence that knew the extent of his ignorance.

Socrates' inquisitions became a debacle of public disgrace for many of the men he tested, which moved them to exact revenge. Socrates was proud of and welcomed the hostilities in part because it validated his prediction that one day he would become the gadfly of Athens, which indeed he had.

But Socrates' embittered peers wanted a pound of flesh, and answered the scandal he caused by charging him with corrupting the youth and irreverence toward the gods. He stood trial but didn't seek to persuade the jurors of his innocence. Instead, he lectured and provoked them. The jury responded with a guilty verdict, to which he replied that he wasn't convicted for a lack of a convincing argument in his defense, but a lack of willingness to grovel to the jury for his life.

When asked what his punishment should be, Socrates mocked his accusers by suggesting free meals at the city's sacred hearth and fire—an honor reserved for city benefactors and winners of the Olympic games. He then offered to pay a paltry fine as proof that he wasn't a man of wealth. The prosecutor wasn't amused by Socrates' proposals and countered with his own: the death penalty. The jury, offended by Socrates' shameless behavior, was easily persuaded and voted that Socrates be put to death.

The night before his execution, Socrates could have escaped his demise. His lifelong friend of great means, Crito of Alopece, arrived at an early hour to save him. Crito had arranged to bribe the guards to allow Socrates to escape, but Socrates politely declined. He would accept his punishment with dignity and poise, and would not be exiled for Athens' ignorance. Crito tried many earnest appeals, but Socrates was immovable.

In his seventh and last dialog, *Phaedo*, Socrates revealed why he was unintimidated by death. He explained that death is merely the end of his body, which is a vessel, and that he is an immortal, unchanging soul that is the cause of life. He would not dissolve into nothingness, he promised his followers, but instead would bring life to a new vessel.

"Either death ends all things, or it is the beginning of a happy life," he asserted.

In Jacques-Louis David's famous painting of Socrates' execution, the philosopher was surrounded by grieving friends including Plato and Crito. A red-robed man is handling Socrates a goblet of lethal hemlock, who's defiantly pointing to the heavens.

Socrates believed that the more knowledge one had, the better he could act reasonably in life and attain happiness. Similarly, Leonardo da Vinci believed that the acquisition of knowledge is always good for the intellect as it helps drive out the useless things and retain the good.

Like every other element of the genius code, however, there's more to knowledge than meets the eye. One of Socrates' most famous sayings is, "I only know that I know nothing." He recognized that a great hindrance to our capacity to learn is not what we don't know, but what we *do* know. An unwavering certainty that one *already knows* when he doesn't—a trap of false knowledge—is indeed an insidious barrier to further learning in any subject.

When Socrates' followers would approach learning a new subject, the first lesson he insisted they learn was acceptance of how little they actually knew about it. He wanted them to begin studying with the assumption that they, in fact, knew nothing.

This profound observation about the spirit of humility and open-mindedness became one of the most important doctrines of Western thinking, and has been echoed by many great thinkers and scientists. James Clerk Maxwell, whose achievements concerning electromagnetism have been called the "second great unification in physics," said that, "thoroughly conscious ignorance is the prelude to every real advance in science." Claude Bernard, who pioneered the use of the scientific method in medicine, wrote that, "those who do not know the torment of the unknown cannot have the joy of discovery." Plato said that "the learning and knowledge that we have, is, at the most, but little compared with that of which we are ignorant." And Benjamin Franklin stated that the "doorstep to the temple of wisdom is a knowledge of our own ignorance."

There's nothing shameful about conscious and professed ignorance. Only an enlightened mind is aware enough to know the boundaries of its knowledge, and the vast wisdom that lies outside. This is a basic prerequisite of genius. They know what they know, and they know what they don't know.

Only a humble recognition of ignorance makes one aware that there is something he doesn't know. That's the first step. There's more to knowledge and the genius, though.

"All things are subject to interpretation," philosopher and cultural critic

Friedrich Nietzsche wrote. "Whichever interpretation prevails at a given time is a function of power and not truth."

Socrates was infamous for questioning everything, even the perfection of the gods themselves. He assumed nothing and wasn't afraid to not only reject the status quo if it was untrue to him but also proclaim the exact opposite.

For over 1,500 years, doctors "knew" that the liver was responsible for circulating blood around the body and that organs consumed blood, which had to be constantly replaced. But then came Dr. William Harvey who, in the 1620s, conducted extensive research into the mechanics of blood flow in the body and determined that the heart was, in fact, the pump that moved blood throughout the circulatory system, and that the organs were not in fact consuming blood.

Harvey's conclusions were not only scientific heresy but also career suicide. The existing beliefs about blood flow, production, and consumption dated back to the luminous Greek physician Galen and were considered absolutely unquestionable. Harvey didn't let this stop him from asking simple, pointed questions about the foundations of Galen's theories, however.

After over a decade of painstaking research, Harvey released his groundbreaking findings, which were immediately rejected by many of his peers. Twenty years later, his work became generally accepted and is today considered the foundation for all modern research in heart and cardiovascular medicine. In fact, Harvey's discovery of the continuous circulation of the blood within a contained system was the 17th century's most significant achievement in physiology and medicine.

Similar stories lurk behind every major paradigm shift in our knowledge of our planet, our universe, and ourselves. Can you imagine what we will know in the centuries to come? Who knows what current dogmas of science and religion will be shattered and transformed by future generations? They'll laugh about our ignorance just as we laugh at our ancestors' superstitions and assumptions. But geniuses know better.

Geniuses know others don't have it all figured out. They know that there are radical discoveries just waiting to be made in every field of human interest. That's what knowledge means to them—observation, original thinking, and application. Einstein said that knowledge isn't *information*—that true learning only comes from *experience*; that knowledge has a dynamic factor.

The advancement of our civilization depends upon people like Socrates who are bright enough to ask "what if?", curious enough to start looking for answers, passionate enough to chase them down no matter where they hide, and brave enough to share what they've learned and insist on its truth.

When you take up such a charge, you awaken a new series of challenges in your journey. Socrates said that to find ourselves, we must think for ourselves. Such self-awareness is the path to individualism, the next powerful element of the genius code.

8

INDIVIDUALISM AND
THE VIRGIN QUEEN

"I hold it to be the inalienable right of anybody to go to hell in his own way."

-Robert Frost

No adventure is without temptations to stray, which can come in many forms: threats, offerings, expedients, distractions, pleas, requests, and demands. In the face of these lures, the weak give in and lose their way; the strong remain true to their purposes.

"Tell me Harry, would you like to see your mother and father again?" Lord Voldemort asks, as apparitions of Mr. and Mrs. Potter appear. "Together, we can bring them back. All I ask is for something in return." Harry knows exactly what Voldemort wants. He reaches into his pocket and pulls out a magical relic. "That's it Harry. There is no good and evil, there is only power and those too weak to seek it. Together we'll do extraordinary things. Just give me the Stone!" As much as Harry yearns to meet his parents, he knows that an alliance with their murderer will bring nothing but pain, misery, and likely, death. "You *liar!*" Harry cries. Voldemort realizes his ruse has failed, and orders his minion to kill the young wizard.

Charles Darwin is fascinated by natural history, but his father insists that he become a doctor. Darwin, however, finds medical school boring and distressing, so he spends his time studying marine life and plants instead. Annoyed, his father then decides that Darwin is to become a parson and sends him to the University of Cambridge. Before long, Darwin is engrossed with collecting and classifying beetles and studying the works of leading naturalists of his time. Darwin then receives an invitation from his mentor to depart on a two-year expedition around the world to study nature. His father vehemently objects, calling it a waste of time, but eventually gives in. The voyage lasts for five years instead of two. Darwin returns with vital research that helps him develop his groundbreaking theory of evolution.

Adam and Eve can eat the fruit from any tree in the idyllic Garden of Eden except the Tree of Knowledge. A serpent visits Eve one day and seduces her with news that the fruit doesn't bring death, as God said, but godliness instead. She eyes the beautiful, succulent fruit, and gives in to temptation. She then convinces Adam to do the same, and they're suddenly shocked to realize they're naked. They cover themselves with fig leaves and hide, and when God finds them and asks what they've done, Adam blames Eve, and Eve blames the serpent. For their disobedience, God condemns the man to the role of laborer to sustain life, and the woman to the role of creator of life through the agony of childbirth. The disgraced couple would no longer enjoy the utopia of Eden.

Whenever someone sets out into the world to do something important or visionary, it's not long before her ideas are challenged, motives are questioned, and actions are disparaged. Invitations to wander from the proper path come quickly and invariably. The more you push to discover your unique self, the more the world tries to make you the same as everyone else. There is but one universal antidote to this perilous tug of war: an unimpeachable commitment to individualism.

A commitment to greatness is an inflexible commitment to independent thought and action. Individualism is a genius' armor against the social pressures of conformity, criticism, and ostracism. If your armor—your dedication to being *you*—is strong enough, you can survive just about anything, just as Elizabeth Tudor did.

Throughout London, heads were thrust upon pikes and corpses hung from gibbets. These were the morbid remains of Sir Thomas Wyatt and his cohorts, a gang that conspired to overthrow the English queen, Mary I, and place in her stead her half-sister, Elizabeth Tudor.

Elizabeth kept the curtains of her litter pulled back as she entered the city so the citizens could see her sickly, frightened face. Mary had ordered her to the London Tower, a royal prison widely known as a place of torture and death, to be interrogated as to her involvement in the treasonous plot. The interrogation was unlikely to be fair; Mary and many of her councilmen were determined to extract an incriminating confession, which they would use to behead her and, thus, remove what they saw as a threat to their seat of power.

Elizabeth was only 21, but this wasn't her first interrogation, and certainly wasn't her first taste of ostracism and abandonment. In fact, from her very first breath, Elizabeth was subjected to a life of rejection and manipulation.

Elizabeth was to be the daughter of King Henry VIII and his second wife, Anne Boleyn. During her mother's pregnancy, Henry defied the papacy by annulling his marriage to Mary's mother and his first wife, Catherine of Aragon, and declared himself the head of the Church of England, which conveniently allowed the dissolution of his matrimony. He then stripped Catherine of title and declared that the young Mary had no claim to his throne. Instead, his new marriage to Anne was valid, and the child she bore—which was prophesied to be male—would be the rightful heir. Thus, Mary's hostility for Elizabeth began with her in the womb.

Then Elizabeth was born, a girl. The king and his court viewed her birth as a great disappointment and sorrow. Henry's anxiety to produce a male heir immediately swelled, exacerbated by the fact that public opinion turned further against Anne, who was widely regarded as the "king's whore"—an invalid wife who spent extravagant sums on gowns, jewels, furniture, to maintain the image of a queen.

Anne was soon pregnant again but miscarried around Christmas 1534. Henry began to worry that his second marriage was just as cursed as his first, which was marred by a stillborn son and daughter, two sons that lived no longer than two months, a daughter that died within a week of birth, and Mary, the only surviving child.

By October 1535, Anne was pregnant yet again. In January, Anne miscarried a male child after only four months of gestation. Henry was enraged. While she was recovering, he alleged that he had been tricked into the marriage by evil magic, and a band of courtiers were rounded up, accused of adultery with the queen, and tortured to extract confessions. Anne was herself accused of incest with her brother, an act of high treason, and of plotting with her other "lovers" to kill the king.

Despite unconvincing evidence of wrongdoing, all of the accused were found guilty and condemned to death. Anne was beheaded on May 19, 1536. Elizabeth was about to turn three years old, and with her mother's marriage annulled, she joined her half-sister Mary as a princess removed from the line of succession. Mary, however, was regarded by Europe and most Englishmen to be the legitimate heir, whereas Elizabeth was viewed as an illegitimate daughter, and perhaps not even the king's.

Henry then married his mistress, Jane Seymour, just 12 days after Anne's execution. Soon after, in October 1537, Jane died in childbirth delivering the long-awaited son, Edward VI. Henry's next marriage to Anne of Cleves was short-lived, ending in divorce. Catherine Howard was next for Henry, a cousin of Anne Boleyn, who resumed an affair with a former lover after a year of marriage, and was executed for it in 1542. Henry's sixth and final wife, Katharine Parr, was a kind woman who believed passionately in education and religious reform. She was a devoted stepmother, and arranged for Elizabeth to have the most distinguished tutors in England.

Thanks to her new stepmother, Elizabeth was educated as well as any legitimate prince, unusual in an age where women were considered inferior to men, and quickly displayed a precociousness and aptitude for her studies that earned Henry's admiration.

Elizabeth further cultivated an image of composed stateliness as an adolescent. She always carried a book with her, dressed with an austerity that was virtually absent in the Tudor court, and used her position to pay for musicians, instruments, and a variety of books.

It's no surprise that we find education at the forefront of Elizabeth's childhood and adolescent life, as it is with the formative years of many geniuses. Individualism is a vast web of experiences, perspectives, interests, attitudes, memories, and values. How these factors combine to make us who we are is completely relative to where we've been, what we've seen, thought about, and accepted or rejected, and what we've done. By cultivating a deep interest in, and knowledge and understanding of the world around her, Elizabeth's sense of identity was remarkably intricate for her age, and her self-esteem reflected this.

King Henry VIII died when she was 13. Henry's will stated that Edward would reign, and if he were to die without heirs that Mary would inherit the throne, and if she were to die without heirs that Elizabeth would become queen.

The now-widowed Katharine took Elizabeth into her home in Chelsea, and married quickly to the dashing brother of the Lord Protector, Thomas Seymour. Little did she know, however, that Seymour had ambitions beyond the Queen Dowager. He planned to win the affections of Elizabeth, only fourteen years old, and eventually win her hand in marriage, thus upstaging his brother's position by placing himself in line to inherit the throne.

Elizabeth had little experience with men and was flattered by Seymour's attention and charm. Before long, however, this gave way to fear. Seymour would tickle and wrestle with her in early morning raids to her room with his wife. He soon had keys made for all the rooms in the home, and visited Elizabeth while she slept. Eventually, Katharine had enough of Seymour's improprieties, warned Elizabeth of the vulnerability of her position, and sent her to live with a prominent member of the Privy chamber.

Later that year, in September 1548, Katharine died giving birth to a baby girl. Her death meant that Seymour would be looking for a new wife, and he again turned his affections toward Elizabeth. He was a man of incredible charm and Elizabeth couldn't help but feel a flutter of excitement in having such a man for a husband. Her governess, Katherine Ashley, was also taken by Seymour's allure, and supported the young princess's whimsical fantasy.

Marriage to Elizabeth was only one of Seymour's many wild schemes, however. He worked to undermine his brother's influence with the young king and to build up a following among the nobility. He also abused his new position as Lord Admiral by extorting bribes from all ships going to Ireland, and even offered protection to pirates in return for a portion of their loot.

Seymour's grandiose plans collapsed before fruition, however, when Edward's council learned of various frauds that he was implicated in. This launched a full-blown investigation, which also examined his past relations with Elizabeth. The Council suspected that Seymour's plans to usurp the throne were abetted by Elizabeth's comptroller and governess, and by Elizabeth herself.

An agent of the Council, Sir Robert Tyrwhit, subjected all to intense interrogations. It's hard to imagine a more traumatic experience for the 15-year-old Elizabeth. Tyrwhit made it clear that she would not be punished for confessing due to her age and assumed naiveté. Elizabeth knew, however, that her answers could result in the trial and execution of some of her most trusted associates, who were supposed to protect her from such intrigues.

As Tyrwhit questioned Elizabeth, he was astonished at her wit and circumspection. She considered and answered his questions carefully, and he was unable to extract any condemning confessions or admissions. The inquisition continued for nearly three weeks, with Elizabeth's story being checked again and again for holes or incongruities, but she remained defiant.

Despite being confronted with her comptroller's confession of Seymour's intentions toward Elizabeth, she maintained that no criminal activity had occurred. She refused to implicate herself or her attendants in any plot to wed the Lord Admiral without the Council's approval, told Tyrwhit that she cared nothing for Seymour, dismissed his playful romps in Katharine's house as harmless, and demanded a public apology from the Lord Protector along with the release of her loyal servants.

In the end, Tyrwhit concluded the investigation convinced that he had not been told the whole story, but the Council accepted that they had been told the truth. Nevertheless, Mrs. Ashley and Mr. Parry were dismissed for irresponsible and foolish, but not illegal, actions. This didn't sit well with Elizabeth, however, who wrote the Lord Protector on their behalf and pleaded for their return to her household. Her wish was granted on the condition that they would never even whisper a word of marriage again.

The Lord Admiral didn't fare so well. He was beheaded for treason without trial in the end of March 1549, much to Elizabeth's sorrow.

This experience left an indelible impression upon the young princess, and taught her an important lesson: her position demanded great responsibility, and her actions carried great weight. Seymour's schemes aside, Elizabeth participated in what she thought was good-natured, albeit slightly flirtatious, play, and a man lost his head because of it. While she felt his execution was unjustified, her cool, judicious nature served her well; instead of using the misfortune to fuel teenage angst or rebellion, she extracted from it a deeper understanding of the politics of the world in which she lived. If she were going to thrive in such an environment, she rightly concluded that she was going to have to play her cards very close to her chest. This shift of her personality would prove invaluable in the trials that were to come.

Elizabeth took great pains to regain the favor of the Lord Protector and Council and prove that she would never betray their trust. She dressed and spoke soberly, cared nothing for indulging in the extravagances of her station, and kept the Council continually informed of even her most insignificant activities.

Her prudence had the desired result, and her life resumed its normal course of studies. She rectified her precarious financial situation by taking over the bookkeeping herself, maintaining meticulous records of expenditures and income, and engaging a trusted adviser to help her manage her estates. The court looked favorably on Elizabeth's actions. Few girls her age and in her position would take a direct interest in such affairs, but in her they saw a bright, strong-willed woman, clearly capable of managing her life. Tensions eased.

By her 17th birthday, Elizabeth was a well-respected, popular princess with considerable intelligence, income, and land. She had grown into a striking girl, tall and slender with fair, unblemished skin, and a famous mane of red Tudor hair that she wore loose. When she traveled the countryside, crowds gathered to see the Protestant princess so renowned for her virtue, learning, and modesty.

As Elizabeth grew into a woman, she ignored the noise of the English court. But when Edward fell ill in 1553, and it became clear that he would not survive, the problem of succession had to be confronted. The shifty new Lord Protector, John Dudley, and other Council members feared that if Mary rose to the throne, her loyalty to Catholic Rome would jeopardize the English Reformation; if Elizabeth were to rule in her stead, however, she would certainly not be the puppet they desired.

Dudley succeeded in convincing the dying prince that to save the throne, he had to alter Henry VIII's order of succession by disinheriting both Elizabeth and Mary, and to then name his cousin Lady Jane Grey, who was married to Dudley's son, as the successor. Edward followed Dudley's advice, which made the scheming Duke the de facto ruler of the realm.

Immediately following Edward's death, Dudley had Lady Grey declared queen, despite her protests. The English people refused to recognize Grey as the proper heir and thousands rallied to Mary's cause every day. The Council learned of Dudley's attempt to place the Crown upon his head, and arrested him and Grey only nine days after she became queen.

With Dudley and Grey removed from power, the Council pronounced Mary as the rightful heir and ruler on July 19, 1553. Mary was enthusiastically received in London, with Elizabeth at her side. But public support of the Tudor queen didn't last long.

The economy was in shambles, harvests were bad, prices rose across the board, and Mary was determined to crush the Protestant faith and English Reformation. Her popularity plummeted further when, in 1554, she announced her intentions to marry King Philip II of Spain, a zealous Catholic like herself, and thus bring the entire weight of the Holy Roman Empire to bear upon the heretics of England. Anxiety and outrage immediately spread amongst the English Protestants and those Catholics that didn't want their country to become a powerless annex of the House of Hapsburg, which controlled both the Holy Roman Empire and the Spanish Empire.

Predictably, whisperings of rebellion spread throughout the lands. Elizabeth was fundamental to these schemes whether she liked it or not. She was the only alternative to Mary's reign and, as a modest Protestant and discreet, learned woman, was considered by many as a more worthy ruler. Mary was no stranger to these rumors and, consequently, grew increasingly hostile toward and distrustful of her sister. She publicly dismissed Henry VIII as Elizabeth's father, allowed distant cousins precedence at court, and blamed Elizabeth's mother for her own mother's tragic fate. Elizabeth's response was characteristic: instead of embroiling herself in such petty hostilities, she retreated to her favorite country house in Hatfield and focused on her studies, safely removed from London's turbulent politics.

In January 1554, however, Elizabeth was dragged into the undercurrent of treason. Sir Thomas Wyatt, a young aristocrat, conspired to prevent Mary's betrothal to Philip of Spain, and planned a movement to march on London and depose the Queen, thus opening the throne to Elizabeth.

Wyatt gathered 4,000 men and led them to the capital, but was turned back by Mary's army and arrested. His men deserted or surrendered. Thereafter, it was uncovered that Wyatt had written a letter to Elizabeth before rebelling to inform her of his intentions, but the letter was intercepted by Tudor agents. Also intercepted was a letter from the Duke of Noailles, a French nobleman, to the king of France, which implied that Elizabeth knew of the revolt in advance, and which repeated rumors that she was recruiting armed supporters. Elizabeth would be subjected to yet another alarming accusation, and would have to find the strength to face it, as well as her sister's bias.

Although Mary's council could find no hard evidence that such accusations were true, they decided to summon Elizabeth to London for questioning. She was first taken to the Palace of Whitehall and held for several weeks while the ringleaders of the rebellion were interrogated. Mary and several of her councilmen were firmly convinced that Elizabeth was guilty, and just needed concrete proof to gain the rest of the Council's agreement to try and convict her of treason. Mary's Lord Chancellor, the Catholic bishop Stephen Gardiner, was particularly eager to see Elizabeth permanently removed from the realm. He questioned her vigorously, but she wasn't intimidated. She steadfastly denied any involvement in the plans and revealed nothing of import, and demanded to speak to her sister. Gardiner denied her request.

Gardiner was frustrated but not defeated. He convinced the Council to relegate Elizabeth to the infamous Tower of London, where he believed he could browbeat her into revealing evidence that would establish her guilt beyond doubt. Upon hearing the news, terror gripped her stomach. This move was, Elizabeth assumed, merely the preliminary to a formal trial in which she would be railroaded, and she begged to be allowed to write her sister. The Earl of Sussex granted her wish, and provided a pen and piece of paper for her to compose the letter on which she believed her life depended.

She chose her words very carefully, not wishing to appear too craven or bold, and ventured to strike a personal tone. She reminded Mary of her promise to never punish her "without answer and due proof," and begged the Queen to not leave the fate of her own flesh and blood to councilors. She scored the remaining space on the page to prevent forgery, and ended it, "I humbly crave but one word of answer from yourself. Your Highness's most faithful subject that hath been from the beginning and will be to my end. Elizabeth."

Elizabeth's composure and humility was more than a desperate attempt at arousing pity in her sister. Through her persistent studies and reflection, she had cultivated a refined sense of ethics, and believed, as Marcus Aurelius put it, that "the best revenge is to be unlike him who performed the injury." She wanted Mary to know that she truly had no intention of threatening her reign.

The letter was delivered late in the night. The next gloomy, rainy morning, Elizabeth was escorted to the grim fortress. Meanwhile, Mary was livid that the letter was allowed and delivered, and refused to read it through. To add further insult to the disgraced princess, Gardiner had arranged for her to enter beneath Traitor's Gate via a barge—the traditional entrance for prisoners returned to their cells after trial. Just a few months earlier, Lady Jane Grey and her husband, Guildford Dudley, had entered through these gates and were subsequently executed to please the emperor of Spain.

Elizabeth initially refused to enter the edifice as a public demonstration against her wrongful arrest, but was eventually taken to her lodgings, which was a small room with a fireplace and a few windows. It wasn't the dingy cell she was imagining, but she was a prisoner nonetheless.

Before long, however, Gardiner's hopes of obtaining further evidence against the princess were all but dashed. His colleagues were reluctant to press Elizabeth too hard, with murmurings that such actions might one day bring grievous consequences. The Queen's judges were emphatic that there was inadequate evidence to convict Elizabeth of treason, and even if more evidence came to light, it was not likely to be acted upon as Elizabeth had won a strong ally in the Lord Admiral William Howard.

With execution an impossibility, Gardiner and Mary conspired to have Parliament disinherit Elizabeth and thus remove her from the line of succession. Her time in the Tower—nearly two months in all—greatly increased her popularity amongst the people, however, and any such move against her would be widely disfavored. Out of options, Mary reluctantly acknowledged that pursuing such a contentious measure would be most unwise.

Ironically, Elizabeth's release from captivity was at the behest of the Spanish king, Philip, who was to visit Mary. Philip knew that his impending union with the Queen had the sizable and influential faction of English Protestants on edge, and that Elizabeth embodied their greatest hope. Any further mistreatment of her, he said, would only make him more unpopular in England, and the marriage more dangerous. Furthermore, he planned to find a suitable husband for Elizabeth—a man sympathetic to the House of Hapsburg—and ensure that the English throne remained in his family.

Mary still refused to accept her sister's innocence and was loath to free her, but she was desperate to please Philip and complied. Elizabeth left the London Tower on May 19, 1554, the anniversary of her mother's execution. She was placed into the care of Sir Henry Bedingfield, a Catholic supporter of Mary, and a man that Elizabeth feared was under orders to assassinate her. Elizabeth calmly pressed her guards for any information that might hint at such a plot, but discovered nothing to cause alarm.

Eventually, plans were made to relocate Elizabeth to a dilapidated manor in Woodstock where Bedingfield would place her under house arrest. Upon leaving the city, the citizens of London turned out in force to wish Elizabeth well, and throngs of people professed their love for her along the journey to her new, albeit more comfortable, jail.

While at Woodstock, Elizabeth quickly learned that Bedingfield was no killer. He was a timid civil servant who prided himself on his diffidence and moderation. Nevertheless, he exasperated her to no end by referring even the most minor requests of hers to the Council for decision, and for extrapolating many new restrictions from their answers. She was at the mercy of a man so afraid to make a mistake that he was happy to play the part of unthinking pedant.

After several vexing months, Elizabeth pleaded with her sister and the Council to either charge her with a crime and try her, or grant her liberty to visit the court and discuss her imprisonment. This meant risking another clash with Mary's courtiers, and a chance for them to concoct another scheme against her, but Elizabeth didn't care. She was certain that she could win her sister's approval. Mary had other matters on her mind, however.

On July 25, 1554, Mary wed the handsome, 27-year-old Spanish king despite early signs of trouble. Anonymous pamphlets condemning foreigners and the marriage were distributed, and Philip's entourage was upset over petty insults by their English hosts.

Elizabeth hoped that the marriage and her sister's high spirits would improve her circumstances, but she was mistaken. Months dragged by as Beding-field continued to deny her quests for certain books and refused to deliver her letters to the Council. Meanwhile, Gardiner still quietly pressed for her execution on the grounds that Protestantism could never be completely eradicated while she still lived.

Philip again came to Elizabeth's defense, however, wishing to know his sister-in-law before making an enemy of her and, as Mary was with child, possibly harboring plans of a new marriage should Mary die in childbirth. In April 1555, almost a year since being sent to Woodstock, Elizabeth was invited to court to witness the imminent birth of her sister's first child.

Two weeks after Elizabeth arrived, Mary sent Gardiner and the most powerful members of the Council to demand that her sister admit her past wrongdoing and seek her queen's forgiveness. Elizabeth stoutly refused and declared that she didn't want mercy, but the law instead. Gardiner then tried to bait Elizabeth into criticizing her sister, but she proved too shrewd. Gardiner was foiled yet again.

Then, one night, a message was delivered to Elizabeth that the queen would see her. She had been begging for this interview for more than a year. Mary was uncharacteristically amicable, and although there was mild sparring at first, she made a peace of sorts. Elizabeth would remain at Hampton Court under light guard, but with her own household and permission to receive certain guests.

While Elizabeth enjoyed her newfound liberty, her fellow Protestants' fears of Philip and Rome proved justified. The new king persuaded Parliament to repeal Henry VIII's Protestant religious laws, thereby placing England fully under the jurisdiction of the Roman Catholic Church. With this reversal came the revival of the Heresy Acts, which allowed for the execution of non-conformists and undesirables. The killing began immediately; prominent Protestants were burned at the stake or beheaded while many others chose exile and left the country.

Famine and poverty were also spreading throughout the lands, which provoked worry among the courtiers that the monarchs were courting revolt. Nevertheless, the slaughtering continued, and the queen earned the nickname "Bloody Mary."

A tragedy much greater than a damning moniker then occurred for Mary. By July 1555, Mary still hadn't given birth to her child, and her abdomen receded. There was no baby. Mary had long suffered from digestive and menstrual troubles, and her swollen stomach and lack of cycle led her to believe that she was pregnant. One month later, Philip drove his wife into deeper despair when he announced that he would be leaving to France to lead his army. He had spent over a year in a country that he disliked, married to a woman seven years his senior whom he pitied but didn't love and suspected was too ill to bear a child. Thus, there was no reason for him to remain in England.

Mary's love for her husband was true, and she pleaded for him to stay. He was adamant, however. Before leaving, he left explicit instructions that Elizabeth was to be treated well. Upon his departure, Mary was heartbroken and desolate.

Dark days followed for Mary. Her popularity had collapsed. And later that year, another conspiracy to depose and replace her with Elizabeth was uncovered. She didn't even attempt to punish Elizabeth for she knew her sister had no involvement, and any actions against the princess would antagonize the Council and risk a popular uprising. In July 1556, yet another rising against Mary failed, this time led by an adventurer named Cleobury.

With her sister barren and of precarious health, Elizabeth's eventual accession was becoming a political reality. Philip began cultivating a relationship with her, suggesting suitors from his family and allies so as to keep England under Hapsburg control. The princess, who plainly stated that she would marry nobody—not even the King's son or any greater prince, rejected them all. Such independence and defiance infuriated Mary, but there was little she could do. Every day Elizabeth gained supporters, even among the Lords of the Council, and any attempt at striking her from the succession would be negated.

Spain went to war with France later in the year. Philip convinced Mary to involve England on Spain's side in June 1557. Her concession brought nothing but heartache, however; the reward was Philip's immediate departure, never to return, and the addition of military defeats to England's now lengthy list of misfortunes and hardships. Six months later, in January 1558, England lost the town of Calais, an English possession since the 14th century, to the French. The surrender was heralded as a supreme failure of Mary's reign. Following this failure plus the anguish of another false hope of pregnancy, the Queen fell seriously ill. As Mary's death approached, Elizabeth began plans to protect her accession from being thwarted, and the Spaniards made plans of their own to secure her goodwill.

On November 6, 1558, with not much longer to live, Mary named Elizabeth as her successor. Eleven days later, Mary took her last breath and Elizabeth, now 25 years old, fell to her knees in humility and awe, and said in Latin, "This is the doing of the Lord; and it is marvelous in our eyes."

Although the day of Elizabeth's crowning was widely celebrated with bells ringing, bonfires burning, and people reveling, it was muted in comparison to the grand displays that Mary had received. Elizabeth was keenly aware of why: Under the rule of a woman, England had become religiously divided, embroiled in war with the Scottish and French, racked by famine, and buried in debt. There was no standing army or efficient police force to ensure order, and the nation had no foreign friendships to call upon for help. The conviction of many was that men were rational and fit for authority, whereas women were impulsive and sentimental, and therefore emotionally, intellectually, and morally unfit to rule.

Apologists for the queen countered with significant exceptions throughout history, but the fact remained: Elizabeth had inherited a crumbling, disgraced nation, and the English people were watching their young, inexperienced queen's every action with skepticism.

Knowing this, Elizabeth developed a strategy to overcome her perceived weaknesses of gender, one that focused on her love for her people and her desire to rule by good advice and council. Her intelligence and willpower had enabled her to weather the storms of her past unscathed—no small feat—and she faced the challenges to come with equal composure and resolve.

Almost immediately after her accession, a new familial feud—one that would prove far more dangerous than the first—began to take shape: Elizabeth's cousin, Mary Stuart, Queen of Scotland and the wife of the French dauphin, announced herself as the rightful heir next in line. Mary had been denied a place in the Tudor succession by Henry VIII's will—an affront that she clearly meant to rectify, but exactly how, was still a mystery. Elizabeth knew that she would have to keep a close eye on her Scottish relative.

Elizabeth's first order of business was selecting men for her government. She dismissed those who had conspired against her under Mary's reign, and rewarded the loyalty and friendship of several intelligent and moderate men who had proved themselves worthy during the trials of her past. At the head of her government she placed longtime friend and faithful servant to the crown, William Cecil, who would become her most trusted adviser and confidant.

In her first round of meetings with her council, the Queen addressed the religious turmoil of the realm. The councilors were pleased to hear that she would adopt a policy of tolerance of both the Catholic and Protestant faiths. She made it clear that no one religious party would receive her preference and that her subjects were Englishmen first; their religious loyalties were of no concern to her as long as they lay secondary to the loyalties to her as queen.

Thus, Elizabeth sought a solution that would not seriously offend the Catholics, but would also meet the desires of the Protestants. As a result, the Parliament immediately began to legislate for a Protestant church, but with many Catholic elements. In May 1559, the new Act of Supremacy became law, and the Church of England was formally established with Elizabeth as the Supreme Governor—a title she chose carefully, as the customary position of Supreme Head was deemed inappropriate for a woman. All heresy laws were repealed to avoid persecution of either Catholics or Protestants, and a law was passed to compel the attendance of church, although the penalties for failure to attend were minor.

Militant factions of Protestants denounced these measures as cowardly and inadequate. They wanted Catholicism purged from the religious hierarchy and from their church's forms of prayer and ritual, and they wanted recusants to be vigorously searched out and persecuted.

Such demands were out of the question for Elizabeth, however, who felt that reforms had gone far enough, and who didn't want to provoke public turmoil. She had no interest in uncovering and judging the inner beliefs of her subjects so long as they kept the peace and remained obedient to her authority—a remarkably enlightened policy in such an age of religious fanaticism and cruelty.

This is a shining example of how one person's strength of character and individualism can shepherd millions into a higher, more civilized plane of existence. The easier choice for Elizabeth, and actually more acceptable one to many, would've been to follow the usual course of history: to smash the pendulum back into Catholicism with a vengeance. But she was willing to try a new approach, one founded on respect and understanding, not disdain and mutual fear. She wanted Protestants and Catholics to adjust to their differences, not war for the souls of England.

With a church of broad appeal established, Elizabeth next had to deal with a personal matter of much anxiety among her council. The question on everyone's minds was whom she would marry and what it would mean for England. There was currently no male heir in the Tudor family, which could lead to a civil war over succession should Elizabeth die an untimely death. England was a poor and militarily weak nation in dire need of major alliances that, many believed, only marriage could bring. The European powers were convinced that she wouldn't last a year as an unwedded queen. She would either marry or lose her throne to revolt or invasion.

Her council was anxious to begin diplomatic negotiations for her marriage, and the first to offer his hand—albeit dejectedly and only for the purpose of bringing England back into the Catholic fold—was Philip II of Spain. Many believed that her acceptance of such a powerful man was a foregone conclusion, but she surprised Philip's agent by saying she had to reflect on it before giving answer.

She had no intention of marrying the Spaniard, but the pretense served a diplomatic purpose. England was still technically at war with France due to her sister's alliance with Spain, but peace talks were underway. Elizabeth needed Spanish support in the negotiations and knew that their belief that she would become Philip's wife was sure to help her objective. By the end of March 1559, the truce was on the verge of being completed, negating the need to maintain the ruse. She graciously rejected Philip II's offer, who gladly married a French princess instead. The war was ended soon after.

Philip was only the beginning of many more suitors that would vie for Elizabeth's affections. She had good reasons to avoid marriage, however. While it would secure her a protector, her husband would expect assistance in furthering his own agendas, and such obligations could not be taken lightly. She also feared that England would be of secondary importance to the European royals that pursued her; they would, she was sure, view the marriage as an opportunity to exploit her nation for their own ends. She intended on remaining safely disconnected from continental rivalries, and marriage to a foreigner would likely make that impossible.

Furthermore, an arranged marriage came with no guarantee of personal happiness. In most cases, the pledge to marry was made without even an in-person meeting. Few princes were willing to present themselves to be judged and potentially rejected, exposing them and their countries to ridicule. Instead, flattering portraits and words were exchanged, but appearances and tales often proved embroidered. Thus, Elizabeth didn't trust paintings and praises, and refused to marry someone she had never met.

Elizabeth's diverse, intensive education and early tangles with court politics had prepared her well for the game of courtship and international affairs. Although still an inexperienced girl in many people's eyes—one that sorely needed the strength and wisdom of a man at her side—she had quickly matured into a shrewd, cultivated woman with an embracive understanding of the world and her place in it. From these deep, branching roots grew her convictions and worldview, and her genius. Her court mistook her distrust of matrimony as narrow-minded tenacity and egocentrism, which can be, by definition, an expression of individualism. It's hardly the type that empowers one to achieve greatness, however. Only the truly depraved dream of "success" that involves themselves only, and unfortunately for them, leaning on such a fantasy is like trying to ask power of a machine wrecked with rust. One of the dominant traits that define history's greatest geniuses is their genuine interest in, love for, and dedication to the well-being of other people—a rare commodity that would guide Elizabeth through her tumultuous, and ultimately triumphant, reign.

In spite of her marital misgivings, Elizabeth planned on using her singleness as a political and diplomatic expedient. She played the game well, skillfully dragging on marriage negotiations and leading each to believe that she would accept their offer. The courtship games went on for years, increasingly agitating her councilors. They wanted a king, and an heir. But Elizabeth wanted independence and control, claiming that she would rather be a "beggar-woman and single, far rather than Queen and married." Her aversion to marriage clearly had more than political considerations at its core, which is hardly surprising given the conjugal difficulties of her immediate family.

She did, however, display a particular fancy for her courtier Robert Dudley. He was two months her senior and, by all measures, an ideal companion: he was tall, dark, handsome, and fit; well-educated and intellectual; a keen patron of the arts; and had a particular ability to make Elizabeth laugh. But her love for him wasn't enough to bring nuptials. She knew that choosing him over his peers would cause animosity and jealousy in those passed over, and they would also resent the elevation of a former equal to such eminence. With the nobles united in their hatred for the parvenu, bitterness would creep down the social ladder until all of England was divided and feuding.

Ever thoughtful and calculating, Elizabeth again forewent her own happiness for the benefit of her people. Look no further than her sister Mary's selfish capitulation to Philip II's hand and will to glimpse how disastrous consequences can be when one acts, as the poet Donne warned, as an island, entirely of itself.

Such was Elizabeth's predicament, and it was exacerbated by the fact that she also refused to name a direct heir. Her own experiences in Mary's reign had shown her that an heir waiting in the wings inevitably became the focus of schemers. Settling the succession, she believed, would bring the appearance of calm and stability, but would, without a doubt, provide the means for enemies to undermine her sovereignty.

Elizabeth's forestalling continued into 1568, ten years into her reign. Europe was now plunged into bloody turmoil. Philip II had dispatched a large army to the Netherlands to crush a Protestant rebellion, and Elizabeth's council worried that the massive force would turn to England next. Further complicating matters was the fact that Mary Stuart, the true queen of England in the eyes of Catholic Europe, was forced out of her throne in Scotland by Protestant rebels, and was now in England. Just as Elizabeth was the focus of conspiracies against Mary I, Mary Stuart's arrival would be seen as an opportunity for discontented Catholics to take the country back. If Elizabeth were to die, Mary had the strongest claim to the throne.

History began to repeat itself when rumors began to spread that the intransigent Catholics in the north were planning a campaign to free Mary and take the crown. There was already talk of Mary and the wealthy and influential Duke of Norfolk marrying afterward, a union that would give England the native king that its people so desired.

The rumors proved true in 1569 when a rebel force gathered under the banner of the Earls of Westmoreland and Northumberland, and the Sheriff of Yorkshire. The situation was immensely dangerous as the Queen's hold over the north was never more than tenuous. She was deeply hurt by the popular movement against her. On the verge of tears, she lamented to the French ambassador that she found it hard to believe that the northern Catholics could so easily forget the honorable treatment they had received from her. Nevertheless, she ordered the Earl of Sussex to raise an army and crush the rebellion.

While Sussex was struggling to recruit soldiers from northern shires, the ranks of the Northern Rebellion quickly grew to over 5,000 troops. The Queen was dismayed at the news, but responded by authorizing the Earl of Warwick and Lord Clinton to muster 10,000 men from their counties. Relations between England and Spain were more strained than ever, and leaders of the insurrection reached out to the Spanish for support in overthrowing the Tudor queen. While Philip was now in favor of a regime change, he was reluctant to materially support the revolution as his military forces were focused on pacifying the Netherlands. He was not ready to go to war with England...yet.

Within a month, Elizabeth's army was strong enough to confront the insurgents, but it proved unnecessary. The leaders of the revolt knew that their under-trained, underfed army would stand no chance against the reliable, well-armed soldiers of the crown, and so they abandoned their cause and fled to Scotland. Hundreds of rebels were captured and executed, including the Earl of Northumberland, to send a message to anyone else that harbored such traitorous desires.

Thus, the Northern Rebellion fizzled, but the stability of the kingdom would always be at risk while Mary Stuart remained in England. Elizabeth had contemplated having her cousin executed after learning of her role in the breakdown of the north, but when the uprising crumbled, such talk ceased. Instead, Elizabeth took the high road: she began negotiations to return Mary to the care of the leader of the Protestant party in Scotland, the Earl of Moray. This plan quickly fell apart, however, when the Earl was assassinated. The French then announced that they would regard Mary's cause as their own, and that if Elizabeth didn't return her to the Scottish throne, they would declare war.

As if the Queen didn't already have enough to worry about, the summer of 1570 brought another new and dangerous challenge. Pope Pius V issued a bill that excommunicated "Elizabeth, the pretended Queen of England, the servant of wickedness," and absolved all of her Catholic subjects of any allegiance to her. Furthermore, any Catholic who obeyed her orders would be faced with excommunication themselves. The Pope had effectively sanctified treason and declared it impossible to be both a good Catholic and a good Englishman.

Elizabeth couldn't afford to ignore this latest development, which forced a dilemma of her own: should she give in to the admonitions of her council and begin purging Catholicism from the realm entirely, or should she continue her course of gentle coexistence and hope that the majority of her Catholic subjects would, in essence, ignore the decree?

Up until now, the Queen had refused to treat English Catholics as enemies of the state, a strategy she chose to continue despite the threat. She responded to the Pope's challenge by reminding her people of her love for them and that she had no intention of invading their faith so long as they maintained social order and followed the laws of the realm. She knew who she was, and she was willing to stand for it, even if it meant her demise. She would rather be deposed than despotic.

Her trust in her Catholics was repaid by continued loyalty, for the most part. While some Catholic incorrigibles denounced their Queen, the vast majority rejected the Papal claim that allegiance to their sovereign and to their spiritual leader were mutually exclusive. They loved their queen, had become accustomed to Anglican services, and Elizabeth suspected that, in time, their attachment to the customs of their ancient faith would wither. Perhaps this was the fear that drove the Pope to issue the bull in the first place.

By the spring of 1571, the negotiations to restore Mary to her Scottish kingdom ground to a halt. The Scottish lords that participated in her deposition rightfully feared that they would be executed with great rapidity and prejudice should she be allowed to rule again, so they plied their considerable influence in the realm to derail the plans of her return.

Mary's patience was finally exhausted. She concluded that her freedom would only be possible by intrigue, and so she enlisted the help of a Florentine banker by the name of Robert Ridolfi. Ridolfi had been secretly involved in fomenting the failed Northern Rebellion, and as a papal agent, was ready to work on Mary's behalf.

The plan was simple enough: convince Philip and his notoriously cruel general, the Duke of Alva, to join the conspiracy and provide an army. Mary promised that many English nobles would raise militias of their own and join the campaign. This wasn't exactly true, but Ridolfi drew up forged papers purportedly from the Duke of Norfolk and others endorsing the plot, which he used to gain further audiences in Spain and Rome.

The Pope blessed the invasion of England, but declined to offer troops. And while Alva doubted the "babbling Italian's" claims, Philip swallowed it eagerly. He decided that he must take this opportunity to punish Elizabeth for her heresy, and the Spanish council began deliberating on how to place Mary on the throne. There was talk of using a Spanish agent to assassinate Elizabeth, but this was ultimately overruled in favor of an outright military attack using forces stationed in the Netherlands.

The first hints of such a plot reached the Queen in April, when a man carrying a packet of ciphered letters was caught. Under the duress of the rack, he confessed that the letters were from Ridolfi to a mysterious English nobleman known only as "40," and that they essentially communicated that Philip would provide the assistance so desired. Elizabeth and her chief adviser, Lord Burghley, now knew that a conspiracy of some kind existed, but nothing more.

Three months later, a fortunate discovery linked the Duke of Norfolk to the scheming. Burghley was alerted to Norfolk's involvement in the transportation of money from Mary to her Scottish supporters—a task unrelated to the treasonous plans, but a connection that set Burghley on Norfolk's trail. The Duke's secretaries were arrested and threatened with the rack, prompting their confession that Norfolk was indeed involved in much more than transporting gold for Mary. The truth was Ridolfi had met with Norfolk to enlist his support, and although the duke approved of the plot, he refused to sign papers to that effect. Ridolfi was undaunted, however, and drew up the forged letters regardless.

Norfolk was sent to the Tower, where interrogations ensued. He confessed that Ridolfi came to meet with him, but claimed that he had no knowledge of a foreign invasion of England. Instead, he said, Ridolfi was merely looking to raise money for Mary to use to bolster her party in Scotland. However, an English Bishop Burghley discovered as intimately involved in the conspiracy exposed Norfolk's lies. A threat of the rack was all it took to loosen the bishop's tongue and expose the entire plot.

Norfolk was tried by his peers in Westminster Hall, and despite his continued insistence of innocence, his arguments failed to convince. A unanimous verdict of guilty was returned accompanied by a sentence to death. Elizabeth balked, however. Norfolk was England's last duke, and a man she admired. Her council insisted that such treason deserved nothing less. And yet, she vacillated several times, signing death warrants, and then retracting them before they could be carried out. Her failure to take action against the duke raised tensions with her ministers, which reached a fever pitch when she refused to punish Mary for her role in the conspiracy.

Mary denied any knowledge or involvement, of course, but everyone knew better. The Council agreed almost unanimously that the traitorous heiress should be executed. In a Commons debate of May 15, Mary was flayed as "a Scot, an enemy to England, an adulterous woman, a homicide, a traitor to the Queen, a subverter of the state." The final speech against her was interrupted with cries of approval from the listeners.

So why did Elizabeth refuse to assent to her execution? She detested Mary and knew her to be unscrupulous to the core, but she felt that the monarchal order as a whole was more important than her personal feelings. Mary was a rightful member of the royalty, and to punish her like a common criminal was a severe action that, Elizabeth felt, undermined the very principles of sovereignty itself.

Some dismissed this sentiment as a cover for a doddering will; a woman over her head, incapable of taking tough, decisive action when necessary. While weak knees may or may not have been a factor, there's still a worthwhile lesson that can be extracted from how Elizabeth handled her dilemma. We often hear how people buy, decide, act, and react based on emotion, not logic, and no emotions bend our wills like love and hate. The lofty peaks and cavernous valleys of our species' history are testaments to the power these forces wield over the human psyche. Elizabeth already faced a dilemma of love in the young Dudley, and despite being a sovereign who answered to nobody but God, she chose what she felt was the greatest good. She looked beyond her selfish interests and considered all circumstances and people involved. In Mary Stuart,

Elizabeth was confronted with a dilemma of hate. A swift execution of her cousin was expected, and from many, demanded. But again Elizabeth's innate sense of responsibility to something much greater than herself took precedence over her personal feelings. As much as she wanted to dispose of Mary, her conviction that it would do more harm than good prevented it.

By May 19, a committee of both houses resolved that Mary could be dealt with in one of two ways: beheading or removal from the line of succession. The former was clearly favored by Parliament, but Elizabeth authorized the latter to be carried out. The Commons were sorely disappointed, and petitions were immediately drawn up asking the Queen to reconsider. She was immovable, though. Mary was not to be executed.

Norfolk was allowed only one fate, however. Parliament would not allow both traitors to escape the rightful punishment, and their demands for the duke's head were so strong that Elizabeth prudently gave in. She signed the final death warrant for Norfolk, and would not rescind it.

When Parliament subsequently drafted a bill stating that Mary should never enjoy the crown of England, Elizabeth's approval was assured, they thought. They were shocked, however, when an agent of the queen announced that it wasn't entirely to her liking, and that she would withhold her consent for the time being. This was understood to mean that it would never be approved, and anger quickly spread. The Queen's fickleness was taken as a mockery of all the work that had been done to preserve her power, and her loyal courtiers couldn't believe that she would allow the threat of Mary to persist. Nevertheless, Elizabeth was adamant—the bill would remain in limbo for the time being.

Many historians have echoed Elizabeth's courtiers and called this a serious lapse in her judgment. It's hard to argue to the contrary. By not only letting Mary live, but leaving her in a position to take the throne, Elizabeth was practically encouraging her own assassination. And once Mary had ascended to the crown, Elizabeth's courtiers—who had bayed for Mary's blood—would be at the usurper's mercy. Herein lies the brutal paradox of individualism: if we are to rise to greatness, it will be a direct effect of our firm dedication to our sometimes unpopular beliefs and courses of action. Consequently, we must be willing to experience the sometimes negative effects of our causes. We must accept that, like Elizabeth, we aren't perfect, and our bold strides toward greatness create ripples. Some will grow into raging whitecaps. And while ardent individualism inevitably causes the storms, only it can subdue them. Just as greatness doesn't require transcendent intelligence, it doesn't require perfection of character—it simply asks that, by hook or crook, we find the wits, strength, and means to complete our journeys. That is, we don't have to call every play right, but we have to devise a game plan flexible and dynamic enough to win. Elizabeth would soon learn this lesson, because her misstep with Mary would quickly swell into a violent typhoon that threatened to smash her into pieces, and ravage the very foundations of England.

The next matter to be addressed was Spain's role in the planned coup. According to certain advisers, this clearly signaled Philip's intentions to declare war on England once he was finished with the Netherlands, and they implored the Queen to join with France to expel the Spaniards from the neighboring lands. Elizabeth knew that such an arrangement was perilous, however. France wanted to claim the Netherlands for themselves, which would present its own host of problems for England, and if the Anglo-French alliance failed, Spain would surely retaliate by invading both France and England. Instead, the Queen authorized a thousand volunteers to go fight on the side of the rebels, more for the purpose of keeping an eye on what was happening than anything else, and then denied any knowledge of the force when confronted by the Duke of Alva.

Continental strife continued to mount. English relations with France sank into an uneasy uncertainty after a genocide of Protestants broke out in France in the fall of 1572, which lasted for several months and resulted in the death of tens of thousands of Huguenots. Spanish forces continued to slaughter Protestants in the Netherlands, and English privateers continued to conduct raids on Spanish ships and harbors, the most successful of which being secretly sponsored by the Queen and led by the legendary captain Sir Francis Drake.

Fears of an assassination attempt against Elizabeth flared up after Pope Gregory XIII proclaimed in 1580 that it would be no sin to rid the world of such a miserable heretic. This led to the second serious plan to murder Elizabeth and empower Mary, who was still held captive in England.

An agent of Sir Francis Walsingham, Elizabeth's astute spymaster, intercepted letters in 1582 from Spain's ambassador, Bernardino de Mendoza, to contacts in Scotland. The letters spoke of plans for a coordinated Catholic invasion of England and Scotland with the objective of displacing Elizabeth in favor of Mary, but had little details. Walsingham immediately deployed spies to uncover who was behind the plot. He had his answer several months later when an informer in the French embassy learned that Sir Francis Throckmorton, a well-born Catholic Englishman, was involved.

After six months of surveillance, Walsingham was sure of Throckmorton's complicity and had him arrested. After meeting the rack, Throckmorton made a full confession, admitting that his French contacts had told him that the French prince was planning to invade England with the support of Philip of Spain and the Pope. Mendoza was directing the conspiracy from within England, and Mary was aware of and supported it.

Throckmorton was executed for his treason. Mary professed innocence once again. And once again, Elizabeth refused to have her executed. Instead, Mary was moved to more secure quarters. Elizabeth then attempted once more to negotiate terms under which the Scottish Protestants would accept Mary's return.

Soon after this plot was foiled, one of the other great Protestant leaders of Europe, William of Orange, was assassinated by a Catholic Frenchman, leaving Elizabeth as the only great pillar of Protestant strength in Europe. She refused to let the clear and present danger alter her many public appearances, but began sleeping with a small sword beneath her pillow.

The failure of the Throckmorton plot only served to increase Mary's desperation for attaining her freedom. By December 1585, Walsingham knew that yet another plot was underway that, like the last, entailed a Catholic invasion of England and assassination of Elizabeth. He lured Mary into the plot by arranging for unauthorized communications to reach her via two double agents in his employ. Each letter between Mary and her conspirators was intercepted and deciphered before being resealed and passed along. Walsingham would simply wait for the plans to unfold and for Mary to fully incriminate herself.

The fatal correspondence came in the summer of 1586. With the plan nearly complete, Mary wrote to one of the plotters, a man named Sir Anthony Babington, explicitly condoning the murder of the Queen. Walsingham had what he needed, and moved in.

The ringleaders were arrested, interrogated, and executed. Elizabeth was then presented with Mary's letters, which brought the Queen's benevolence to an end. Mary went on trial and defended herself vigorously, arguing that as a sovereign queen she wasn't liable to the laws of England. She denied plotting Elizabeth's death, but her correspondence was irrefutable evidence. She was sentenced to death, and Elizabeth signed the death warrant with a heavy hand. She then balked, and favored the idea of eliminating Mary through a stealth assassination, which would be publicly announced as a natural death. In this, she could avoid backlash from other European sovereigns and Mary's son, James, King of Scotland. Elizabeth's courtiers took matters into their own hands, however. They had a signed death warrant, and they would put it to purpose. On February 8, 1587, in front of 300 witnesses, Mary, Queen of Scots, was beheaded.

When news of the execution reached Elizabeth, she flew into a rage. As she expected, European Crowns denounced Mary's demise as unconscionable, and James spoke of exacting revenge. Nevertheless, the Council breathed a collective sigh of relief, believing that Mary's consignment to the grave removed the greatest threat to the Queen's reign and stability of the realm, but they were wrong.

For years now, English pirates had been plundering Spanish ships. Although Elizabeth publicly disavowed the practice, she privately encouraged it and even knighted her greatest marauder, Sir Francis Drake, in 1581. England's recent support of the Dutch rebellion also drew Philip's ire, and Mary's execution pressed upon him the need to end the Protestant menace in Europe. Consequently, he decided that peace with England was no longer possible, but his advisers believed that he could ill afford a new war. The Spanish army and navy were the largest and best prepared in the world, but they were also weary after years of fighting. Morale was low and leadership was lacking.

Nevertheless, Philip believed that Mary's execution provided the perfect opportunity to depose Elizabeth as it had united much of European opinion against her. And so he spent the majority of 1587 preparing a massive invasion fleet. The Pope officially approved the invasion and even told Philip that he could freely choose the next English ruler.

When word reached Elizabeth that the Spanish forces in the Low Countries were growing, and that a formidable armada was amassing in Spain, she knew that she had to ready her people for war. Fortunately, she had paid attention to the maintenance of her fleet since the beginning of her reign, which, as a result, was in its best condition in England's history. On land, defensive preparations were set in motion, which included the training of thousands of able-bodied men as well as the erection of ramparts, earthworks, and parapets; the digging of ditches; and so on.

Despite their preparedness, many Englishmen were doubtful of their chances of success. What could their small nation possibly do against the might of the great Spanish forces that had defeated the Turks, cowed France, conquered Portugal, and cut through the Low Countries?

The massive Spanish fleet, now known as the "Invincible Armada," set sail for England on May 20, 1588 in a grand procession of 130 ships carrying over 30,000 men. They would sail to Flanders to rendezvous with the Duke of Parma, who waited with more soldiers and transport ships. From there, the assault upon Elizabeth's realm would begin.

After a lengthy delay refitting in Corunna due to a shortage of provisions and inclement weather, the Armada continued its course through the English Channel unimpeded. The English skirmished with the Spanish warships but were unable to destroy a single ship. But the tides of war would soon change.

On July 27, Philip's grand Armada anchored off Calais to await Parma. The anchorage was the opportunity the English had been waiting for. They loaded up eight relatively insignificant vessels with all manner of combustible materials and, on the following night, set them ablaze and floated them toward the Armada. The Spaniards panicked, wrongly assuming that the ships were loaded with explosives, and scrambled out to sea, weakening their disciplined formations.

The next morning, off the coast of Gravelines, the Armada turned to face the English despite its scattered ranks and lack of weather gauge. The ensuing battle is now known as one of the greatest naval victories of all time for the astute High Lord Admiral Charles Howard, whom Elizabeth had wisely appointed in 1585. The English used the superior maneuverability of their ships and weather advantage to provoke Spanish fire while staying out of range, and then dart in close to deliver devastating broadsides.

After eight hours of battle, the English ships began running out of ammunition. Once they had fired their last shots, they were forced to pull back, but the Spanish had taken a severe battering. Five Spanish ships were lost and many others were severely damaged. The victory was a great boost to English morale, but the Armada's presence in the Channel still posted a serious threat, and Parma's invasion was still looming.

The next day, at Tilbury, Elizabeth appeared before a large assembly of inexperienced troops that would be the first to face the fearsome duke and his renowned soldiers. Several councilmen had urged her not to go before masses of armed men, fearing assassination, but Elizabeth trusted her people and wanted to show it. She wore a silver breastplate over a white velvet dress, carried a truncheon, and rode by the marching ranks atop a majestic steed.

"My loving people," she began. "We have been persuaded by some that are careful of our safety, to take heed how we commit ourself to armed multitudes for fear of treachery; but I assure you, I do not desire to live to distrust my faithful and loving people.

"Let tyrants fear. I have always so behaved my self, that under God, I have placed my chiefest strength and safeguard in the loyal hearts and goodwill of all my subjects, and therefore I am come amongst you, as you see, at this time, not for my recreation and disport, but being resolved in the midst and heat of the battle, to live or die amongst you all, to lay down for my God, and for my kingdom, and for my people, my honour, and my blood, even in the dust.

"I know I have the body but of a weak and feeble woman, but I have the heart and stomach of a king, and of a King of England too, and think foul scorn that Parma or Spain, or any Prince of Europe should dare to invade the borders of my realm; to which, rather than any dishonour shall grow by me, I myself will take up arms, I myself will be your general, judge and rewarder of every one of your virtues in the field. I know already for your forwardness, you have deserved rewards and crowns; and we do assure you, in the word of a Prince, they shall be duly paid you."

As she came to the end of her most celebrated speech, thousands of troops shouted in unison, impassioned by their queen's words.

Days passed and the Armada didn't return, and Parma didn't invade. The Queen hoped that, for the time being at least, the Spaniards had been deterred in their campaign. As it turned out, the conquest had already collapsed.

Much of the Armada was ordered to sail back to Spain, but horrible storms, battle damage and the rocky shores of Ireland and Scotland sent scores of ships to the bottom of the ocean. Parma had lost thousands of troops to disease and was unable to cross the Channel due to poor weather and unexpected raids by the Dutch navy. Against all odds, England stunned the European powers by defeating the greatest naval power in the world.

A sort of renaissance ensued in England. The English took their victory as a symbol of God's favor and of the nation's impregnability under a virgin queen. Elizabeth had now ruled for 30 years, and in stark contrast to the political turmoil that preceded her, she brought peace and general prosperity to the realm.

Even the Pope, who hated Elizabeth, declared, "She is certainly a great Queen and were she only a Catholic she would be our dearly beloved. Just look how well she governs! She is only a woman, only mistress of half an island, and yet she makes herself feared by Spain, by France, by the Empire, by all… Our children would have ruled the whole world."

Elizabeth ruled for another 15 years, and had to face more difficult challenges. Her most trusted advisers died and were replaced by rivalrous heirs, the war continued with Spain, another assassination attempt was foiled, a revolution in Ireland was put down, and the economy was stricken by poor harvests, unscrupulous monopolists, and the costs of war.

Not all was grim, however. English literature flourished thanks to men like William Shakespeare and Christopher Marlowe. England continued its maritime explorations—something that Elizabeth had long supported—adventures that grew the prestige of the English navy and led to the establishment of the American colonies. Trade and diplomatic relations were established with the Barbary states and Ottoman Empire.

Elizabeth died quietly in her bed on March 24, 1603, at 69 years old, but not before passing her throne to her cousin James, King of Scotland. She'll be forever remembered and celebrated for her passionate individualism, which not only renewed her nation's self-confidence and sense of sovereignty but also afforded it a national identity of its own.

Nearly every great advance of mankind is an expression of passionate individualism—each began as one person's idea, which usually was rejected by many as stupid, impossible, impractical, heretical, dangerous, or shameful. Newton's first law of motion—the law of inertia—stood in direct opposition to more popular ideas of his time, and caused much uproar and debate. When the Athenian statesman Cleisthenes began to reform Athens according to his ideas of democracy, he was vehemently opposed by the aristocracy, which denounced it as a way for the abundant poor to tyrannize the rich minority.

We're fortunate that these great visionaries and their brethren didn't lose their nerve to defy their peers and the masses. Imagine what path England might have taken if Elizabeth had been more like her sister, Bloody Mary, and married her country off to a foreigner. The Reformation probably would've been crushed, and with it the Church of England. England would've wound up a mere appendage of France or Spain, preventing the formation of the mighty British Empire. This, in turn, would've certainly changed the course of American history, as the colonies would've fallen to the French or Spanish, thus changing the evolution of Western civilization in more ways than we can imagine.

Thousands of years of thinkers have known that the multitude never create anything extraordinary. Emerson said that the masses "have no habit of self-reliance or original action." Seneca said that "nothing is so contemptible as the sentiments of the mob." Thoreau said the mass "never comes up to the standard of its best member, but on the contrary degrades itself to a level with the lowest."

If it weren't for the indomitable individualism of history's greatest men and women, who fearless championed their radical ideas and dreams, the human species would still be wandering the wilds, struggling against the crude forces of nature, mystified by the stars, and bludgeoning animals and each other with clubs and stones.

As your adventure grows, it will necessarily involve you in the lives and machinations of more and more people, which will necessarily bring more and more criticisms, recommendations, warnings, and guidance. Some of these suggestions will benefit you, and some will be invitations to disaster, and like Elizabeth, you'll have to know when to seek advice, and when to impose your will.

If you care too much about what other people think, say, or do, you'll be pulled away from your path in every other direction imaginable. You'll simply hand over your destiny to those you desperately seek approval from. Geniuses don't fall into this trap. They are, as the Indian philosopher Osho said, "just a little more stubborn than ordinary people." They just "go on hammering."

Elizabeth, for example, made it clear that while she intended to rule by good counsel, she was more intelligent than most men and would not allow her council or government to bully her into becoming a figurehead. This was wildly unpopular with many powerful men in her country, but she didn't care.

Your unique view of the world and your right to act on those views is more valuable than the comforting confirmation of others. This is the only way greatness is achieved, actually. "If the single man plants himself indomitably on his instincts, and there abides, this huge world will come around to him," Emerson wrote.

Thinking and acting originally comes with risks, however. You're going to make mistakes. You're going to find out that things were not as you thought. The genius knows that self-confidence doesn't come from always being right, but from not fearing to be wrong. The learning of a valuable lesson and the progression of your thinking and understanding can easily offset the temporary discomfort of realizing that you're wrong. In fact, the best lessons in any endeavor and indeed in life are often learned through failure, and can only be learned that way. Sometimes a thousand words can't convince you of something like a mere moment of failure can.

Positive, powerful individualism doesn't necessarily come easy, however. Every great genius relied on the same process to formulate new, powerful ideas.

One of the simplest common denominators of every genius is their voracious appetite for learning. They place enormous value on books and reading, and on the pursuit of knowledge at large. They also found it incredibly easy to get interested in just about any subject, no matter how mundane or obscure it might seem to others.

Sir Francis Bacon, philosopher and creator and champion of the scientific method, said that we should read "not to contradict and confute, nor to believe and take for granted," but to "weigh and consider." Voltaire said that "what we find in books is like the fire in our hearths."

The essence of individualism is not just having a unique point of view, but one that you stand by with certainty and conviction. Beliefs or opinions based on little actual knowledge are flimsy, or worse, ignorant. They are usually little more than shallow summaries of other people's thoughts, which can be shaken by equally shallow counterpoints and specious reasoning. Ideas grounded in a rich understanding of the matter, however, are deep, multi-faceted, and an expression of your unique insights. They constitute true enlightenment and burrow into your soul. These are the type of ideas that support entire movements and define eras. And this is the way of geniuses.

Today's entertainment-soaked society gives us a million different ways to avoid learning, thinking, and making decisions. Between TV and the Internet, it's never been easier to fill our lives with meaningless distractions, and it sends a clear, subtle message: that we're dumb, trivial, and that this is all we can comprehend or do.

If you want to experience a marked shift in your views and understanding of any subject or aspect of life, commit to reading one book per week on it. Each book you finish is like a cobblestone that you get to add to your road to greatness. The more thoroughly you pave this road, the easier you can travel it in your journey. Don't treat it like school homework, either. You don't have to remember dates, names, and places for a test. You're reading to learn the lessons—those are what matter.

"We haven't time to spare to hear whether it was between Italy and Sicily that he ran into a storm or somewhere outside the world," Seneca wrote, "when every day we're running into our own storms, spiritual storms, and driven by vice into all the troubles that Ulysses ever knew."

The point: Look for how you can apply the information to help you forward in your journey. If it has no application, it doesn't matter.

If you come across words or concepts you're unfamiliar with, get them clarified with a dictionary or encyclopedia. You'll never fully comprehend what you read if you don't fully understand the words used to communicate the concepts.

Use a highlighter when you read to mark the passages that you think are most interesting, insightful, or useful. If something striking occurs to you, note it down in the book. These things make it easier to review the book in the future, and they encourage a more active, thoughtful style of reading.

Reading this way isn't "easy." But it's incredibly rewarding. It will enable you to leap past your peers and is, I believe, one of the simplest and most powerful ways to awaken your inner genius.

"Insist on yourself; never imitate," Emerson wrote. "Your own gift you can present every moment with the cumulative force of a whole life's cultivation."

Elizabeth had a radical vision of what England could be, and her gift to her people was a resurgence of English strength, pride, tolerance, independence, and prosperity—the very foundation of the great empire that would follow.

Who are you, and what gifts will you present to the peoples of the world? Striving, fighting, deliberating, and pressing to discover answers to those questions, as Elizabeth did, is the essence of individualism, and of your journey to greatness.

9

JUDGMENT AND THE GREAT MEDICINE REVOLUTION OF ANCIENT GREECE

"Our senses don't deceive us; our judgment does."

-Johann Wolfgang von Goethe

All adventures force heroes to make tough decisions. The irrevocable, inescapable types that set off a three-alarm fire in your gut, because you know that your journey will be forever defined by these fleeting moments.

While war ravages Europe, the cynical American expatriate Rick Blaine spends his time quietly tending to his nightclub and gambling den in Casablanca, Morocco. Through a chance encounter with an acquaintance, Blaine comes into possession of two invaluable letters of transit—documents that grant the bearers freedom to travel throughout Nazi-occupied Europe without inspection. A deal is arranged to sell them for a small fortune, but when Blaine meets the buyer—a leader of an anti-Nazi rebellion—and his beautiful wife, Ilsa, he's stricken; she's his former love who, years ago, left him mysteriously. Old wounds re-open, old passions flare, and Blaine ultimately faces an agonizing dilemma: does he help the woman he loves escape and lose her forever, or secretly betray her honorable husband to the Germans and attempt to rekindle their romance? His loyalty to the greater cause trumps his selfish desires, and Blaine not only delivers the papers, but convinces Ilsa to continue supporting her husband, and puts his life on the line to help the couple escape.

Robert E. Lee is a decorated war hero who opposes slavery and denounces the growing secession as "revolution" and a betrayal of the founders of America. After his home state of Virginia secedes, President Lincoln offers him the command of Union forces as a major general. But there's a problem: accepting means he will have to lead soldiers to slaughter his own people. His heart is torn, but Lee's ties to his family and state are too strong. He resigns from the Union army and three days later, takes up command of Virginia state forces.

It's been three years since Fred Smith put all of his money into founding Federal Express to specialize in the "impossible": the overnight delivery of packages. The company is on the verge of bankruptcy—it's losing a million dollars per month—and Fred can't persuade investors for another penny. At week's end, the company is down to its last $5,000, which isn't even enough to get planes into the air come Monday. Smith needs tens of thousands of dollars to appear out of nowhere, or FedEx goes under. What to do? He takes the $5,000 to Vegas, spends the weekend at the tables, and returns with over $30,000. The payoff is just enough to keep the company afloat for a few more days, which are all Smith needs. In that time, he manages to raise $11 million to keep operations going. Two years later, the company turns it first profit of nearly $4 million.

Like Blaine's predicament in Casablanca, some decisions stretch the strings of morality to their limits: choosing the lesser of two evils, sacrificing one to benefit many, contemplating an opportunity to boost self to the detriment of others. Other decisions, like Lee's, represent cosmic wedges driven into your path, creating a fork that forever changes the nature of your journey. And then there are those decisions, like Smith's, that demand every ounce of horsepower, and every strand of toughness your wits, imagination, and heart can muster.

Awakening your inner genius and harnessing your potential for greatness requires developing your sense of judgment because the final outcome of every journey is nothing more than a collection of decisions, both big and small. Choose unwisely and you crash on the rocks; choose wisely and you can navigate even the most treacherous waters, just as the father of Western medicine did.

A distraught mother carried her sick child, delirious with fever, into a sacred temple of Asclepius, the Greek god of medicine.

She gave her boy to robed priests, who laid him upon a large, marble altar and beseeched the gods to cure him of his suffering. Opium was then administered to induce a "dream state," in which the great healer Asclepius would visit the boy in a vision and heal him, or so they hoped. The mother brought offerings of gold and silver coins, which were cast into the sacred spring to gain the favor of the Divine Physician.

But as the night wore on, the boy's condition worsened: his breathing was shallow, his skin cold and pallid. The priests informed the mother that the gods would not lift their punishment, and Asclepius would not answer their call. The only chance for her son, they said, was surgery to release the evil spirits that the gods summoned into him. Upon the mother's permission, the priests drilled a hole into the boy's skull and punctured his brain. He was dead by morning. The priests consoled the despairing mother, ensuring her that she shouldn't place any blame on herself—it was merely the will of the gods.

Such tragedies were common in ancient Greece. Superstitions, evil spirits, and disfavor of the gods were widely thought to cause poor health, illnesses, and disease. Thus, "cures" often relied on divine intervention, dangerous surgeries, bloodletting, and other procedures that often worsened conditions or proved fatal. One man had a different vision of medicine, however. He believed that natural forces caused poor health, illnesses, and disease, and therefore that such issues could be understood with observation and treated with gentle, non-invasive methods that allowed the body to heal itself. Such blasphemous views—in the eyes of his contemporaries anyway—earned him a reputation as a heretical outcast that opposed the religious infrastructure of Greece. But despite the popular outcry, Hippocrates remained convinced of his sound judgment on matters of health, a decision that later earned him the honorable distinction of father of Western medicine.

Hippocrates was born in 460 BC. As a young man, he traveled the lands of Greece to treat patients and educate people on what he called the "healing power of nature." Hippocrates insisted that one must treat the body as a whole, and thus centered his therapies around keeping the patient clean and sterile, and on restoring the body's ability to heal itself through the use of diet, herbs, rest, cleanliness, and exercise. He shunned the common practices of drugs and surgery and instead emphasized that one should "let food be thy medicine and medicine be thy food."

Word soon began to spread of the effectiveness of his treatments and the audaciousness of his theories. When such news reached the ears of governing authorities—who claimed that they were the spokespeople for the gods of health—they ordered Hippocrates to cease his teachings at once. Hippocrates ignored their threats and continued to travel, treat patients, and teach the healing powers of nature. His defiance soon caught up with him when, upon arriving in small rural city to treat citizens, he was arrested for disrespecting the gods. He was quickly sentenced to indefinite detention in state prison. But detention couldn't dissolve his will to heal others through his teachings. So, while incarcerated, he wrote one of his most famous works, *The Complicated Body*, which contains many physiological conclusions that we know to be true today.

Hippocrates spent nearly two decades in prison before finally being released. Once free, he resumed his work with greater vigor than ever, determined to end the age of superstitious medicine that relied on magic, not reason, and that often did more harm than the disease it attempted to treat. "Wherever a doctor cannot do good, he must be kept from doing harm," he wrote.

Throughout his treatments of patients, Hippocrates diligently catalogued illnesses as acute, chronic, endemic, and epidemic. His relentless work ethic and keen sense of judgment catalyzed a wide range of medical breakthroughs that we still rely on today, such as the identification of asthma and pneumonia by their symptoms; the medicinal and cosmetic value of bee honey; the importance of traction, counter-traction, and splinting in treating bone fractures; the healing power of fever; the prognosis of thoracic empyema, a form of lung disease; and even the use of positive imagery to improve convalescence, which he argued was connected to the brain, not the heart as was commonly believed. He was also the first documented chest surgeon, whose findings are still relevant to pulmonary medicine today.

To value Hippocrates' contributions to modern medicine only by such breakthroughs (the ends) would be woefully incomplete, however. His methods (the means) are equally valuable and relevant today. His use of all the senses—touch, smell, sight, hearing, and even taste—to carefully observe patients was a major medical innovation. And unlike any other physicians of his day, he kept meticulous, individualized patient records that consisted of detailed accounts of all symptoms including complexion, pulse, fever, changes in the feel of organs, movement, skin color, eyes, and excretions. He even took the pulse of a patient while conducting a case history to detect if the patient had lied. Hippocrates' purpose for keeping such extensive records was to establish a clinical profile of facts and histories that could be passed down to and employed by other physicians, a standard we largely take for granted today.

"Conclusions which are merely verbal cannot bear fruit, only those do which are based on demonstrated fact," he said. "For affirmation and talk are deceptive and treacherous. Wherefore one must hold fast to facts in generalizations also, and occupy oneself with facts persistently, if one is to acquire that ready and infallible habit which we call 'the art of medicine.'"

This perspective reveals an important lesson about judgment. Hippocrates wasn't quick to jump to conclusions before gathering, reviewing, and carefully considering all the relevant facts. He was constantly scouring his data for patterns, correlations, and discrepancies. He would draw out and emphasize insights and weed out and scrap red herrings. This methodical and objective approach to collecting and analyzing data is necessary to developing extraordinary judgment. We can judge only as well as our data will allow.

It wasn't long before aspiring doctors began flocking to Hippocrates to learn his methods and develop a similar sense of judgment. The demand became so clamorous that he founded the Hippocratic School of Medicine. In his school, Hippocrates taught more than just the diagnosis, prognosis, and treatment of illness and disease; he also taught the importance of strict professionalism, discipline, and rigorous practice. He recommended that physicians always be well-kempt, honest, calm, understanding, and serious. A Hippocratic physician was to be clean and pleasant smelling without foul odors or long and dirty fingernails. When in an operating room, he was to pay special attention to lighting, personnel, instruments, and the positioning of the patient. And outside the operating room, he was to remain cheerful to keep the patient in good spirits, as Hippocrates found that this helped recovery.

Hippocrates' teachings spread far and wide as his followers multiplied across Greece, treating patients, gathering information, and educating people on the foundations of good health. Within several years of its founding, Hippocrates' school was championing a veritable revolution in Greek medicine. Its medical discoveries were many, such as the connection between clubbed fingers and lung and heart disease; the facial symptoms forewarning of death; the effective treatment of hemorrhoids; the distinction of foodborne and airborne illnesses; the description of many illnesses including tetanus, tuberculosis, arthritis, mumps, and malaria; and the value of citrus fruit in counteracting lethargy.

Many fundamental observations about general health also resulted from Hippocrates' work, including the fact that growing bodies have the most innate heat and thus require the most food, that too much or too little sleep is bad for health, that spontaneous exhaustion can indicate disease, that obesity leads to premature death, and even that idleness and lack of occupation "tend one toward evil."

Improving the methods of medicine and educating society on the healing powers of nature were phenomenal achievements. But Hippocrates wasn't fully satisfied because the profession he loved was rife with charlatans who, despite having no formal training or expertise, billed themselves as competent physicians and fleeced customers by making incorrect diagnoses, prescribing worthless or harmful "treatments," and even performing dangerous surgeries that often resulted in mutilation or death. He detested these frauds and resolved to remedy this widespread problem.

"Medicine is of all the Arts the most noble; but, owing to the ignorance of those who practice it, and of those who, inconsiderately, form a judgment of them, it is at present far behind all the other arts," Hippocrates wrote. "Their mistake appears to me to arise principally from this, that in the cities there is no punishment connected with the practice of medicine (and with it alone) except disgrace, and that does not hurt those who are familiar with it. Such persons are like the figures which are introduced in tragedies, for as they have the shape, and dress, and personal appearance of an actor, but are not actors, so also physicians are many in title but very few in reality."

To combat such egregious medical malpractice, Hippocrates developed the first ethical code of medical conduct, which became known as the Hippocratic Oath. The oath read as follows:

"I swear by Apollo, the healer, Asclepius, Hygieia, and Panacea, and I take to witness all the gods, all the goddesses, to keep according to my ability and my judgment, the following Oath and agreement:

"To consider dear to me, as my parents, him who taught me this art; to live in common with him and, if necessary, to share my goods with him; to look upon his children as my own brothers, to teach them this art; and that by my teaching, I will impart a knowledge of this art to my own sons, and to my teacher's sons, and to disciples bound by an indenture and oath according to the medical laws, and no others.

"I will prescribe regimens for the good of my patients according to my ability and my judgment and never do harm to anyone.

"I will give no deadly medicine to any one if asked, nor suggest any such counsel; and similarly I will not give a woman a pessary to cause an abortion.

"But I will preserve the purity of my life and my arts.

"I will not cut for stone, even for patients in whom the disease is manifest; I will leave this operation to be performed by practitioners, specialists in this art.

"In every house where I come I will enter only for the good of my patients, keeping myself far from all intentional ill-doing and all seduction and especially from the pleasures of love with women or with men, be they free or slaves.

"All that may come to my knowledge in the exercise of my profession or in daily

commerce with men, which ought not to be spread abroad, I will keep secret and will never reveal.

"If I keep this oath faithfully, may I enjoy my life and practice my art, respected by all humanity and in all times; but if I swerve from it or violate it, may the reverse be my life."

As Hippocrates put his oath's moral code and system of accreditation of new physicians via an apprenticeship into wider use, medicine became established as a legitimate profession that the people could trust. The oath proved so well structured that it served as a foundation for later pledges and laws that define good medical practice and morals, and it continues to serve as a model for many other professional codes today.

Hippocrates' outstanding judgment is again evident in his code. He knew that great men act for the benefit of all, not just for their selfish interests, and think with the long term while meeting the needs of the present. He always considered the ethics of his choices, and knew that his integrity was more important than immediate gain.

The Hippocratic teachings grew so powerful that, in time, they effectively divorced the subject of medicine from religion and philosophy, and placed it in the realm of a natural science. Aristotle referred to Hippocrates as "the Great Physician" and described him as a "kind, dignified, old country doctor" who was also, at times, "stern and forbidding." Plato concurred, praising his scientific approach to medicine.

By the end of his life, Hippocrates and his followers had revolutionized the practice, ideals, and ethics of medicine. What has survived of their legacy includes over 70 written works, called the Hippocratic Corpus, which are simple, direct, and earnest in their desire to help others. In these writings you can find annual records of weather and associated diseases, treatises on how to set fractures and treat wounds, how to feed and comfort patients, and how to take care of the body to avoid illness. Included are works on the symptoms, prognoses, and treatment of serious diseases as well as works on the care of children and on childbirth. Also included are some of the first recorded arguments that medicine is indeed a science based on firm principles and methods.

Although the exact year of his death is unknown, Hippocrates lived to be at least 80, with some accounts claiming that he lived well past 100. His teachings only grew in influence after his death. The Romans eventually adopted Hippocratic medicine partially due to the exalted physician Galen's praise and application of it. Hippocratic and Galenic texts all but disappeared in the early Middle Ages but were adopted by the Arabs in the 18th century, and were resurrected in Europe after the Renaissance.

Hippocrates' work formed the backbone of modern medicine and the series of revivifications of it have been said to make up the whole history of internal medicine. It also sharply highlights the transformational power of one man's decision to follow his judgment over all, even the hue and cry of the misguided or miscreant—and even when they're the sacred "authorities."

The esteemed medical historian Fielding Garrison wrote that Hippocrates was "above all, the exemplar of that flexible, critical, well-poised attitude of mind, ever on the lookout for sources of error, which is the very essence of the scientific spirit."

As the dissection of human corpses was outlawed in ancient Greece, little was known about how the body actually functioned. Hence, many inaccurate theories had gone in and out of vogue as to what organs did what, what caused disease, and what regulated overall health. Hippocrates was acutely aware of this shallow reshuffling of theories. More importantly, he knew what was knowable and unknowable about the body. So, instead of arguing about bodily humors or other—at that time—unprovable hypotheses about physiology, he focused his efforts on the practical: on the careful observation, diagnosis, and prognosis of illness and disease, and the effective restoration of health. Although he wasn't sure as to *why* illnesses could be cured with herbs, nutrition, rest, and mild exercise, he knew that they could and devoted his entire life to developing the empirical side of medicine. He was only interested in what he could know with certainty, and what was workable, and one day, medical theory would catch up and explain exactly why his methods healed.

The Webster's Dictionary defines *judgment* as "the process of forming an opinion or evaluation by discerning and comparing; discernment." To *discern* means to "perceive or recognize; to have knowledge of" and "to see the difference between two or more things."

Hippocrates' rational nature showcases how important pragmatism is to developing a keen sense of judgment. In your quest for greatness, you're going to have to sort through mountains of possibilities, ideas, opinions, and facts. Your judgment will serve as your filter; its first job is to separate (discern) what will serve useful in your journey and what will be a dead end. Or, as Nietzsche put it, "...the imagination of the good artist or thinker produces continuously good, mediocre, or bad things, but his judgment, trained and sharpened to a fine point, rejects, selects, connects... All great artists and thinkers are great workers, indefatigable not only in inventing, but also in rejecting, sifting, transforming, ordering."

You've probably heard that the ability to judge only comes with experience, and that mistakes and failures are invaluable in developing this ability. While there may be some truth in that, experience alone is a harsh, inefficient teacher that can be very expensive, time-consuming, and heartbreaking. That reality demands that we ask: what can we do to better develop our ability to judge the many situations and circumstances we will face in our journeys, and thus be able to make more good decisions than bad? To attain our answer, let's first look at one of the biggest enemies of sound judgment: our power of mental distortion known as *cognitive dissonance*.

A FOX, SOME GRAPES, AND THE END OF THE WORLD

Christian radio broadcaster Harold Camping had predicted that the world would end on May 21, 2011. Many believers sold their possessions and anxiously awaited Jesus Christ's return, only to be disappointed as that Saturday came and went without incident. This wasn't their first letdown. In 1992, Camping declared that the world would end sometime in September 1994. After that prophecy failed, he "corrected" his numbers and said that March 31, 1995 was the actual Day of Judgment. After that too proved incorrect, he again amended his numbers to indicate that May 2011 would indeed bring the Rapture.

Failed doomsday prophecies have been around for centuries. They date back as far as many Europeans' hysterical fear of the year 1666, and continue to crop up in modern society. The most baffling aspect of all such prophecies is the number of people that refuse to face the duplicitous nature of false prophets like Camping, and the rationalizations they invent to buy into the next declaration, and the next, and the next.

While you and I aren't gullible enough for such an obvious deception, we've all fallen prey to the "glitch" in thinking that allows people to be so thoroughly deluded. Aesop, the famous Greek slave and storyteller, recognized it thousands of years ago and immortalized it in one of his fables. Known as "The Fox and the Grapes," the fable goes like this:

> *The fox who longed for grapes, beholds with pain*
> *The tempting clusters were too high to gain;*
> *Grieved in his heart he forced a careless smile,*
> *And cried, 'They're sharp and hardly worth my while.'*

The moral of the story is that when the fox's expectation didn't meet the result, he had to rationally justify his failure to feel better about it. This illogical reasoning is commonly referred to as *cognitive dissonance*, which boils down to the fact that people hate to be wrong. When people desire things and then fail to accomplish them, they often diminish the importance of the thing so desired or the desire itself. When compelling evidence to the contrary refutes people's convictions, they often irrationally argue against the evidence by inventing strange, baseless harmonies between their beliefs and the opposition, or simply altering or purposely misunderstanding conflicting factors.

When someone has closed his mind to the possibility of any other reality, he can exhibit extraordinarily irrational judgment, which predisposes him to making disastrous decisions. Case in point: William Orton.

Orton, president of the Western Union Telegraph Company in 1876, had over $41 million dollars in cash and a monopoly on the world's most advanced communications technology. One day, a man named Gardiner Hubbard approached Orton to sell him the patent for a new invention that he helped fund called the "telephone" for $100,000. Orton immediately saw the device as a threat to his empire and, consequently, applied a most inopportune method of "unknowing" what he glimpsed. He convinced himself that the telephone was nothing more than a gimmick, writing directly to the inventor, Alexander Bell, to tell him that Western Union had no need for such an "electrical toy." Bell kept the patent and, within a few years, his telephone company was the largest corporation in America. Meanwhile, Orton died of a stroke.

Poor judgment literally killed poor Orton, and it also nearly killed one of the greatest hallmarks of American industrialism: the Ford Motor Company.

The Ford Model T debuted in 1908 as the first affordable quality automobile, and quickly revolutionized American culture. In 1912, after Henry Ford returned from a family vacation to Europe, his engineers presented to him an improved prototype of the Model T to compete with automobile innovations from companies such as General Motors and Chevrolet. Much to their dismay, Ford proceeded to rip the car apart with his bare hands. Customers should not need anything more than basic transportation, Ford believed, and thus there was no need for new products. The American automobile buyers felt differently, however; Ford's misjudgment of what people should or shouldn't need or want would cost him and his company dearly.

In 1923, Ford's automobile market share slid to 57 percent; the decline continued to 45 percent in 1925, 34 percent in 1926, and a dismal low of under ten percent in 1927. Finally, with his company in near shambles, Ford faced the fact that he had to adapt or die. A replacement to the Model T was announced in 1927, but it was too late. Ford had lost his dominance in the marketplace forever, and allowed competitors like General Motors, Chevrolet, and Dodge to rise to prominence.

Winston Churchill wrote that the truth "is incontrovertible." He said, "malice may attack it, ignorance may deride it, but in the end; there it is." Orton and Ford, lacking objective and pragmatic judgment that valued truth above all else, learned that lesson the hard way.

If we are to sharpen our ability to judge, we must think less like Orton and Ford and more like Hippocrates: we must remain open to new or opposing ideas, facts, and theories; we must not irrationally avoid them in fear of discomfort, embarrassment, or confusion. The consequences of willful delusion can far outweigh the discomfiting nature of realizing that things are not as you thought, or that they've changed. Be careful, though. While a certain measure of open-mindedness is present in all geniuses, they also know when to seal the hatches, as we can see in the philosophical feud of the celebrated philosopher and mathematician Gottfried Leibniz, and the brilliant Enlightenment writer Voltaire.

The rejection of ideas, practices, and philosophies considered sacred or inviolable by peers, authorities, and societies is a hallmark of many of history's greatest thinkers. Such astute minds, however, didn't offhandedly reject counter-arguments but rather met them with cogent arguments of their own based on reason, evidence, and insight. They invited debate and carefully considered other positions and viewpoints.

Leibniz was a Lutheran and believed that the apparent flaws of our world can be justified by the theory that our world must be the best and most balanced of worlds, because it was created by an all-powerful and all-knowing God that would not have created anything less. By contrast, Voltaire believed that a supreme being must exist, but rejected the notion of one that intervenes in human endeavors.

Voltaire criticized Leibniz's theory in *Candide*, in which the protagonist witnesses war, disease, death, slavery, torture, and many other barbarisms, and concludes that God must have abandoned this globe to some evil creature. "Who in his right mind could think that this is the best God could have done?" Voltaire asks. Leibniz had anticipated this objection, however, and countered it elegantly in an essay, *Ultimate Origination*:

"*We know but a small part of the eternity which extends without measure, for how short is the memory of several thousand years which history gives us. But yet, from such meager experience we rashly make judgments about the immense and the eternal [...].*

"Look at a very beautiful picture, and cover it up except for some small part. What will it look like but some confused combination of colors, without delight, without art [...]. But as soon as the covering is removed, and you see the whole surface from an appropriate place, you will understand that what looked like accidental splotches on the canvas were made with consummate skill by the creator of the work. What the eyes discover in the painting, the ears discover in music.

"Indeed, the most distinguished masters of composition quite often mix dissonances with consonances in order to arouse the listener, and pierce him, as it were, so that, anxious about what is to happen, the listener might feel all the more pleasure when order is soon restored [...]. He who hasn't tasted bitter things hasn't earned sweet things, nor indeed, will he appreciate them. Pleasure does not derive from uniformity, for uniformity brings forth disgust and makes us dull, not happy: this very principle is a law of delight."

Leibniz's response is equally compelling, and opens your mind to new possibilities. Both of these men had evolved their own truths, both were aware of and took into account alternate and opposing theories, and both continued to investigate, study, and accept challenges so they could further expand and refine their truths.

The lesson here is that you have the right to invent your own truths and defend them, even when others disagree. You are under no universal mandate to conform to groupthink or authority. Buddha told his followers that they should "believe nothing, no matter where you read it, or who said it, no matter if I have said it, unless it agrees with your own reason and your own common sense."

Hippocrates personified this mindset, maintaining that the gods didn't cause illness and disease, even though the entire aristocracy of Greece cried blasphemy. Similarly, Copernicus asserted that the Earth revolved around the Sun and, thus, wasn't the center of the universe, an informed opinion in direct defiance of the powerful Catholic Church and its considerable influence over the minds of many Europeans.

"All truth passes through three stages," Arthur Schopenhauer wrote. "First, it is ridiculed. Second, it is violently opposed. Third, it is accepted as being self-evident."

Just because your views aren't widely held or agreed upon doesn't mean they're wrong. The climax of your journey to greatness might very well depend on their dissemination and acceptance. To achieve that end, you must not run from opposition; you must be willing to accept objective evidence to the contrary and to think through and debate between shifting points of view. Greatness demands that you devote yourself to the narrow intellectual path that winds between crippling agnosticism on one side and reckless solipsism on the other—the path of resolute but well-founded opinions and beliefs that yet remain pliable. This is simply a psychological manifestation of the foundation of evolution—the minds that can adapt, thrive; those that can't, succumb.

Confucius said, "no matter how busy you may think you are, you must find time for reading, or surrender yourself to self-chosen ignorance." Thomas Jefferson collected over 10,000 books and considered them vital to his well-being. Mark Twain said, "The man who does not read good books has no advantage over the man who cannot read them."

Studying the ideas and lives of other accomplished people is an incredibly effective shortcut to improving your judgment, awareness, and understanding of any field, and of life itself. By exposing yourself to a wide variety of schools of thought, experiences, decisions, and consequences, you gain insights that might never have occurred to you otherwise. By reading voraciously, you get to vicariously experience and sort through a wide range of circumstances and situations to find useful lessons and data that will help you successfully navigate your adventure. What you can learn in a handful of the right books would literally take you lifetimes to discover and evolve yourself.

Use the research and conclusions of past geniuses as jump-offs for your own hypotheses and discoveries. This might lead you to forward the findings and philosophies of others, but don't be afraid to modify or refute them in your own ways. As Einstein once said, "Any man who reads too much and uses his own brain too little falls into lazy habits of thinking."

Continuous education is a sure path to wisdom and a keen judgment; and by *education*, I don't mean it in the sense of modern schooling, which has students memorize a sea of facts but gives little importance to the ability to think for themselves. William Butler Yeats, the Nobel Prize-winning writer and poet, said that education is "not filling a bucket, but lighting a fire." As we saw with Hippocrates, it only takes one such fire to extinguish millions of shadows of ignorance, superstition, and deceit, and reveal to all the path to wisdom, reason, and truth.

There exists unlimited tinder for your fire: your ideas and experiences, and those of others, and your ability to understand, experiment with, accept, reject, and evolve them. It takes persistent vigilance and diligence to keep your fire alight, however. Hippocrates said that "life is short, and art long; opportunity fleeting, experience perilous, and decision difficult."

Your journey to greatness won't be easy. You will be faced with frustrating dilemmas, puzzling mysteries, and decisions that can only be made on instinct. While you can seek counsel, you can never shed your responsibility as the captain of your ship. Be like Hippocrates—purposefully cultivate your sense of judgment and energetically exercise it to chart a bold course in your journey. If you do, you'll find the strength to weather the storms of your mistakes, and keep your bow pointed toward greatness; and the prudence to make the most of the full sails and smooth waters of your successes, and gift humankind with a wonderful new way to comprehend and navigate the universe.

10

HONESTY AND THE RAPIER WIT OF THE RENAISSANCE

"Honesty is the best policy. If I lose mine honor, I lose myself."

-William Shakespeare

Only heroes with honest hearts can emerge from the fires of their journeys unscathed. True greatness is never bestowed on the deceitful or deluded.

Roderigo, a dissolute playboy, and Iago, an officer in the Venetian army, conspire to destroy general Othello's life. Roderigo wants his wife, Desdemona, and Iago wants revenge for being passed over for promotion by Othello. Their plan is simple: convince Othello that his wife is having an affair with the man who got Iago's promotion, first-lieutenant Cassio, which will drive Desdemona into Roderigo's arms, and Cassio into resignation. The duo's machinations work too well, and things quickly spiral out of control. Othello is tricked into believing Desdemona is cheating, but vows to kill her. Roderigo tries to kill Cassio at Iago's urging, but fails. In a desperate bid to prevent a confession, Iago stabs his cohort to death. But the freefall doesn't stop. Othello smothers his innocent wife to death on charges of adultery, Iago's scheme is discovered and revealed by Cassio's wife—whom Iago kills—and Shakespeare's grim play ends with Othello committing suicide and Iago being dragged off for torture and imprisonment.

Abraham Lincoln doesn't have the advantage of going to the right schools, cultivating the right connections, scoring well on tests, or the opportunity to exploit social trends and fads. What he does have, however, is a willingness to work incredibly hard and an outstanding integrity. While practicing law for 20 years before becoming president, he earns the nickname "Honest Abe" by reducing fees for the poor, persuading clients to settle out of court to save money that they would have to pay him, and even offering his services for free. His colleagues rank him at the head of his profession, partly because they're certain that he never told a lie. His advice to those studying law is to "resolve to be honest at all events; and if, in your own judgment, you can not be an honest lawyer, resolve to be honest without being a lawyer." His renowned honesty helps him win support as an Illinois state legislator, then a member of the United States House of Representatives, and finally as President of the United States.

Socrates said the greatest way to live with honor is to be what we pretend to be. Individualism alone isn't enough—honesty is the glue that holds it all together and gives you the strength to endure the worst the world can throw at you. And as you're about to see, when the pressure is on in the journey to greatness is when honesty with others, and with yourself, matters most.

May 16, 1717 was a bad day for François Marie Arouet. It was the day he was imprisoned for a crime he didn't commit.

A year earlier, he had been exiled from Paris for criticizing Phillip II d'Orleans, the Regent of the French Kingdom, for alleged incest with his daughter. Shortly after Arouet's return from banishment in 1717, two anonymous pamphlets were published that again ridiculed the regent.

Phillip fumed over the mockery and immediately blamed Arouet, who was a rising star of the aristocratic literary circles. Despite having no evidence of authorship, Phillip ordered Arouet to the Bastille—an infamous fortress used to hold criminals and other undesirables—for 11 months. Arouet was given no trial or say in the matter—he was simply arrested and jailed and locked away in the Bastille's dank, vermin-infested dungeons. He was allowed a couple of books, a night cap, and two handkerchiefs.

The egregious injustice of his imprisonment impressed upon Arouet the need for wholesale social reform in France. This time in the fetid, dark underbelly of the citadel marked a turning point in his life. He shed his birth name and assumed a new one, Voltaire, and dreamed of freeing Europe from its traditions of superstition, injustice, intolerance, cruelty, and war.

Quite some time passed before Voltaire could obtain a pen and some paper and ink. Once he did, he spent his time in jail crafting his first play, *Oedipe*, which was an adaptation of Sophocles' famous tragedy, *Oedipus the King*. After completing it, he then began an epic poem, *Henriade*, in which he praised King Henry IV for ending France's wars of religion, and promoted the ideal of tolerance.

Upon his release from the Bastille in April 1718, Voltaire arranged for the debut performance of *Oedipe*. It was a runaway hit, playing to packed theaters for 45 consecutive days. At the young age of 23, *Oedipe* earned him a sizable sum and won him great recognition, even from the young queen Marie. Consequently, the regent gave him a pension and a position that would allow him a leisurely, luxurious life in amongst the elite, but he would soon learn that it came with a steep price: complete censorship of his writings. This was Voltaire's first major test of honesty. Were his radical ambitions for sale, or would he choose his integrity, instead? His answers would set him on a crash course with the French aristocracy.

Voltaire was united with other thinkers of his day in the belief in the supreme importance of reason. Through his writings, he challenged the dogmas of Catholicism and preached deism—the belief in a supreme being, but not one that interacts with humankind. "If God did not exist, he would have to be invented," he later wrote. "But all nature cries aloud that he does exist: that there is a supreme intelligence, an immense power, an admirable order, and everything teaches us our own dependence on it."

He became more interested in England, a country that tolerated freedom of thought, and began learning English to study the works of philosophers like John Locke and Isaac Newton. This was the beginning of a new stage of intellectual development for Voltaire, and it was accelerated by another clash with nobility.

While at an opera in 1725, Voltaire was insulted by an arrogant aristocrat from the powerful Rohan family for not belonging among the elite. Voltaire turned the insult back on the young nobleman, who flew into a rage and charged at him. Voltaire drew his sword, but the two were broken up before any violence. Only days after the incident, Voltaire was lured outside while dining at the Duke of Sully's estate. Waiting was a gang of lackeys hired by Rohan, who savagely beat Voltaire while the young aristocrat watched on from his carriage, laughing and jeering.

Over the next three months, Voltaire practiced his swordsmanship in anticipation of challenging Rohan to a duel to the death. He finally issued the challenge, but the aristo's family wouldn't have it. Instead, they quickly obtained a *lettre de cachet*—a penal decree signed by the king, often bought by members of the wealthy nobility to dispose of enemies—that caused Voltaire to be arrested and sent to the Bastille, again without trial or even formal charges.

While imprisoned, Voltaire received a steady stream of admiring visitors, but fandom didn't change his circumstances. Fearing indefinite detention, he offered an alternative punishment to the French authorities: exile from France. His offer was accepted, leading Voltaire to set out for London with a fiery determination to one day reform the French judicial system, which vested ultimate power in judicial officials and allowed for arbitrary arrests, torture to extract confessions, indefinite detention without trial, trial without a jury, complete confiscation of property upon being found guilty, and the justification of any ruling by the citation of confusing, contradictory laws.

Voltaire arrived in London in 1726 knowing nobody but one merchant. He immediately installed himself in the literary circles and won the respect of some of the great English dramatists of the time. He parlayed his new friendships into audiences with the nobility, and soon found a friend in Queen Caroline, who loved poetry. She welcomed him into the British high society. In return, he astutely published an English edition of his poem *Henriade*, dedicating it to the queen, which not only strengthened his relations with the English royalty but also made him a healthy sum of £1,000.

Voltaire continued to be fascinated by all things English. He was intrigued by Britain's constitutional monarchy as opposed to the French absolute monarchy. He respected England's belief in freedom of speech and religion. And he admired the Quakers for their tolerance and simplicity. Further, he devoured English philosophy and literature, achieving fluency in the new language within six months of arriving in London.

He kept writing, of course, during this time. In 1727, he published two essays and began work on his groundbreaking biography of Charles XII of Sweden. In it, he rejected the sacred cow that divine intervention alone guided history. Instead, he suggested that humans control their own destinies, a proclamation that marked the beginning of his energetic repudiation of religious dogmas. "Superstition is to religion what astrology is to astronomy, the mad daughter of a wise mother," he wrote. "These daughters have too long dominated the earth."

Historians describe these English years as Voltaire's first great transformation, both intellectually and morally. It's during these times that he cemented his convictions that freethinking, democracy, and equality would mark the next great social evolution. Further, it taught him a valuable lesson in honesty with himself; it invigorated him to rise up in the name of what he knew to be true—to live in accordance with his conscience, regardless of the forces that were sure to strike back. The explosion of energy in his Bastille cell was now a refined, focused beam, and it had a purpose: purging the cultural gloom of France.

After nearly three years of exile, in 1729, Voltaire was invited back to Paris, devoid of pensions and banned from the royal court at Versailles. He returned to his home with a vision of bringing English enlightenment to his people, and to spread the message of personal liberty.

He knew, however, that his mission would require financial independence. Thankfully, a perfect opportunity presented itself. The French government was staging a sort of lottery to help reduce the public debt, for which many tickets still remained. While at a dinner party, Voltaire overheard a distinguished mathematician claim that the scheme was so poorly organized that if one were to buy all the remaining tickets, he would be guaranteed to win a huge profit.

While others dismissed the comment as absurd, Voltaire immediately investigated it and concluded that the man was indeed correct. He then convinced several friends to pool their money together to buy every remaining lottery ticket. Voltaire put everything he had into the investment. It would either make him a rich man free of the restrictions imposed by wealthy patrons, or break him financially and force him to work through the filters of others. On the surface, such exploitation can be easily stamped as dishonest. But, considering the circumstances, was it? Voltaire faced two extremes: write under the yoke of oppressive censorship that would squash his radical ideas, or win in a game of gambling and be free to pursue his humanitarian goals. Voltaire knew that the former was the true betrayal of not only himself, but of millions of his countrymen. Just as a cure that kills one but saves a thousand is an acceptable cure, the scheme was a legal and acceptable means to his end—an act that was, he felt, for the greater good.

Much to the disgust of the Minister, the ploy worked: Voltaire's syndicate earned a staggering sum of £40,000, much of which went to Voltaire as the organizer and principal investor. His father's inheritance also became available to him soon after the lottery coup. From this point forward, Voltaire never again struggled financially. While many other writers were forced to appeal to powerful men of means for their livelihood, and thus defer to their editorial demands or prejudices, Voltaire answered to nobody.

By 1732, through a combination of artfully written plays, poems, and essays, Voltaire had fully redeemed himself in the eyes of the Parisian elite and was residing at the royal court of Versailles. This reprieve would be short lived, however. His next work of controversy, *Letters Concerning the English Nation*, was first published in English in 1733. In it, Voltaire openly praised the more tolerant English society and its constitutional monarchy, which he claimed was a better, more progressive form of government than France's.

"The English are the only people upon earth who have been able to prescribe limits to the power of Kings by resisting them," he wrote, "and who by a series of struggles have at last established that wise Government where the Prince is all powerful to do good, and at the same time is restrained from committing evil; where the Nobles are great without insolence, though there are no Vassals, and where the People share in the government without confusion."

In the same publication, Voltaire espoused Newtonian science over the Cartesian principles that many French thinkers held sacred, and rejected Pascal's claim that the purpose of life is to reach heaven through penitence. Instead, he offered that the purpose of life is to assure happiness to all men by progress in the sciences and the arts, in accordance with their nature.

Voltaire's unabashed honesty about the state of French politics and society stimulated an uprising of new discussions among the elite and commoners alike, but also brought great personal risk. Years earlier, France had instituted royal censorship that required the review of any and all written works before publication. Anything that was deemed contrary to religion, public order, or sound morality was denied publication rights. Much to Voltaire's dismay, a publisher took it upon himself to publish *Letters Concerning the English Nation*—the manuscript of which censors probably would've burned on the spot—in French as *Lettres Philosophiques sur les Anglais* in 1734. Voltaire was again embroiled in scandal and uproar.

The book was banned, the publisher sent to the Bastille, and all copies in Paris were gathered and burned publicly by the executioner, denounced as "scandalously contrary to religion, morals and society." The aristocracy clamored for Voltaire's arrest and imprisonment, and a warrant was issued in the same year.

Consequently, Voltaire was forced to flee once again. He found refuge in the estate of the Chateau de Cirey, which was owned by the Marquis Florent-Claude du Chatelet and his wife, Emilie du Chatelet. The couple used the sovereignty granted by their aristocratic title to create a safe haven for Voltaire, and a base for the next stage in his life.

Emilie was 27 years old, 12 years Voltaire's junior, and married with three children. She was an intelligent, educated woman who studied Greek and Lat-in and trained in mathematics. The two quickly realized that they were on the same wavelength and set forth on a voyage of discovery together, studying the natural sciences, history, and philosophy. Together they collected over 21,000 books on myriad subjects, which they studied and discussed day and night. It wasn't long before they began an affair, which was openly tolerated by Emilie's husband, who visited from time to time. Never one to care much for rules, it's interesting to note how Voltaire conducted himself with Emilie. Upon falling in love, he informed her husband of their intent to be lovers, which he approved of, and they flouted social conventions by regularly appearing in public together, unashamed of their extramarital relations. Ironically, and for what it's worth, Voltaire had an affair in the most honest way one could.

Voltaire's and Emilie's work was instrumental in propagating the new ideas in natural philosophy to continental Europe. Emilie translated Newton's *Principia*, and they wrote *Elements da la Philosophie de Newton* (Elements of Newton's Philosophy) together. The latter was a layman's introduction to Newton's groundbreaking ideas. Voltaire considered it a "machine of war" against the "backward Cartesianism" that dominated the minds of the French. It wasn't long before a bona fide culture war erupted in France between Newtonian and Cartesian philosophies, with Voltaire forming the tip of the Newtonian spear.

By the early 1740s, Voltaire's brand of honesty had reached critical mass, and his genius was widely recognized throughout Europe. In a grand recognition and acknowledgement of his love for the dissemination of truth, no matter how heretical, many hailed him as the greatest poet and playwright of all time. He was inducted into Germany's Hall of Fame, and was elected a member of the Royal Society in England. Even the prestigious *Academie Française* could no longer keep him from their ranks; with the king and pope behind him, he was admitted to the institution. To nobody's surprise, his inaugural paper was witty, sarcastic, and sacrilegious.

Tragedy would strike in 1749, however. Emilie, his lover of 15 years, went into labor with her fourth child. Voltaire was present and witnessed her death during the childbirth. He was devastated and lost, unsure of where to go. He spent time in Paris to mend his spirits, but decided that settling again in the capital was imprudent as he never stayed out of trouble for long. So instead, he took an offer from Fredrick, the King of Prussia, to join his court, but got himself kicked out within a few years due to escalating spats and quarrels with Fredrick and his courtiers.

Voltaire planned on returning to Paris, but learned that Louis XV had banned him largely because of the publication of his monumental historical work, *Essai sur les moeurs et l'esprit des nations* (Essay on the Manners and Spirit of the Nations), which uniquely focused on the story of human progress instead of the deeds of monarchs and religious leaders. In it, Voltaire used history to argue that persecution and intolerance were not only unjust but useless, and that the greatest advancements in knowledge were always accompanied by the greatest freedom of thought.

Instead of living elsewhere in France, he turned to Switzerland and bought a large estate just outside of Geneva. He was welcomed and honored as a champion of human rights and tolerance, but it wasn't long before he wore out this warm reception. First, there were the plays he was writing and performing at his estate despite the fact that Genevan law forbade private or public theatrical performances. Then there was his involvement in the 1757 publication of a controversial encyclopedia that criticized Geneva for banning theater, and that praised Calvinist pastors that doubted Christ's divinity.

"Virtue supposes liberty, as the carrying of a burden supposes active force," he wrote. "Under coercion there is no virtue, and without virtue there is no religion. Make a slave of me, and I shall be no better for it. Even the sovereign has no right to use coercion to lead men to religion, which by its nature supposes choice and liberty. My thought is no more subject to authority than is sickness or health."

The encyclopedia's publication rights were revoked in France, and Swiss intellectuals decried it a subversive work meant to undermine social and moral order.

French censorship intensified when, in 1757, a man named Damiens attempted to assassinate Louis XV. The king's response was an edict that decreed death for "all those who shall be convicted of having written or printed any works intended to attack religion, to assail the royal authority, or to disturb the order and the tranquility of the realm." This promise of death didn't stop Voltaire from continuing his program to advance the Enlightenment and defeat what he felt were the enemies of philosophy and the truth, the ecclesiastical and aristo-monarchal establishment. His efforts were encapsulated in his famous motto, "Ecrasez l'infame!" ("Crush the infamy!"), which referred to the royalty's and clergy's historical and prevalent abuses of the people.

By the end of 1758, Voltaire no longer felt safe in Geneva, and bought an even more extensive property in Ferney—a city on French soil bordering Lake Geneva. He continued to entertain friends and acquaintances with theater, and wrote what is considered some of his best work. This included one of his most loved and widely read publications, *Candide*, which is a satirical story that outright attacks religious and philosophical optimism that was popular at the time.

Five years later, he released his greatest work of philosophy, the *Dictionnaire Philosophique* (Philosophical Dictionary), which vigorously attacked the perceived injustices and absurdities of the Old Regime life, and elegantly explained concepts of tolerance, morality, equality, and friendship. "What is tolerance?" he wrote. "It is the consequence of humanity. We are all formed of frailty and error; let us pardon reciprocally each other's folly—that is the first law of nature."

Now in his 70s, Voltaire spent much of his time campaigning on behalf of the oppressed. He meddled in Genevan politics, taking the side of the workers who had no civil rights, and built a factory and watchworks on his property to help them. He also stuck to his characteristic themes of religious tolerance and respect for the rights of man, attacking the use of torture and heinous punishments. The case of Jean Calas was particularly illustrative of Voltaire's staunch pursuit of civil liberties.

Calas was a Protestant who tried to cover up his son's suicide to prevent his body from being drawn and quartered for committing a mortal sin. Rumors circulated that Calas had in fact killed his son because he wanted to convert to Catholicism, the state religion, and the whisper campaigns erupted into a frenzied scandal.

Calas was convicted of murder on the flimsiest hearsay evidence, and was subsequently brutally tortured to extract a confession. Since he wouldn't admit guilt to a crime he didn't commit, he was sentenced to death on the wheel, a form of punishment that consisted of being tied to a large wooden wheel and having one's limbs broken with an iron cudgel, and then being left for hours or even days to die of shock or dehydration. Calas was shown "mercy," though, as the executioner publicly strangled him to death after breaking his limbs. Calas maintained his innocence until his last anguished breath. The state then confiscated his property, leaving his widow homeless and penniless, exiled his surviving son, and turned his daughters over to a Catholic convent.

Voltaire heard about the grotesque affair and, livid, decided to investigate. He called for one of Calas' sons to visit him in Ferney, and after learning what happened, set out to clear the poor father's name. He wrote dozens of letters to powerful allies throughout Europe, including Catherine of Russia and Frederick the Great. He hired a lawyer and raised money for the family to prepare a case to vindicate Calas. After two years of tireless work, Voltaire secured a unanimous vote of Calas' innocence in the parliament of Paris, which resulted in the returning of his estate back to the family, and the children back to the mother. Voltaire even gave them an estate to live in once the case was won.

This was one of many such cases taken up by Voltaire while living in Ferney. Many victims were sadly proven innocent after execution, but scores of innocent lives were saved thanks to Voltaire's efforts. He conducted these crusades against injustice and barbarity at no small risk to himself. "It is dangerous to be right when the government is wrong," he said.

In 1778, after living in exile in Ferney for nearly 20 years, Voltaire longed to return to Paris. He was now 83 years old and had just completed his tragedy *Irene*. The performance's debut was to take place at the National Theater in Paris, and he wanted nothing more than to oversee its production.

Voltaire was granted entrance to the capital city in February 1778, and received a hero's welcome as the undisputed leader of the Enlightenment. Parisians lined the streets, cheering his return, swelling Voltaire with rapturous joy. The affair proved too much for him though. He quickly fell ill and, by the end of the month, believed he was going to die. "I die adoring God, loving my friends, not hating my enemies, and detesting superstition," he wrote.

As fate would have it, however, he made a partial recovery and used what borrowed time he had left to resume preparations for the opening of *Irene*. At the end of March 1778, he attended a performance of the play and was overwhelmed by the effusiveness of the audience, who demanded that he speak from the box, and crowned him with a laurel wreath.

He decided to remain in Paris, bought a house, and began work on another tragedy. Several weeks later, however, he became seriously ill and was soon on his deathbed. According to one story, when a priest admonished him to renounce Satan before passing, his reply and last words were, "Now is not the time for making new enemies."

Voltaire's written legacy included works in almost every literary form, including plays, poems, novels, essays, and historical and scientific works. He wrote under at least 178 pen names, and produced over 20,000 private letters, and over two thousands books and pamphlets before passing away.

He will forever be remembered as a courageous polemicist who dauntlessly fought for human rights, including the right to a fair trial, and freedom of speech and religion; who condemned the hypocrisies and injustices of the despotic French aristocracy; and who helped steer philosophy, theology, and science away from superstition and toward progressive rationalism. His ideas greatly influenced important thinkers of both the American Revolution, which was underway at his death, and the French Revolution, which broke out 11 years after his passing.

Voltaire's spirit is best summarized by his words that "to hold a pen is to be at war," and his philosophy is best summarized by his conviction that no authority, no matter how sacred, should be immune from challenge by critical reason.

"I have never made but one prayer to God, a very short one," he said. "'Oh Lord, make my enemies ridiculous.' And God granted it."

The duality of honesty and dishonesty color every aspect of your journey to greatness. Frank, forthright behavior allows you to remain in the light, whereas duplicity casts an ever-growing shadow over you and your path. Most forms of immorality and evil are sustained by lies, and stories like *Anna Karenina, Madame Bovary,* and *Othello* have endured for generations as grim warnings of the cataclysms that can begin with simple dishonesties.

Honesty and genius have a deeper relationship than this, however—one that Voltaire's life and teachings give incredible insight into. A genius' honesty starts with the realization that the first person we must stay true to under any and all circumstances—the person we must never cheat, deceive, or delude—is ourselves.

OUTWARD BEHAVIOR IS ONLY A REFLECTION OF WHAT'S WITHIN

Honesty with ourselves is also called *integrity*. It entails calling things as we see them and standing by our perceptions of right and wrong and true and false, regardless of what others think.

In his book *The Way to Happiness*, L. Ron Hubbard explains it like this:

"Many want you to believe things just to suit their own ends.

"What is *true* is what is true for *you*.

"No one has any right to force data off on you and command you to believe it or else. If it is not true for you, it isn't true.

"Think your own way through things, accept what is true for you, discard the rest. There is nothing unhappier than one who tries to live in a chaos of lies."

Voltaire knew the injustices and tyrannies of his time were inexcusable, even though they were deeply ingrained in the European social and religious traditions. His resolute honesty and integrity compelled him to fight aristocratic and religious oppression despite continuous persecution and ostracism. He wasn't afraid to expose and denounce evil, regardless of its pretenses or power. As a result, he inspired the masses to find their own voices and act on what they too knew to be true. Thanks to the proliferation of his ideas and those of a small group of his peers, political and intellectual despotism was overthrown, and the world was forever changed.

This unwavering loyalty to ourselves is the first lesson of honesty that we must embrace in our own journeys. We may not have to face the same pressures to conform or simply shut up as Voltaire did, but we will all have to face moments where we have to decide: do we make a prayer, grit our teeth, and push forward, staying true to our beliefs? Or do we warp our perceptions and conclusions and tell ourselves why it's okay, or that something else entirely is actually happening? "Life is bristling with thorns, and I know no other remedy than to cultivate one's garden," Voltaire wrote. That is, we can only overcome the dangers of the world by fully knowing ourselves.

Ayn Rand spotlights this inner struggle of self-honesty in her opus *Atlas Shrugged*, a tale of how society collapses when nobody is willing to confront reality and deal with things as they are, not as they wish them to be. It takes courage to speak up and be right when popular opinion is wrong. Voltaire lamented how difficult it is to "free fools from the chains they revere." All great moral, religious, intellectual, scientific, and philosophical advances were led by a small group of brave visionaries whose honesty awakened minds, one by one, until their ideas reached the tipping point and were finally accepted as valued truths. "Love truth, but pardon error," Voltaire said.

These geniuses valued honesty over all—even their lives, in many cases. They passionately strived for truth with themselves, a devotion that enables us to be truthful with others. We've all heard that "honesty is the best policy," but how do we find the strength to stay true when faced with the consequences of fessing up, or the lure of shady shortcuts?

Studies of human relations, such as the one done by Wellesley College, have shown that people who are generally honest with others are happier, more optimistic, have higher self-esteem, and have better relationships with others.

Some people consider honesty with others as a difficult burden, a habit that creates unnecessary problems and conflicts with others. Conflicts are inherent in any close relationship, however, and are actually healthy if dealt with openly. Would you avoid a conflict or moment of embarrassment if you knew that dodging it would contribute to long-term depression, stress, guilt, and delusion? Doubtful. But that's exactly what happens when you lie to others—you add darkness to a cloud that can eventually blot out the light of life.

Lies, even "white lies," have deeper, more insidious and toxic ramifications in your quest for greatness. Lies create an alternate reality that must be maintained with even more lies. Those lies, in turn, require supporting lies of their own. Aristotle warned of the exponential nature of lies when he wrote that "the least initial deviation from the truth is multiplied later a thousand-fold." Eventually, this web of deceit becomes so entangled and restricting that you'll feel like Gulliver in Lilliput—a prisoner immobilized by an army of ants and their bonds.

Furthermore, lies must be carefully juggled to avoid confrontations with reality. Abraham Lincoln said, "No man has a good enough memory to make a successful liar." Fooling people is just much harder than most liars think; while listeners may not challenge dubious claims, many people easily pick up the scent of a liar. Eventually someone finds a claim or comment out of place, and like nudging a quavering Jenga tower, it all comes toppling down. The truth, however, doesn't need to be tracked and protected. Things are what they are. The world is your memory and proof. If questions arise, you can just point to the incontrovertible.

Like a pebble thrown into a pond, the ripples of one lie can reach the farthest shore. When you lie to someone, you are, in fact, denying them an understanding of the matter at hand, small or large. The choices that they make based on your lies are your responsibility, and can be quite unpredictable, as we saw in *Othello*.

Honesty begets simplicity, which da Vinci called "the ultimate sophistication," and which will serve you very well in your journey. The self-imposed complexities of deceit are like a straitjacket that tightens and disfigures you, inch by inch. Eventually, you forget what it's even like to be able to think and act freely.

Your adventures are going to require that you reconsider facts, change views, discuss confusions, reconcile conflicts, and resolve doubts. Dishonest people work to mask and mutate truth and reality, and thus are inherently incapable of performing these vital functions successfully. Their thoughts are merely used to, as Voltaire said, "justify their wrongdoings," and their words to "conceal their thoughts." Only an honest heart and open mind is flexible enough to know when to be humble, when to be adamant, when to be skeptical, and when to be trusting.

11

ABILITY TO COMMUNICATE AND THE PEN OF REVOLUTION

"If wisdom were offered me with this restriction, that I should keep it close and not communicate it, I would refuse the gift."

-Seneca

No journey to greatness is traveled alone. Without the help of allies, the hero can never complete his quest.

Odysseus is trying to return home to Ithaca having escaped the insidious Lotus-eaters; defeated the tyrannical Cyclops; evaded the giant, cannibalistic Laestrygonians; defied the witchcraft of the goddess Circe; skirted the Sirens; survived the six-headed Scylla; and gained freedom from the amorous Calypso. His adventures have cost him his entire fleet and crew. Soon after, he finds himself stranded alone on the shores of a strange land. With the help of Athena, however, Odysseus meets the people that rule the land—the Phaeacians—and wins the favor of their king and court by sharing the stories of his adventures. They agree to ferry him home. After 20 years of absence, Odysseus returns to the loving arms of his wife, Penelope, and the rest of his family.

Political power in China is split between three contentious families: the clans of Jisun, Mengsun, and Shusun. Dismayed by rampant immorality and injustice, Confucius desires to dismantle the oligarchy and establish in its place a centralized government based on law and natural morality. Lacking any military power, Confucius' only option for a successful revolution is diplomacy. Through his teachings, he builds a peaceful army of disciples that spread his message of equality, ethics, self-improvement, sincerity, and the cultivation of knowledge. Confucius and his following work tirelessly for a year and a half before they successfully convince the ruling clans to agree to their reforms. They raze the first of their fortified cities to prove their sincerity. Confucius' teachings continue to grow in influence through his students, and eventually, they become the backbone and official imperial philosophy of the legendary Han Dynasty, and remain so for nearly 2,000 years.

Muhammad visits a cave near Mecca to spend several weeks alone, in prayer, as he did every year. This time, however, the angel Gabriel visits him in his sleep and commands him to recite several verses praising God. Muhammad awakes deeply disturbed. Is he possessed by a demon or was the revelation real? Even if it were, who would believe him? He considers throwing himself down the mountain, but is stopped by a divine voice claiming he's an apostle of God. He returns home and tells his wife, Khalidjah, what happened on the mountain, distressed and unsure of what she will think. She consoles him and accepts his revelation as true. Further revelations occur, and Khalidjah encourages her husband to preach the word of God to his fellows. He follows her advice, but is ignored and mocked by Meccans as a deluded false prophet. Khalidjah stands by him as his first convert, however, and helps him in his work. Together, they recruit the first followers of Islam, and she remains at his side until her death, nine years later.

Without a willingness and ability to communicate, our potential for genius will never fully develop. While many would measure genius by internal criteria—intelligence, eloquence, creativity, and so forth—the true measure and bottom line is external: sphere of influence. Virtues of character only become genius—and greatness—when exercised, and when their use stimulates change in the minds, lives, and societies of our fellows. This can't be accomplished alone. No man or woman, no matter how special, gets very far without allies and advocates. No movement, no matter how righteous or inspired its leader, rises to power without the tireless, shoulder-to-shoulder effort of its disciples to win acceptance with others.

Communication is the catalyst that makes it all possible. It's the force that enables you to export your brand of consciousness into the world. The ideas, philosophies, and actions that fill the annals of history are, in essence, manifestations of effective communication. True or false, good or evil, persuasive communication shapes our world.

The ability to communicate is the *weapon* of the genius code, and what a weapon it is. History has proven it stronger than armies and empires. And as you're about to see, the pen is not only mightier than the sword, but without the pen, the sword has no purpose or place in this world.

Thomas Paine was thirty-seven years old, and he had failed at everything he had ever tried.

His first business as a staymaker flopped. Shortly thereafter, his first wife and child died in childbirth. He was fired from his next job as an excise officer, one of the most hated government officials in England, for negligence. He then found employment as a servant and even tried preaching as an ordained minister of the Church of England. Several years later, he was reinstated as an excise officer and remarried, but was fired again within three years, this time for being absent without permission. His second wife left him soon after. Like a cosmic kick while he was down, he was then forced to sell all of his belongings and declare bankruptcy.

The future looked scarcely promising for Paine, but buried among the ashes was a single ember of hope, one that would eventually fuel a fire that would transform the world. This ember took a simple form: a pen.

During his second stint as an excise officer, Paine had written and actively distributed thousands of copies of a treatise that argued for a pay raise as the only way to stifle corruption among his peers. In 1772, he moved to London to continue lobbying on behalf of the excise officers, and was introduced to Benjamin Franklin by the Commissioner of the Excise, George Lewis Scott. Although his dissemination efforts collapsed and led to his second termination as an excise offer and bankruptcy, the chance encounter with Franklin set the stage for a call to adventure that would forever change Paine's fortunes.

Franklin saw something unique in Paine and suggested that he start anew in colonial America. Franklin wrote a letter of recommendation for Paine to his son-in-law to employ him "as a clerk, or assistant tutor in a school, or assistant surveyor."

With nothing to lose, Paine boarded a ship to America the next month. He barely survived the voyage. The ship's water supplies were tainted and typhoid fever broke out among the passengers. When the ship pulled into port in Philadelphia in November, Paine was too weak to disembark. Fortunately, Franklin's physician was waiting to carry him off the boat and attend to his care. It took six weeks for Paine to fully recover his health.

Back on his feet, Paine's first job in America was as an editor for the *Pennsylvania Magazine*, a position in which he did remarkably well. In addition to his regular duties, he began writing articles and poetry for the magazine and other newspapers. One such article was entitled "African Slavery in America," in which he excoriated the African slave trade and signed as "Justice and Humanity."

"That some desperate wretches should be willing to steal and enslave men by violence and murder for gain, is rather lamentable than strange," he wrote. "But that many civilized, nay, christianized people should approve, and be concerned in the savage practice, is surprising."

As fate would have it, Paine had arrived to America just as the tensions between the colonies and England were reaching their boiling point. Paine had no love lost for King and Country; the decades he had spent at the bottom of English society in poverty and obscurity had seen to that. In fact, his plights in England primed him to voraciously champion the colonial cause. After the first blood of the Revolutionary War was spilled in Lexington and Concord, Paine argued that the colonial revolutionists should not only revolt against taxation, but should demand independence from the scurrilous English monarchy. His fiery diatribes won him many friends in the taverns, and he got an idea. If his brand of revolution was as persuasive as it seemed, what would happen if he placed his soapbox before the entire nation?

The answer came in January 1776, when he suddenly burst into the limelight with his pamphlet *Common Sense*, and his life and indeed the world would never again be the same.

Despite its brevity—less than 50 pages—*Common Sense* was the most important pamphlet written during the American Revolution, paving the way for the Declaration of Independence. It went through dozens of editions and quickly spread among the literate, selling over 100,000 copies in three months. Throughout the course of the war, over 500,000 copies were distributed. With only two million people living in the colonies at the time, *Common Sense* is the most circulated book in American history.

In *Common Sense*, Paine flayed the monarchal system of government, declaring that hereditary succession is no proper claim to honor or power, and that one honest man is worth more to society than "all the crowned ruffians that ever lived."

"But where, say some, is the King of America?" he said. "I'll tell you, friend, he reigns above, and doth not make havoc of mankind like the Royal Brute of Great Britain... so far as we approve of monarchy, that in America the law is king."

Paine also attacked the alleged virtues of the British constitution and de-

clared his belief that reconciliation was unacceptable. In his e...
plete dissolution of British power in America was desirable.

"We have every opportunity and every encouragement before us," wrote, "to form the noblest purest constitution on the face of the earth. We have it in our power to begin the world over again."

Although the ideas expressed in the tract were not new, Paine's communication style of those ideas differed greatly from the other revolutionary leaders from whom he borrowed thoughts, such as John Adams, Thomas Jefferson, and John Dickinson. The latter were rational, educated men who wrote for each other. That is, they wrote in an erudite, highly stylized fashion that followed rhetorical rules and included numerous Latin quotations, historical citations, and classical allusions, all of which resulted in text that was nearly incomprehensible to the average American.

Paine, on the other hand, had an uncanny ability to extract the most important concepts from the great Enlightenment thinkers of his time and communicate them in such a way that anyone could understand. He pioneered a new style of political writing by deliberately rejecting the rhetorical traditions of persuasion and, instead, used clear, concise language to imbue his writing with passionate feelings that formal writing conventions made impossible. He scorned "words of sound" that only "amuse the ear" and instead chose simple, direct language drawn from the commonplace world as known by even the most uneducated person. "As it is my design to make those that can scarcely read understand," he said, "[I] shall therefore avoid every literary ornament, and put it in language as plain as the alphabet." The result was the boldest and most eloquent expression of what many Americans felt about their ties to the British Crown.

In this we learn the first major lesson of effective communication and winning allies: that above all our communications must be easily understandable by the recipients, and must meet their agreement. We must speak in terms they understand, and it's not on them to agree, it's on us to persuade. Eloquence must not obscure meaning, and verbiage must not delay its delivery.

Paine didn't write ten words when five would do, and didn't allow a love of his words to compel him to fill a tome when a tract would better serve his ends. He knew that true sophistication in writing isn't achieved by ransacking the thesaurus and filling pages with hollow, meandering words. Quite the opposite; true sophistication in writing is only achieved by paring down your ideas and words to their bare, expressive minimum—no more, and no less. Paine's words, clothed in everyman's attire, found welcome homes in the hearts

and those same words, sharpened to a razor's
ways guns and cannons never could.

like wildfire. Its future vision offered a solution to
o were disgusted with English tyranny, compelling
ediate and momentous choice: England or America;
Common Sense was read in taverns across the colonies to
sp. publicanism, arouse enthusiasm for a split from Britain,
and rec into the Continental Army.

There's no question that, as Benjamin Rush said of *Common Sense*, "its effects were sudden and extensive upon the American mind." It sparked a public debate about independence that had been previously muted or hushed. Its magnetism was irresistible, and it was quickly recognized for what it was: a work of genius.

After *Common Sense* had effectively made Paine an American celebrity, he came to know all the political leaders of the Revolution. He desired to help his fellow patriots further and, thus, continued to write on behalf of the American cause. His next great contribution to liberty was his series of essays titled *American Crisis*, which were published and distributed throughout the war.

The first article—published on December 19, 1776—opens with the famous lines, "These are the times that try men's souls: The summer soldier and the sunshine patriot will, in this crisis, shrink from the service of their country; but he that stands it *now*, deserves the love and thanks of man and woman." Paine was referring to the very real possibility that the Continental Army was going to disintegrate within the month if the tides of war didn't change. Washington read this essay to his troops at Christmas 1776 on the eve of their first major victory in the war, the Battle of Trenton.

"It matters not where you live, or what rank of life you hold, the evil or the blessing will reach you all," Paine warned Americans in this first essay of *Crisis*. "The far and the near, the home counties and the back, the rich and the poor, will suffer or rejoice alike. The heart that feels not now is dead; the blood of his children will curse his cowardice, who shrinks back at a time when a little might have saved the whole, and made them happy. I love the man that can smile in trouble, that can gather strength from distress, and grow brave by reflection. 'Tis the business of little minds to shrink; but he whose heart is firm, and whose conscience approves his conduct, will pursue his principles unto death."

In the essays that followed, Paine continued to denounce the cowardly, exalt the patriotic, and inflame the hearts of Americans with visions of a definitive and final separation from Britain. "We fight not to enslave, but to set a country free," he declared in *Crisis No. IV*, "and to make room upon the earth for honest men to live in."

In 1779, Paine was appointed clerk of the General Assembly of Pennsylvania, where he witnessed firsthand the dismay of American troops due to lack of pay and supplies. In response, Paine started a subscription for the relief of the soldiers, and was the first to fund it with $500 of his own money, which was scarce due to his refusal to accept any monies for his writings to ensure that cheap editions could be widely circulated. Two years later, he arranged for himself and John Laurens, an aide-de-camp to Washington, to travel to France. They returned with a "gift" of six million dollars, a loan of ten million dollars, and clothing and ammunition that proved vital to the final success of the Revolution. Paine "positively objected" to Washington's offer to propose payment by Congress for his services.

Paine wasn't without detractors, however. Something about him bothered members of America's gentry. His appearance was careless and bedraggled. His large nose was usually reddened from too much drink. His dress was dingy, his wig frayed. While serving the government in various capacities, he became embroiled in one political dispute after another, increasingly at odds with everyone. While he mingled with the likes of Washington, Jefferson, and Lafayette, he was never fully accepted as a gentleman.

Further, Paine was criticized as a man without fortune, family, or connections—a mere piece of debris that had washed up on American shores and that continued to float loosely in the American hierarchy. Paine embraced his lack of connections, however. He boasted that he could "view the matter rather than the parties, and having no interests, connection with, or personal dislike to either, shall endeavor to serve all." He referred to himself as a "citizen of the world," one who had no personal interest to promote.

At the end of the war, Paine was poverty-stricken and petitioned Congress for financial assistance. Washington endorsed the plea, but Paine's opponents in Congress buried it. Pennsylvania gave him five hundred pounds and a farm in New Rochelle, New York. He accepted the offer, relocated, and began focusing his time on inventions, conceiving plans for an iron bridge without piers and a smokeless candle. It was a listless time for Paine, one that was not long endured, however, because his next calling soon presented itself: the French Revolution. Enraged by Edmund Burke's renunciation of the movement in his *Reflections on the Revolution in France*, Paine left for France shortly after telling Washington, "a share in two revolutions is living to some purpose."

Paine replied to Burke by rushing to write and publish *The Rights of Man*, which became one of the most celebrated and important works of political thought in the history of the Western world. The book exploded onto the European scene and summed up what he had learned about constitutionalism and political theory while in America. To this day, *The Rights of Man* is widely recognized as the most cogent expression of American revolutionary political thinking ever written.

The Rights of Man analyzed the basic reasons for European discontent and provided a remedial alternative to arbitrary government, widespread poverty and illiteracy, and frivolous war. Paine argued that the age of hereditary monarchy and aristocracy was over; that people were no longer subjects but equal citizens born with inalienable, natural rights; that the people had the right to define and limit their governments with constitutions; that these constitutions could not be arbitrarily altered by governments; that nobody had a right to rule beyond the rights granted by the sovereign people; that because people are naturally sociable, society doesn't need a restrictive government to regulate every aspect of it; and that people were free to pursue their own happiness. If Jefferson had codified his political beliefs, much would have resembled *The Rights of Man*.

"I speak an open and disinterested language, dictated by no passion but that of humanity," he wrote in chapter five. "To me, who have not only refused offers, because I thought them improper, but have declined rewards I might with reputation have accepted, it is no wonder that meanness and imposition appear disgustful. Independence is my happiness, and I view things as they are, without regard to place or person; my country is the world, and my religion is to do good."

The publication of *The Rights of Man* caused pandemonium in the British nobility, who feared it spelled "bloody revolution" in England. Consequently, Paine was told to publish it in an expensive edition "so as to confine it probably to that class of readers who may consider it coolly," and was warned that if it were published cheaply for dissemination among the populace, he would be prosecuted. Paine ignored the advice, of course, as his mission was to make political criticism accessible to the common people, and to express the rage of the lower classes of society that were tired of being ridiculed and held in contempt by their aristocratic superiors. Paine was again in his element, communicating the innermost problems of his people—the poor, disfranchised, and oppressed—in a way that showed he understood their plight better than even they did.

Consequently, the book was banned and the publisher jailed, and government agents instigated mobs, hate meetings, and burnings in effigy. Paine, who was by then living in Paris, was charged with treason and tried in absentia, found guilty of seditious libel, and declared an outlaw to be executed should he ever return to England. The book was ordered permanently suppressed.

"If, to expose the fraud and imposition of monarchy," he answered, "to promote universal peace, civilization, and commerce, and to break the chains of political superstition, and raise degraded man to his proper rank; if these things be libelous ... let the name of libeler be engraved on my tomb."

Like Voltaire, Paine learned that bold, radical communication wasn't without consequences. But he also knew that critics, no matter how vehement, must never stop him from continuing to put his pen to paper. Fortified with this resolve, he wielded his words like a sledgehammer and, counting on the strength of his armor of popularity, kept on communicating in the voice of the people, for the people.

As an enthusiastic supporter of the French Revolution, Paine was granted honorary French citizenship and was elected to the National Convention. He voted for a French Republic, but alienated many extremists by opposing the execution of Louis XVI on the grounds that revenge killing was immoral, suggesting exile to America instead.

In December 1793, Paine fell victim to the Reign of Terror. A decree was passed that excluded all foreigners from the Convention, and he was arrested and imprisoned. Before his arrest, however, he had begun penning another book, *The Age of Reason*, which he finished while incarcerated (and under the belief that he would die in prison). This was the work that would ultimately destroy his reputation among not only his peers but also his true power base: the common people.

The Age of Reason was a blistering attack on Christianity, the Bible, and orthodox religion. Further, it served as a tribute-of-sorts to deism and the belief that nature was the only form of divine revelation. Unfortunately for Paine, most of those who had grown to love him were as religious as they were anti-aristocratic. In their eyes, *The Age of Reason* advocated ideas that were simply unforgivable.

"The most detestable wickedness, the most horrid cruelties, and the greatest miseries, that have afflicted the human race have had their origin in this thing called revelation, or revealed religion," he wrote. "Whenever we read the obscene stories, the voluptuous debaucheries, the cruel and torturous executions, the unrelenting vindictiveness with which more than half the Bible is filled, it would be more consistent that we call it the word of a demon rather than the word of God. It is a history of wickedness that has served to corrupt and brutalize mankind; and, for my part, I sincerely detest it as I detest everything that is cruel."

Paine's extraordinary ability to inflame and unite would turn against him, and not even his inestimable contributions to the progression of political and social thinking could save him. His words would again prove more destructive than any worldly weapons.

Although *The Age of Reason* led people to call him, as Theodore Roosevelt famously said, "that filthy little atheist," Paine was certainly no atheist. In fact, he dedicated large portions of the text to explaining his deistic beliefs in God as the great creator and harmonizer of the universe.

"I believe in one God, and no more; and I hope for happiness beyond this life," he declared. "I believe the equality of man; and I believe that religious duties consists in doing justice, loving mercy, and endeavoring to make our fellow creatures happy. ... The word of God is the creation we behold and it is in this word, which no human invention can counterfeit or alter, that God speaketh universally to man."

Regardless of *The Age of Reason's* deistic message, most Americans saw only infidelity. Thus, Paine's "atheist" label stuck. Ironically, his religious views were actually common among liberal-thinking gentlemen of the era, such as Franklin, Jefferson, and other elites. They had the discretion to keep their deistic religious views out of the public eye, however, whereas Paine did what he did best: he spoke openly to the people in the streets. And he learned that the weapon of words can cut both ways—and deeply, at that.

The Age of Reason went through 17 editions between 1794 and 1796, causing many to fear that Paine's radical, offensive views were undermining the moral fabric of society. Paine narrowly escaped execution and was released from French prison in 1796, thanks to the fall of Robespierre, leader of the militant Montagnards that locked him up, and the efforts of the new American Minister to France, James Monroe, who backed Paine's claim that he was an American citizen.

When he returned to America in 1802, however, he quickly discovered that his services to the country had been all but forgotten. He was attacked by the public and press as a "lying, drunken, brutal infidel," and was abandoned by his former friends. He continued to write despite the ostracism, denying that he was an atheist, but it was to no avail. He lived by the pen and, in the end, would die by the pen.

The demise of Paine's good standing in the eyes of his countrymen presents the antithetical lesson to what we learned when his explosive debut as a Revolutionary thought leader won their love and loyalty. In the beginning, with *Common Sense*, he used his brilliant talents as a communicator to give the common people a collective voice, and they rallied to him in droves. But here, with *The Age of Reason*, he used those same talents to slap their faces, and they loathed him for it. As we proceed in our own adventures to make lasting impacts on the world, we must always consider how our communications will be received, and must always endeavor to make even the most unpalatable ideas compelling, not repulsive. A great ability to communicate enables you to galvanize and electrify others, and thus persuade them to your side in your journey. But, without an equally great sense of responsibility to temper and moderate what gets communicated and how, it can easily become chain lightning that shocks and scars everyone it touches.

"With all the inconveniences of early life against me," Paine wrote, "I am proud to say, that, with a perseverance undismayed by difficulties, a disinterestedness that compels respect, I have not only contributed to raise a new empire in the world, founded on a new system of government, but I have arrived at an eminence in political literature, the most difficult of all lines to succeed and excel in, which aristocracy, with all its aids, has not been able to reach or to rival."

Paine died on June 8, 1809 in Greenwich Village, New York City, at 72 years old. Only six mourners attended his funeral. The writer and orator Robert G. Ingersoll said that with Paine's name left out, "the history of liberty cannot be written," and summarized his life thus:

"Thomas Paine had passed the legendary limit of life. One by one most of his old friends and acquaintances had deserted him. Maligned on every side, execrated, shunned and abhorred, his virtues denounced as vices, his services forgotten, his character blackened, he preserved the poise and balance of his soul. He was a victim of the people, but his convictions remained unshaken. He was still a soldier in the army of freedom, and still tried to enlighten and civilize those who were impatiently waiting for his death. Even those who loved their enemies hated him, their friend—the friend of the whole world— with all their hearts."

In a letter he wrote to Benjamin Waterhouse in 1805, John Adams doubted "whether any man in the world has had more influence on its inhabitants or affairs for the last thirty years than Tom Paine."

If Paine hadn't put a pen to paper, the American Revolution might have very well collapsed under the early pressures of skepticism, defeat, and dismay. Through his extraordinary ability to communicate, Paine popularized a vision of a new republican world in which corrupt, dictatorial powers would wither. He heralded the end of the ancient custom of hereditary autocracy and the beginning of a new dawn in political theory and liberty, which captured the hearts and minds of millions.

Paine's influence during this tumultuous period affirms beyond doubt that the ability to communicate is one of the most important traits of the genius code—if not the most important. Regardless of the many virtues one can possess, if he or she can't clearly and persuasively communicate his or her ideas to others, no great impact is possible.

Can you imagine the world today if Newton had failed to convince with *Principia*? If Darwin had given into his fears of religious persecution and social disgrace and withheld *Origin*? If Copernicus hadn't defied religious dogma with irrefutable evidence and reasoning in *Revolutions*?

Indeed, our world has been shaped, and continues to be reshaped, by geniuses that have the courage and ability to communicate the inconvenient truths, radical awakenings, and civilizing reformations that banish oppression and corruption, and enrich our understanding, control, and enjoyment of ourselves, others, and the universe itself. Such communications form our species' entire mental, moral, technical, and aesthetic heritage, which must be learned and preserved by every successive generation. Thus, it's no coincidence that the first great human civilization, the Sumerians, were the first to develop a codified language that sparked an unprecedented outpouring, dissemination, and mingling of ideas and culture.

So, what does it take to be a persuasive communicator? While we've certainly learned much from Paine, let's learn from another of the masters.

ARISTOTLE'S SECRETS OF PERSUASION

Over 2,000 years ago, Aristotle wrote that there are three basic ways to persuade people. So accurate and effective was his formula that it is still used today to sway us to vote, buy, and think as others want. Aristotle said that to convince others that your ideas are valid, you must use three appeals: *ethos*, *pathos*, and *logos*.

ETHOS

Ethos is Greek for "character." Concerning language, Aristotle explained ethos as the trustworthiness or credibility of the speaker or writer. He said that ethos determines the audience's first impression. By showing that you have good sense, a good moral character, or expertise or authority, you can quickly win your audience's acceptance, just as Paine did with *Common Sense* and *The Rights of Man*.

Ethos has been leveraged in many ways in the world of marketing. "I'm not a doctor, but I play one on TV," has opened many commercials, spoken by popular actors that were hired to promote a wide variety of products, ranging from Vicks cough syrup to caffeine-free coffee to cigarettes. You might think that such a tacky appeal to ethos would never work, but think again—many of these commercials were wildly successful and ran for years.

Studies have shown that our culture, which places much importance on deference to authority, has hardwired people to submit to the opinions and orders of those who carry symbols of authority, such as a doctor's white coat, a title such as *professor*, fashionable clothing and trappings, and even physical height. Con men know this and, thus, are a fascinating study in ethos. They speak urbanely, dress impeccably, drive flashy cars, and even wear shoe lifts, all to gain immediate status and authority with their victims.

References to science and history are also incredibly powerful persuasion devices, and can be used to establish yourself as an expert. By weaving science or history, or both, into your communications, you not only greatly amplify the credibility and authority of the message itself but also create the impression that you are intelligent, educated, and in possession of wisdom that most people aren't. Formal writing relies heavily on citations and references to prove scholarly merit; informal writing benefits from the same principle.

Another influential way to create positive ethos is to create the perception of *similarity*. We like people we perceive to be similar to us. Similar opinions, traits, backgrounds, experiences, lifestyles, etc. Studies of human behavior have revealed how strong this simple observation really is. One such study showed that people tended to help those who dressed like them more often than those who didn't. Another showed that people were not only more likely to sign petitions of requesters who were dressed similarly, but also likely to do so without reading the petitions.

Paine used the appeal of similarity very skillfully to create ethos in a way his gentrified peers simply couldn't. Revolutionary leaders that were educated at Harvard and Princeton couldn't really represent the plight of the ordinary people. But Paine, who spent most of his life at the bottom of English society, could. While he spoke of the same ideals and injustices as his refined comrades, he expressed them in a more radical, bitter way that only a commoner could accurately and fully articulate. The result was a democratic revolution among the working folk that grew far beyond the Founders' expectations.

Subtleties like word choice and style of writing and speaking are also used to create ethos. Many influential writers and speakers choose their words carefully to cultivate an image of insightful wisdom and decisive confidence tempered with a humble, altruistic heart and dash of self-deprecating humor, and people eat it up. They also are careful to speak as their audience speaks. Paine was infamous for his coarse and abusive language, which was exactly how the bourgeoisie spoke about the British.

PATHOS

Pathos is Greek for "suffering" or "experience." The appeal to pathos is the appeal to emotion. Many rhetoricians over the centuries have considered it to be the strongest of the three appeals, which explains why so much of today's political discourse and advertising is engineered to move us emotionally.

Most people would like to believe that they weigh every decision in life rationally and only take action accordingly, but even Aristotle knew that powerful emotions such as anger, pity, fear, elation, admiration, and courage inevitably and radically, if subtly, influence our judgments.

An argument that relies only on cold logic will always lose to one that might be light on logic but deep in feeling. Examples abound throughout history: how many populations have been led into disastrous wars by demagogues? How many dictators have come to power by arousing the fear and hate of the people?

Pathos, more than ethos or logos, explains Paine's breakout popularity. Aristotle said that if we want to make an audience angry, we must understand their state of mind, whom they're angry at, and why they're angry with these people. Paine was acutely aware of why the colonists were at daggers drawn with Britain, and he exploited this tension masterfully in his writings.

Throughout history the method of mobilizing people to war has been the same: remind them of their grievances with other nations or people, blame others for their economic difficulties, and focus their thoughts on alleged insults, crimes, and atrocities committed against them. Just as Paine used these methods to inspire the honorable Revolution, others have used them to inspire the infernal: the Holocaust, the Rwandan genocide, and the Yugoslavian ethnic cleansing.

Aristotle taught that one of the most powerful ways to invoke pathos is story. Storytelling has been with us since the earliest times and was the original form of recording historical accounts. Nothing can rouse and change us as easily and profoundly as stories. There's something magical about how they subconsciously persuade us to drop our shields of skepticism, and transform our beliefs and values, sometimes without us even realizing it.

"Forget about PowerPoint and statistics," wrote the *Harvard Business Review*. "To involve people at the deepest level, you need stories."

By including stories in your communications—personal stories, stories of others, or even fictional stories—you will gain open access to your audience's minds and hearts. Stories can be used to motivate employees, teach your children a lesson, build a following, or as Paine did with his vivid stories of English abuse, change the world.

LOGOS

Logos is Greek for "word." Aristotle used *logos* to refer to the clarity and logic of the reasoning behind communication.

People often put too much faith in logic's ability to persuade. While formal logic and scientific reasoning are highly valued among the cloistered academia, look no further than the emotional pandering of mainstream politics to see how little it matters in the persuasion of the masses. That said, the appeal to logic is a fundamental pillar of persuasive communication and is, really, the heart of any position being supported. Aristotle taught two basic methods of logical thinking: *induction* and *deduction*.

Induction is a form of reasoning in which a conclusion or general law is formulated based on observations. That is, giving a bunch of similar occurrences and then drawing from them a general proposition. This is the heart of the scientific method. By contrast, deduction is a form of reasoning in which a conclusion or law is formulated based on the truth of other premises. Socrates' famous syllogism is an example of deductive reasoning: "All men are mortal; Socrates is a man; therefore, Socrates is mortal."

Inductive reasoning moves from the particular to the general; deductive reasoning moves from the general to the particular. Both methods have their uses and pitfalls.

For example, when the bubonic plague decimated Europe and parts of Asia in the 14th century, killing almost three quarters of the population in less than 20 years, the burning mystery was how the disease was spreading. Word began to spread that in each area of major outbreak, hordes of stray cats roamed the streets.

Through faulty inductive reasoning, it was assumed that the Black Death must be spread by cats, and the obvious solution was to eliminate the cats. People began killing cats on sight. It turned out, however, that the plague was spread by fleas carried by rats, and because cats killed rats, wiping out the cats increased the population of rats, which increased the population of infected fleas, which accelerated the spread of the plague. This mistake of concluding more than the premises actually warrant is a common mistake in inductive reasoning.

The validity of the conclusion of a deductive argument, therefore, is dependent upon the validity of the premise and the form of the argument itself. If the premise or form is false, then the conclusion is false.

If I state that all dogs have fleas, this is a dog, and therefore this dog has fleas, this is a valid argument in terms of form. Based on the premise, the conclusion can't be otherwise. But it's not true. Even if I claim that I have observed 10,000 dogs and every one had fleas, and thus I have inductively concluded the premise that all dogs have fleas, my conclusion is still nothing more than a prediction or conjecture. Maybe dog number 10,001 would have no fleas. How could I know unless I had examined every dog in the world?

A deductive argument's form is invalid when something is introduced in the conclusion that is wholly new and independent from the things mentioned in the premise. If I claim that all living creatures have a genetic code and therefore all living creatures are genetically related, my conclusion supposes many things to be true that aren't contained in the premise. The proof of the genetic relation of all living creatures would require a whole other line of reasoning. A valid argument based on the same premise, however, would be, for example, "All living creatures have a genetic code; this is a living creature; therefore, this living creature has a genetic code."

So, when communicating, be conscious of the logical soundness of your arguments. Use agreed upon facts and statistics to support your inductive conclusions, and beware of supposing more than the premise indicates. Think your deductive conclusions through and ensure that they are necessary consequences of your premises. And once you have it worked out, have faith in your premises and conclusions. Logic is meant to serve you and refine your observations, thinking, and communication, not haunt you with nagging doubts and "what ifs."

Paine's life shows us that an extraordinary ability to persuade isn't enough by itself, though. If he had understood the next lesson of communication, he would be remembered quite differently today.

———

Author and inventor Buckminster Fuller once said that you "never change things by fighting the existing reality." To change something, he wrote, "build a new model that makes the existing model obsolete." A cursory review of every great cultural advance in history confirms Bucky's observation.

Galileo didn't simply criticize inconsistencies in the rigid dogmas of geo-centrism. He presented the world with a brand new way to view the physical universe and our place in it, and took great pains to expound and defend his ideas. Einstein later called him the father of modern science.

Pasteur didn't merely join the ranks of intellectuals that undermined the idea of spontaneous generation—the belief that cells magically sprung forth from inanimate matter. He demonstrated through creative experiments that fermentation is caused by micro-organisms, which inspired him to investigate if the same was true of animal and human diseases. Thus, germ theory was finally proven and accepted, and medical science was changed forever.

Even the rise and fall of Paine can be viewed through these glasses. His antimonarchal treatises were scathing damnations of an entire social and political system, yes. But they also provided a viable, welcome alternative that was the greatest expression of equality and liberty in history. He wasn't tearing down the world; he was ushering in a new wave of respect for and faith in humanity.

Paine's anti-Christian rants were different, however. He was attacking not only a deeply ingrained social custom, but in the minds of many, the very core of existence itself. Factually speaking, many of his arguments against Christi-anity and revealed religion were compelling, but he failed to, as Bucky said, "build a new model that makes the existing model obsolete." His deistic beliefs were presented rationally. He even started a religious sect known as *theophilan-thropy*. But no mere outline of deism—the principles of which are in substance very similar to the basic beliefs of Christianity—could have possibly persuaded the common people to reject the religious traditions of their ancestors, and in many cases, abandon the very meaning of their lives. Thus, Paine became known as little more than a sacrilegious muckraker, harmful to the moral order of society.

Changing the foundations of theology will require much more than Paine could muster alone. If the progression of the physical sciences is any indicator, the change will probably come from a most unsuspecting corner of the world, and it will reconcile the mysteries of the divine, the physical, and the spiritual in a way never before conceived.

True genius is not just the ability to recognize, discredit, and disprove the illogical, superstitious, unjust, and immoral, but the ability to conceive of and effectively communicate a new reality of greater value. "He has a right to criticize, who has a heart to help," wrote Abraham Lincoln.

Take the lessons of Paine to heart. Your ability to communicate will, more than anything else, determine the distance you'll travel in your journey to greatness and who you'll travel it with. Use it vigorously and judiciously, and your cause will become the cause of many. Use it unwisely, however, and your cause will become the weapon of your own destruction.

12

OPTIMISM AND SURVIVING THE TIMES THAT TRIED MEN'S SOULS

"Be careful what you water your dreams with. Water them with worry and fear and you will produce weeds that choke the life from your dream. Water them with optimism and solutions and you will cultivate success."

-Lao Tzu

All great quests require that the hero muster his greatest strength in the bleakest times. When all hope seems lost, when the hero is afraid, trapped, and his will is all but broken, he must face the Supreme Ordeal and rise to greatness, or be broken by it.

The Israelites desire to free themselves from Philistine rule, and their armies face off. For 40 days, the monstrous Philistine warrior Goliath terrorizes the Israelites, mocking, challenging, and slaughtering scores of their untrained soldiers in hand-to-hand combat. King Saul and his men tremble in fear at the mighty champion. But then one young teenager, David, volunteers to fight him. Saul tries to forbid the boy from sacrificing himself to the battle-hardened barbarian, but David is certain that their god will lead him to victory. He collects five rocks, grabs his shepherd's staff and sling, and marches to meet what everyone believes will be a quick death. Goliath roars insults and taunts at the puny David and promises to feed him to the animals. David counters with his own promise: to kill and behead the blasphemer. Goliath has had enough and closes in for battle. David is undaunted; he rushes to meet the giant, places one stone in his sling, and fires it directly at the titan. It strikes true, sinking into Goliath's forehead. The Philistines fall silent as their hero stumbles and crashes to the ground. They realize they can't defeat an army with such a powerful god behind it, and flee. The war is over before it even began.

Harland David Sanders is 65 years old. His restaurant failed and he's broke, but he has one chance at redemption. For the last 20 years, he has perfected the art of fried chicken, and so much so that he won state-wide recognition as the "Kentucky Colonel"—an Old Southern gentleman of grace, charm, and good cooking. He travels the state, living out of his car, pleading with owners of run-down diners to use his chicken recipe at a commission of five cents per chicken. He's turned away over 1,000 times before making his first sale. Invigorated, he continues his sales beat, and finds more takers. Ten years later, he sells Kentucky Fried Chicken for $2 million, and collects franchise and appearance fees for the rest of his life.

Optimism is the genius code's test of faith. Can you believe in yourself, your ideas, your decisions, and your abilities when you're given every reason not to? Can you stand your ground when you're faced with your worst fears and difficulties? Can you remain hopeful when the world around you is rotting with despair and chaos?

One genius faced these challenges with the weight of the entire American Revolution on his back. With all the odds stacked against the patriots and his battered army, his unwavering optimism was his—and America's—only chance at survival.

It was Christmas Day 1776, and General George Washington's men had little to celebrate.

The first four months of war were calamitous for the American Revolution. The Continental Army had suffered a debilitating string of defeats, which left the rebels dismayed and despondent. Their numbers had dwindled to 5,000 men fit for duty, and over 3,000 enlistments were expiring at the end of the year. Many were not intending to renew. Troops were even beginning to desert their regiments.

"These are the times that try men's souls," wrote Thomas Paine, who was with Washington's army during one of the retreats. Many Americans feared that the Revolution would die in its infancy.

Although morale was at a low ebb, Washington knew that one bold victory would be enough to reinvigorate the colonials and set the British on their heels. He had carefully considered different offensive actions as one more crushing defeat would likely end the war. The operation that he settled on would be conducted on Christmas night, in Trenton, New Jersey, where 1,400 well-provisioned enemy troops were entrenched. The scheme became known by its password, "Victory or Death."

Washington arranged for 20 large boats to be brought to Trenton. They were to be the essential transports to ferry his entire army across the icy Delaware River to launch a surprise attack on the Hessian forces occupying the city. Washington hoped to catch the loyalists tired and hung over from late night partying.

The maneuver was incredibly risky. Washington was staking the main body of the Continental Army—and the very spirit of the Revolution—on his ambush. While he had a numerical advantage, his troops were desolate from losses and a lack of supplies and food. Additionally, before the battle could even begin, the river itself would have to be conquered. It had a strong, running current with flowing ice, and many of his men couldn't swim. Crucial to the plan's success were the experienced mariners who would be counted on to navigate the treacherous waters.

On the morning of the Christmas offensive, Washington ordered his army to prepare three days' food, 60 rounds of ammunition, and fresh flints. After an afternoon parade, thousands of troops marched off to their designated crossing points. Washington would lead the first group of over 2,000 Continentals across the river. Two other detachments would cross in different locations.

After sundown, the boats pushed off and began their perilous journey. It wasn't long before the weather turned from bad to worse. As temperatures dropped below freezing, the drizzle turned to sleet and snow, and the winds picked up to what one soldier described as feeling like a hurricane. Miraculously, Washington and his forces reached their landing zone safely after almost nine hours of rowing, and immediately set up a defensive line. Nobody was to pass through this perimeter, and the password used to identify fellow soldiers was the familiar "Victory or Death."

The two other crossings didn't fare so well. The inclement weather and logjam of massive ice chunks were only the beginning of the travails to come. The landings that were successful were late by three hours, and by 4 a.m., Washington learned that over half of his attacking force—more than 1,000 troops—had to turn back. This was a crucial moment in the mission. When the rebels learned that they were at half-strength, whispers of despair quickly spread. Washington understood their fears, but in his mind, there was no option but victory. Aborting would crush morale, his troops wouldn't re-enlist, and the Revolution would fizzle. The only way out was through the Hessian forces that lay ahead of him, and like Leonidas' legendary Battle of Thermopylae, Washington knew what his men could achieve on sheer will alone.

He rallied his troops with ardent promises that the element of surprise would allow them to secure a victory despite their vastly reduced numbers. Washington then led the advance of his army toward Trenton through cutting sleet and rain, riding up and down the line to keep his men motivated. Many of his troops didn't even have shoes, leaving behind trails of blood as they marched nearly nine miles to the Hessian encampment.

After only a few miles of marching, two men had frozen to death and many of the rebels' gunpowder had spoiled due to exposure to the storm. Washington informed General Sullivan that they are to rely on the bayonet if necessary. He was "resolved to take Trenton," as he said, at any cost, including his own life.

When Washington and the colonials were only two miles out from Trenton, they came upon a small force of 50 rogue Americans that had just conducted a raid on a nearby Hessian outpost. Washington couldn't believe his bad luck. The marauders were unaware of the impending ambush and their assault of the outpost would likely cause the Hessians to prepare for a larger attack. Once again, Washington was faced with a choice: temporarily retreat and risk a complete collapse of morale, or stay the course despite even further complications and risk a complete collapse of the Revolution. His optimism didn't waver, nor did he. If they had lost their advantage of surprise, they would have to make up for it with raw ferocity and, who knows, maybe a bit of luck.

Ironically, that small raid worked in the Americans' favor. Just a day earlier, the Hessian officer in command, Johann Rall, had been informed by American deserters of Washington's scheming to cross the river. Rall publicly dismissed it as rumor, and then assumed that the small skirmish of Christmas night was the "attack" he was warned about. Thereafter, Rall and his forces relaxed their guard.

The Americans caught another break that night. The terrible weather had in fact presented the opportune moment for the ambush because it dissuaded the Hessians from sending out patrols. Further, they had failed to set up any fortifications in the city despite being advised to do so days earlier, because Rall considered it unnecessary.

While some might view such luck as gifts from the beyond, it's interesting to note how often indefatigable optimism brings luck. Emerson said that "shallow men believe in luck or in circumstances," and strong men "believe in cause and effect." Would circumstances have aligned themselves so perfectly if Washington would have dejectedly led his men to what he thought would be certain defeat? I don't believe so. Optimism creates luck, not vice versa.

At about 8 a.m., the American forces reached the first Hessian outpost in Trenton. Washington led the assault, riding in front of his soldiers. They caught the Hessians by surprise. The battle had begun. Washington immediately ordered a battalion to block the escape route to Princeton, and his generals closed in with their forces to surround the enemy. The Hessians tried to mount a defense but the invasion was too well orchestrated; they were quickly outmaneuvered and overwhelmed.

Street by street, the Americans pushed the Hessians back, capturing cannons and men. Rall decided to attack the American flank in a desperate attempt to break Washington's lines and secure the advantageous high ground. Washington spotted the maneuver and rallied his troops into a battle formation to meet the enemy. The Hessians were soon caught in a deadly crossfire with three separate American contingents firing upon them from entrenched positions.

When he saw the Hessian attack was faltering, Washington led a charge to rout them, crying, "March on, my brave fellows, after me!" After Rall was mortally wounded his troops finally scattered, breaking the back of the defense. The remaining Hessian regiments quickly surrendered. Over 100 Hessians were killed and over 900 captured. Washington lost no men in the battle and suffered only four injured.

Washington had led the Continental Army to its first major victory in the Revolution, and the effects were profound. The victorious operation provided a much needed surge of confidence and optimism to the troops. It proved they had what it took to fight and defeat their fearsome and battle-hardened enemy. But this breakthrough, however potent, wasn't enough to erase the effects of months of low morale. The army at large was still very much on the brink of dissolution, with many soldiers still intending on putting down their arms and returning to their families when their enlistments expired on December 31.

On December 30, with the over 5,000 redcoats at his doorstep, preparing a powerful counter-attack, Washington rode in front of his men and cried out, "My brave fellows, you have done all I asked you to do, and more than could be reasonably expected; but your country is at stake, your wives, your houses and all that you hold dear. You have worn yourselves out with fatigues and hardships, but we know not how to spare you. If you will consent to stay only one month longer, you will render that service to the cause of liberty and to your country which you probably never can do under any other circumstances." At first, nobody volunteered to stay and fight, but then one soldier stepped forward. He was followed by another. And another. Within moments, men were flooding forward. In the end, only a small handful had refused to move.

Washington made good use of his troops over the next ten days, leading them to three back-to-back, momentous victories that culminated in a full British retreat from New Jersey. Consequently, confidence swelled among the colonials, and new enlistments began to pour in. The Revolution was saved.

Washington had delivered hope and optimism to his people when it was needed most, and continued to do so, eventually leading the Continental Army to its ultimate victory over Great Britain. His optimism, and his outstanding ability to galvanize others with it, is interesting when you consider that Washington was very different than his intellectual peers. Unlike Adams, Jefferson, or Franklin, Washington wasn't a learned man; he was a man of affairs. According to Jefferson, Washington had "neither copiousness of ideas nor fluency of words"; he was a practical man who often had little to say, but he was capable of dramatic action. His dynamism produced the type of infectious optimism that mere words, no matter how poignant, can never match, because optimism requires hope, and hope requires inspiration, and nothing inspires like leading from the front, and by example.

In a grand final testament to his character, Washington retired from the presidency after serving for two terms, overseeing the creation of a strong, well-financed government that won the acceptance and confidence of the people of the newly formed republic. Despite many calls from his peers and electorate to become "president for life"—that is, to possess complete dictatorial powers, Washington graciously declined the invitations to immeasurable wealth and influence. He knew that such an appointment would invalidate the republican character of the nation and the Constitution, and he was optimistic that the government and country he had helped to create would flourish under a new leader. And so he chose to live a private life following his departure from the presidency, tending to his businesses and estate.

Congressman Henry Lee, who served under Washington in the Revolutionary War, famously declared at Washington's funeral that he was "first in war—first in peace—and first in the hearts of his countrymen." Upon Washington's death, Napoleon ordered ten days of mourning in France. Thousands of Americans donned mourning clothing, which they wore for months.

While the Supreme Ordeal in your journey to greatness won't pit you against the fearsome armies of a global superpower, it will take an equally frightful form. Like Dante's final gate of Hell in *Inferno*, which taunted him to "abandon hope, all ye who enter here," the only way out of the crucible will be through. And the only way through will be by the light of your optimism. As we saw with Washington, and with many other geniuses analyzed in this book, that light burns on the fuel of unrelenting action. If we stop to doubt, wonder, or reconsider, the flame dies, and our optimism fades.

Helen Keller said that optimism is the "faith that leads to achievement" and that "nothing can be done without hope and confidence." Washington's unlikely success at Trenton is a prime instance of such faith in action and the momentous role it can play in our journeys to greatness.

Optimism has pushed many geniuses through long nights, bitter criticisms, demoralizing failures, and the loneliness of being outside of the status quo. By the end of the war, for example, Washington had become more of a monument than a man, seen as completely unapproachable by many.

What is the secret of people like Washington, though? How are they able to remain hopeful and stick to their visions and beliefs through great trials and tribulations?

Well, to better understand optimism, let's first take a closer look at its ugly counterpart, pessimism, and what it can teach us about how we view ourselves, our undertakings, and the world around us.

IT'S TIME TO GET PESSIMISTIC ABOUT THE PESSIMISM INDUSTRY

The pessimism industry continues to grow as the years tick by.

Pessimism really kicked into high gear with Thomas Robert Malthus's 1798 treatise of doom and gloom, *An Essay on the Principle of Population*. In it, he predicted that all of mankind was doomed because population would inevitably outrun food supply. He thought it would happen sometime within 100 years of his lifetime. Hence, many "Malthusians" welcomed famines and epidemics because they felt it was population "correcting itself."

To this day, Malthus is the foundation and inspiration for much of the contemporary pessimism industry. Paul R. Ehrlich, the author of *The Population Bomb*, predicted in 1968 that hundreds of millions would die of starvation in the 1970s, and that life expectancy would plummet in the 1980s. It didn't happen. Later, the infamous Club of Rome report in 1972 said we'd run out of raw materials by the 1990s. Wrong again. These doomsday prophets all assumed that human beings were like sheep, grazing on the grass until it's all gone. Well, we're a bit smarter than sheep.

The point is there is always a ready supply of despair. Thankfully, more times than not, realities never turn out as bad as such fatalists want us to believe. You would think that we would simply grow tired of it all. Sadly, we don't.

Well, as the former president of Coca-Cola, Don Keough, said in his book, *The Ten Commandments for Business Failure*, we need to be aggressively pessimistic about the pessimism industry. Turn off the news. Stop focusing on failures. A tilt of your head or attitude; it can make all the difference in how you see your world. Whatever our future holds will have a lot to do with what we believe it will hold. Don't underestimate the power of self-fulfilling prophecies. When enough people begin to believe with certainty that things will turn out a certain way, their behavior evolves to match, and the outcome is all but guaranteed. Thus, it's important to envision and share beautiful, believable, achievable visions of what can be as these too can convince people, which starts the process of making them true.

Sometimes, like Washington before his victory at Trenton, all you have to hang onto is your hope and resolve. His army was in tatters. His highly experienced enemy had him outnumbered and outmaneuvered, and had momentum on their side. Objectively speaking, the Revolution had hit bottom, and was, many said, beyond redemption. If it weren't for Washington, their prophecy would have come true.

Herein lies the great danger of the cynical despair that you find every night in the news and every morning in the newspaper. They are ambassadors of hopelessness that work tirelessly to convince people that the future is a cruel prefiguration of sorrow, disappointment, misfortune, and oppression. If people are exposed to this type of thinking often enough, they'll begin to believe it and then act accordingly. In the end, they reap exactly what they unwittingly sow.

If you believe the fearmongers, there never is a good time to start anything. Something is always wrong. There are always holes in the business model, always dangers lying below the surface, waiting to swallow you whole. But if you believe in your inherent creativity and resourcefulness—if you acknowledge your inner genius—then almost any time is a good time to start anything.

Washington's daring crossing of the Delaware River and ambush of the entrenched Hessians could've failed in numerous ways, but he refused to dwell on it. Instead, he focused on how it could somehow be made to work, and against all odds, saw it through.

Before we can be optimistic about our future, we must get pessimistic about the pessimism industry. There's something else to a genius' optimism, though, and it strikes at one of the most fundamental questions humans have ever asked.

Ancient wisdom has long regarded all human activity as play. We're born into the Great Mystery, as Einstein said, and we proceed to love, hate, create, destroy, rise and fall. Here lies the greatest secret of optimism: how we deal with the vicissitudes of life.

An optimistic outlook is easy to assume when everything is going as planned—we're naturally encouraged by our successes. But how do we find the strength to hold our heads up when, like in Washington's plight, we feel like we're on the road to ruin?

Well, we must first realize that, as writer and painter Henry Miller said, "by choosing to live above the ordinary level, we necessarily create extraordinary problems for ourselves." This is as inescapable as any other law of nature—the farther you make it in your journey to greatness, the bigger the barriers you'll have to overcome. The optimistic person is able to acknowledge this and meet problems, no matter how large, with equal vigor. Winston Churchill said that a pessimist "sees the difficulty in every opportunity" whereas "an optimist sees the opportunity in every difficulty." There's more to pessimism, though; the person that despairs at the very thought of difficulties has a fundamental misunderstanding of what it means to be a human being.

The physical, intellectual, and social comforts of modern civilization have softened the reality that life is, and always will be, a never-ending game of *competition* and *selection*. The trials and processes of evolution and survival of the fittest regulate this game. Thus, turmoil is inherent and unavoidable. The romantic notion that the journey to greatness can be shortcut through reliance on honeyed thoughts, candied smiles, and cloying words is nonsense. Only the toughest survive the rigors of existence, and even they have a time of it.

Nature smiles at the economic, political, and social devices that we erect to try to change the rules of biology and escape its commotion. In time, these futile attempts to shift the pressures of life onto the backs of others always crumble. The people that rely solely on the collective effort for their survival eventually find themselves without support, and soon after, at last gasp.

As we've seen, men like Washington imbued themselves with the pugnacity of our forebears that had to chase, fight, and kill to survive. They expected hardship. They were willing to face the worst. They embraced the fact that the universe, in all its apparent tranquility, is a carefully balanced chaos of forces we barely understand. If we're to bear upon its journey, we too must be a force of nature. Positive visions and convictions are the muses of optimism, but their inspiration is fleeting if not supported by a backbone of steel.

13

YOUR INVITATION TO THE BROTHERHOOD OF GENIUS

"Only the individual can think, and thereby create new values for society—nay, even set up new moral standards to which the life of the community conforms."

-Albert Einstein

Because of geniuses, you can wake up every day and brush your teeth with clean water, flip on your coffee machine, and fire up your laptop.

Because of geniuses, you can pray to Allah, Jesus, God, or the universe, or nothing, without fear of persecution.

Because of geniuses, you are not a slave, nor a helpless subject of a crazed or incompetent oligarch, but a sovereign individual free to pursue your own happiness.

Because of geniuses, you have songs to dance to, stories to love, paintings to admire, and architecture to marvel at.

By the time you've left your home for work in the morning, you've benefited from the work of hundreds, if not thousands, of geniuses. You live in a world built and upheld by geniuses. Every piece of culture that you treasure has a long lineage of geniuses. And every hope you have for the future of this world is a hope that geniuses will continue to work to make it so.

The world desperately needs more geniuses, not more intelligent spectators or idle critics muttering in obscurity. Human problems are more complex and dangerous than ever, and we are regularly reminded how fragile the equilibriums of social, political, economic, and religious forces truly are. Humanity doesn't magically survive by the grace of the Unknown; it's borne on the backs of mighty individuals that are often misunderstood, fought, ridiculed, thwarted, and forgotten by most. But there they are, creating legacies that we carry forward every day.

The path to genius is very different from what's sold by mainstream culture as normal and acceptable. If we are to live our lives according to the popular trends, we are to hate our work and cut as many corners as possible, worship glitz and celebrity, escape living with meaningless entertainment, and day by day, endeavor to shed the burden of responsibility for our lives, our fellows, our nation, our species, and our planet.

Although intelligent people make many compelling arguments as to why you should leap into this trap, you know deep inside that it's a lie. You know that convincing people to sleepwalk through life, entranced by pop culture, influencing nothing, and denying their ability and right to make a difference is nothing more than a bald-faced attempt at destroying our civilization. So don't buy into it. "One day you finally knew what you had to do, and began, though the voices around you kept shouting their bad advice," is how Pulitzer Prize-winning poet Mary Oliver described moving away from the profane toward a deep sense of purpose and connectedness in the world.

If you don't like where some aspect of humanity is going, you can do something about it. If you have a stubborn desire to reach out into our culture and write "I was here," nothing can stop you outside of yourself. "It's awfully simple," wrote L. Ron Hubbard. "If you just looked at life this way and said, 'Why, I don't see anything that could offer me any trouble; no obstacles around here that I can see. As far as putting forward my ideas, as far as even thinking up ideas, as far as carrying forward in life at large, I don't see any obstacles,' you wouldn't have any."

There's a catch, however. A simple prerequisite. The only way to really be effective is to pursue greatness at a genius level. "You have to run as fast as you can just to stay where you are. If you want to get anywhere, you'll have to run much faster," Lewis Carroll wrote in *Alice in Wonderland*. The first step to becoming a genius is simply deciding that you are going to endeavor to do so. It's a big decision to make and, ironically, is itself a moment of genius. It takes courage, individualism, honesty with yourself, optimism, and imagination to break from the lockstep of the "now you're supposed to" society and join the ranks of the radicals who think for themselves, pursue lofty goals, and whose responsibility is indeed the survival of our species. And make no mistake—if humankind eradicates itself in one of the ever-growing ways available, it will be because our geniuses were too few, were too marginalized, or too disorganized.

The records of the last 10,000 years have clearly proven that we have no divine guarantee of our continued existence, personally or as a race. Biologist Janine Benyus said that life creates the conditions that are conducive to life. History is a grand struggle between the insane's destructive urge to dominate and smash, and the genius' creative urge to emancipate and enrich.

Every genius throughout history shares a bond that transcends time, location, and ethnicity. They form a brotherhood that doesn't just influence the tapestry of human experience, but that built and maintains the loom, provides the thread, and imagines and weaves the future. Your own journey to greatness echoes the same journey taken by history's greatest men and women. All heroes must leave the known and comfortable world to heed a call to adventure, survive trials, gain wisdom, overcome temptation, win allies, and, through ironbound grit and guts, create a profound meaning in their lives, and the lives of others, that transcends death. The genius code shows you how to take this epic journey, and once embodied, proves that you've done so.

Anyone can join this brotherhood, but it can't afford to send recruiters or limos. It has no grand initiation rites, but you'll know in your heart when you're admitted. It cares little about wealth or fame, but values above all an extraordinary sense of pride, purpose, and self-worth that few understand. It enforces no rules, and your membership is renewed through your continued reverence for the human endeavor and your long, hard efforts to take it forward.

So, is the Brotherhood of Genius right for you? Well, ask yourself the following questions.

Who are you, really, and how many people could benefit from knowing you?

What are you capable of, really, and what might happen in the world if you unleashed it?

Why do you think you're here, and what can you create that nobody else can or will?

If you don't have definitive answers, don't worry. Most people don't. But if those questions ignite a vigorous spark of curiosity, then empower yourself to explore their meaning and magnitude. Become a genius, labor for greatness, and make the world feel your presence.

Regardless of the paths that these questions take you down, you will inevitably arrive at the realization of the fantastic importance and value of contributing to the world to your utmost. If you worry you can't make it or it will be too hard, consider this: Your mind, even on its dullest days, has a baffling computational ability that vastly outstrips anything we can hope to build. Your body, an impossible harmony of trillions of cells and one septillion activities, is engineered with such brilliance and precision that you're free to ignore it. And you, with your ability to perceive, reason, and act, are the most sentient form of life in the known universe. In these ways, you're already a reflection of genius. But will you live up to the spirit of greatness born into your every cell, and stitched into your soul? Will you discover what it feels like to be truly alive? You don't have to be any smarter to start this journey, nor does it require outstanding talents or opportunities for entry. You have no destiny—grim or grand—beyond what you're willing to create.

Einstein said that you can live your life as though nothing is a miracle, or as though everything is a miracle. Well, I believe that it's a miracle of unimaginable proportions that you and I even exist, and that you can read these words, understand their meaning, and contemplate their significance. When you consider the fact that only four percent of the universe is made up of stars, planets, and galaxies, and 96 percent is made up of stuff astronomers can't see, detect, or even comprehend, your miraculous nature becomes apparent, undeniable, and inescapable.

You were entrusted with the most simple, powerful and magical talent in the universe: the talent to create the conditions of life that are conducive to life. I believe this talent carries the responsibility of making the most of it. Do you? Will you?

ABOUT THE AUTHOR

Sean Patrick is a dad, husband, Floridian, author, entrepreneur, slightly off-kilter, hopelessly optimistic, 28-year-old that's obsessed with creation, marketing, storytelling, fitness, and educating.

Founder of Oculus Publishers, Patrick is on a mission to enlighten, entertain, and inspire people through beautiful stories and ideas.

When not writing or building something, you can usually find him lifting heavy things in the gym, trying to make a dent in his never-ending "to-read" list, acting like a fool to make his son laugh…and writing in the third person. Wink, wink.

WOULD YOU DO ME A FAVOR?

Thank you for reading my book. I hope you enjoyed it! I'm positive that if you decide to walk the path to greatness, you can unlock possibilities for happiness and accomplishment that you never believed possible.

I have a small favor to ask. Would you mind taking a minute to write a blurb on Amazon about this book? I check all my reviews and love to get feedback (that's the real pay for my work—knowing that I'm helping people).

Visit the following link to leave me a review on Amazon.com:

HTTP://BIT.LY/AYIG-REVIEW

Visit the following link to leave me a review on Amazon.co.uk:

HTTP://BIT.LY/AYIG-REVIEW-UK

Also, if you have any friends or family who might enjoy this book, spread the love and lend it to them!

Now, I don't just want to sell you a book—I want to connect with as many people as I can and hear their stories, learn from their wisdom, get inspired by their courage, and, well, just enjoy the delights of friendship.

Thus, I'd love to hear from you, and what you thought of this book! All feedback is welcome, and if you have any ideas you'd like to share on how I can improve the book or what you think I should write about next, let me know! You can reach me at sean@yourinnergenius.com, or on Facebook, Twitter, and G+:

Like me on Facebook: www.facebook.com/AwakeningYourInnerGenius

Follow me on Twitter: @ayigenius

Thanks again, I hope to hear from you, and I wish you the best!

Sean

ARE YOU READY TO AWAKEN YOUR INNER GENIUS? THEN YOU WANT TO DOWNLOAD THE FREE AWAKENING YOUR INNER GENIUS WORKBOOK!

You now know things that most people will never understand about how to unlock our potentials and achieve greatness, but you might feel a bit unsure about where to start.

Well, thanks to feedback from hundreds of readers, I was able to create this totally free workbook to help you out. In it, you're going to explore each trait of the "genius code" further and learn how to join the small handful of people who walk the path to greatness.

Inside you'll find a detailed study guide that will expand your understanding of the genius code thought-provoking essays, and get you into action with fun, helpful practical exercises. That's not all though.

I've also included links to some of the most inspiring, spellbinding, and illuminating talks I've seen on each trait from luminaries like Steve Jobs, JJ Abrams, James Cameron, Jeff Bezos, JK Rowling, Seth Godin, and many more. These talks will supercharge your drive to find and follow your bliss, and live a fulfilling, delightful life.

By doing this workbook, you're going to begin your journey to greatness and witness doors opening in your life that weren't even visible before.

My mission is to help you get to that moment. That's what makes me most happy.

Download this free workbook today and make this next year the year where you awaken your inner genius, and let the world feel your presence!

Visit HTTP://BIT.LY/AYIG-WORKBOOK to get this report now!

Made in the USA
Columbia, SC
19 May 2021